THE

CHEATS

AND

ILLUSIONS

OF

Romish Priests and Exorcists.
Discover'd in the
HISTORY OF THE DEVILS
of
LOUDUN:

Being an Account of the Pretended Possession OF THE URSULINE NUNS, AND OF The Condemnation and Punishment of URBAN GRANDIER a Parson of the same Town.

William Turner
1703.

Dedication
TO HIS
GRACE
The Most Reverend Father in GOD
THOMAS,
By Divine Providence,
Ld. Archbishop of Canterbury.

May it please Your GRACE;

THE following Sheets contain an Account of a most Remarkable Passage that happen'd in France during the Ministry of Cardinal de Richelieu; and which gives us a Sketch of the Arbitrariness of that Haughty, Designing Prelate; of the Malice and Revengeful Spirit of Popish Priests; and of the Sinister and Diabolical Methods whereby a Convent of Ursuline Nuns establish'd themselves in the Town of Loudun.

This History, which was originally written in French, has met with a very favourable Reception abroad: And 'tis justly presum'd, That a Translation of it will not only be Entertaining, but likewise Useful to an English Protestant Reader: Especially at this Time of Day, when the Restless Papists, and their Cabal, are secretly endeavouring to undermine our Happy Settlement, and to divert the Course of the Succession to the Imperial Crown of these Realms, from a Lawful Protestant Heir, to a Popish Frenchified Pretender: In

Order to bring in Popery, and its inseparable Companion, Arbitrary Sway, among us.

The Author of this Translation, (who is a Presbyter of the Church of England) having desir'd me to take Care of its Publication, and to procure it a Patron, I thought I could not better discharge this latter Part of my Trust, than by laying these Sheets at Your GRACE's Feet; whose Zeal for the Advancement and Defence of the True Religion did gloriously Shine, notwithstanding the Threatning Storms from a Popish Court, not only in the Erecting a Free-School at St. Martin's, adorn'd with a Choice Library, in Opposition to the College of the Jesuits in the Savoy; but also in Unravelling and Defeating the subtle Diabolical Arts, whereby those Ministers of Hell and Tyranny endeavour'd to lead astray Unwary Protestant Youths. Every Body will easily apprehend, that by this I mean the Famous Conference Your GRACE had with Pulton, the Jesuit; wherein Your GRACE's Learning, Strong Reasons, and Solid Judgment, gain'd an Immortal Triumph over the Obstinacy and Noise of a bold fallacious Caviller.

'Twas this Apostolical Zeal, exerted in the most difficult Times, together with your Exemplary Piety, Goodness, Charity, and Forbearing Temper, that gain'd Your GRACE the entire Confidence and Esteem of Two of the Best Princes that ever sway'd the English Scepter, King WILLIAM and Queen MARY, of ever Blessed and Pious Memory: And which induc'd his Late Majesty to raise Your GRACE to that Supream Station you hold in the Church: That by this very Choice all

England might be convinc'd, how truly he wish'd, and earnestly endeavour'd by all Gentle and Christian, (which certainly are the most Efficacious) Methods to bring Those over to the Establish'd Religion, whose Birth and Education has insensibly led them to Dissent from it. And indeed, as long as your GRACE is alive, that Great and Good King is sure to have, here on Earth, an unexceptionable Witness of his Moral and Christian Virtues; The Liberties of England, a Firm Support; And the Church, a Wise and Vigilant Director, and a most Tender Father.

    That these Blessings may be long continued to this Happy and Flourishing Nation, is the most Fervent Wish of him, who most gladly lays hold on this Opportunity to subscribe himself,

May it please Your GRACE,
Your GRACE's
Most Humble,
most Faithful,
and most Obedient Servant,

THE HISTORY OF THE 𝕯𝖊𝖛𝖎𝖑𝖘 𝖔𝖋 𝕷𝖔𝖚𝖉𝖚𝖓:

Or, an Account of the

Possession of the Ursuline Nuns.

AND THE

Condemnation and Punishment of

URBAN GRANDIER,

a Parson of the same Town.

BOOK I.
Sect. I

THere is no doubt but that particular Relations of the nature of those which are contain'd in this Book, would have been much better receiv'd, and have made more impression, whilst they had the grace of Novelty, than when after a long course of time they seem to have been buried in Darkness and Oblivion. Nevertheless it may not now be thought improper to produce and revive them, since they deserve it, both by their importance, and their Singularity; and the only reason why they were buried in Silence, is, because Arbitrariness and Tyranny have stopt the Mouths of those who would have attempted to entertain the Publick with them, and set the Truth thereof before their Eyes. 'Tis upon this

Motive, that because at this time one may speak freely, and without constraint, that now are publish'd the long and fatal Intrigues of a Convent of Nuns, and a great number of Ecclesiasticks, supported by a party of the Magistrates and Inhabitants of a Town, and favour'd by the Court. These Intrigues have been of great Consequence; forasmuch as they have caus'd a Parish Priest to be Condemn'd to be Burnt alive; and that they tended to establish in France certain Maxims which would subject the People to a real Inquisition. They have been peculiar, and of a strange singularity, seeing that Devils are immediately concern'd, or that 'tis pretended that they did intermeddle, and that they have possest and caus'd all these Nuns to act their part. In fine, this History appears so much the more considerable, that the Facts it relates eave been continued a great many years, that they have had for Spectators and Witnesses, a Number of Persons illustrious by their Rank, and by their Merit; that there was never a Relation of the same Nature, more closely furnish'd with Circumstances, nor better attended with all necessary Proofs; and that it gives a clear and exact Idea of the Sentiments that one ought to have of the pretended Diabolical Possessions, of the Apparitions of Devils, and of the Miracles that were done upon these Occasions. It discovers also at the same time the Obliquity of Mans Nature, and how far 'tis capable to go, when 'tis once engag'd in an evil Design.

Sect. 2.

Although the History of the Martyrdom of Saint Ursula, and the Eleven Thousand Virgins which accompanied her, be liable to many contradictions, and that the greater part of the Learned doubt of its Veracity; This Saint has not been omitted to be Canoniz'd, to whose Honour the Beatified Angela of Bresse founded in the last Age in Italy, an Order of Nuns according to the Rule of Saint Augustine, which was approv'd by Pope Gregory the Thireenth, in the Year 1572. And since, in the Year 1614. Magdalene l'Huillier introduc'd it into France, with the approbation of Pope Paul the Fifth, by a Monastery which she founded at Paris, whence this Order spreading it self by degrees through all the Kingdom, there was establish'd in the Year 1626, a Convent at Loudun, which is a large Town, tho' ill peopled; situated between the Provinces of Poitou, Tourain and Anjou, and which separates them all three, without having anciently made any part of them, or having had dependance upon either of them.

Sect. 3.

In this Place this Society, although as yet very small, was in great want, and very destitute of necessary conveniencies for their subsistance. It was then part of an Order, so little distant from its Birth, that it was not so rich and wealthy, as now it is at this Day, since a few more years has given it the leasure to consider of its Affairs, and to provide more advantageously for its establishment. It was compos'd of Maidens of very good Families, Noble and Ignoble, but who were not rich, or who would not give considerable Portions to those, whom they put out of their Houses to ease themselves of the Charge. Therefore these Maidens were lodg'd in a hir'd private House, which was of no great extent, and according to their Institution, took Boarders to teach them, and from their Pensions drew part of their Maintenance. The House where they dwelt belong'd to Moussaut du Fresne. The Prior Moussaut his Brother, was their first Confessor, but was not long so, for he died some time before the discourse begun, concerning the Diabolical Possession, of which we are to treat.

Sect. 4.

The younger-sort of these Maidens, who were of a very chearful Spirit, and who sought nothing but to divert themselves, as much as the compass of their Confinement would allow; took an Occasion by this Mans Death (and the Conceit which some Persons had, that Spirits haunted the House where they dwelt) to rise in the Night, and make a Noise in the Granaries, and to give themselves the Pastime to fright the young Boarders; Some also of the more simple and aged of the Nuns (to whom the others had not dar'd to discover the sport) conceiv'd a great deal of fear: This encourag'd the Actresses even to get upon the top of the House, which was not difficult at Loudun, where most of the Roofs are built in such a manner, that they admit of an easie access. They came at length to enter into the Chambers of the Boarders, to take their Petticoats off from their

Beds; and at last to practice every thing that might serve to give them a Divertisement, and to befool the Boarders and the other Nuns. One of the Boarders at that time between Seventeen and Eighteen years of Age, nam'd Mary Aubin, who was admitted into the Pleasures and Secrets of these Actresses, serv'd to terrifie the others by the fear which she seem'd to have, especially when these Sprights came into their Chamber, the Doors whereof had been well bolted, but they had since been softly open'd by her, who constantly related this Prank after the same manner, to her most intimate Friends, till she was almost Sixty Five years old, when she died.

Sect. 5.

After the Death of Moussaut, John Mignon, Priest and Canon of the Collegiate Church of Saint Crosse, in Loudun, was chosen to be the Confessor of the Ursulines. The Elder sort of them exprest to him the cause of their Fear, and the Younger made him a Confident of their Sport. This Man was an Intriguer, Malicious and Ambitious, and had then different Passions working in him. He propos'd to himself, not only to suffer the sport to continue, but to Authorize it, and to lend it a helping Hand, and to try if he could not make use of it, which might serve him to revenge himself of his Enemies, and to gain a reputation of Piety and sanctity, to which he was a great Pretender. But that the Designs of the Contrivers of this Tragical Piece, may more throughly be discover'd, we must bring the principal Person on the Stage, who was mostly concern'd in the Tragedy.

Sect. 6.

Urban Grandier was a Priest, Born of an honest Family, the Son of Peter Grandier, and Nephew of Claudius Grandier, who was also a Priest. These Ursuline Nuns, in the time of their being possess'd, said, that Urban Grandier had learnt Magick of his Father, and his Uncle; but the Inhabitants of Xaintes, where they had dwelt, dissipated this slander by the good Testimony they gave of their Lives and Conversation. He perform'd the course of his Studies under the Jesuits of Bourdeaux, who observing in him very considerable Endowments, took an affection to him, and procur'd to him the parsonage of Saint Peter, in the Market of Loudun, which is in the presentation of the Jesuits of Poictiers. He had also obtain'd a Prebend in the Chapter of the Church of Saint Crosse. The uniting of these Benefices in one Person, who was not of that Province, expos'd him to the Envy of many Churchmen, who would have been well satisfied with one of the two. This he was sufficiently sensible of, when he saw himself accus'd, for he often said to his Friends, that one part of those of that Order, who had declar'd themselves against him, had a Quarrel with his Benefices, rather than his Person. He was of a tall Stature, and of a good Presence, of a steady Mind, and subtil Wit, always Comely and well drest, never going but in a long Garment; this outward neatness was accormpanied with a polite Wit;

He exprest himself with much Ease and Eloquence; He preach'd often, and acquited himself in that Employment incomparably better than most of the Monks who went up into the Pulpit. There is a Funeral Oration of his, upon the Death of the Illustrious Scevola of Saint Martha, which is a very Eloquent Piece, and sets forth the fineness of his Genius. He was gentle and courteous to his Friends, but proud and haughty towards his Enemies. He was Jealous of his Rank, and never yielded any thing of his interests, repelling injuries with so much vigour, that he exasperated the Spirits of those whom he might have gain'd by taking other Methods. In the mean while he was expos'd to many Enemies, his haughtiness had rais'd him a great number, and the extraordinary inclination he had to the Courting of Women, had made him still many more: It was not the Rivals that he was to fear, but the Fathers and the Mothers provok'd and enrag'd by the Evil Reputation, which his frequent Visits had drawn upon their Families.

Sect. 7.

In the year 1602 he had a Process before the Official of Poitiers against a Priest nam'd le Mounier, and the Twenty First of April in the same Year, he obtain'd a Sentence against him, which he caus'd to be executed with much Rigour, to the end that he might terrifie those that should attempt to give him Trouble in time to come; whereat le Mounier continued so much provok'd, that when he saw him accus'd of Sacriledge and Irreligion, he became a Witness himself, and even thunder'd out Monitories against him by the Orders of Laubardemont, a Commissary sent by the Court, to take Cognizance of this Affair.

Sect. 8.

Some time after Grandier had another Suit against the Canons of St. Cross, upon the occasion of a House which he contended for with the Chapter; Mignon powerfully oppos'd his Pretensions, who was in Credit for the sake of his Family, and he was well skill'd in Matters Benificiary, and had conceiv'd a great jealousy against Grandier, whose Proceedings he always oppos'd. But although this Canon had sollicited the Suit with much Heat, the Chapter notwithstanding lost their Cause. Grandier triumph'd and insulted over Mignon with so much Pride, that he had a sensible Resentment of it.

Sect. 9.

Barot, the Uncle of Mignon, and President of the General Assessors, a rich Man, and Childless, and by Consequence much respected and caressed by his Heirs, had also a Quarrell with Grandier, who treated him with the utmost Haughtiness, and as a pitiful Fellow, which caus'd Barot's Family to conceive so great an animosity against Grandier, that every one of them put himself forward to shew their Resentments, the better to make their Court to their Kinsman.

Sect. 10.

But all this came nothing near the Displeasure of Trinquant the Kings Attorney and who was also the Uncle of Mignon. He had a Daughter which Grandier had visited too familiarly; she became sickly and languishing; She had an intimate Friend named Marthale Pelletier, whose Fortune being very mean, she engag'd to serve her upon this occasion, and was always near her during her indisposition. This Friend was so affectionate and faithful to her, that at the Expence of her own Reputation, she charg'd her self with the Child, and took care to provide it a Nurse; but this kept not Persons from believing that this Child was rather the issue of her, who had been so long retir'd and languishing, than of her who had been charitable enough to be willing in a Case of necessity, to own her self to be the Mother. Trinquant having a knowledge of the Rumors which ran about to the disadvantage of his Daughter, caus'd Martha le Pelletier to be put in Prison, to oblige her to make a Declaration concerning the Birth of the Child, which she had put into the hands of the Nurse, She own'd her self to be the Mother; and promised to bring it up with much care, that Justice should have no hold of her. The publick laugh'd at this Proceeding, the Declaration was not believ'd, and Trinquant remain'd but the more mortified.

Sect. 11.

This Affair was upon these Terms, when Barot was so ill treated by Grandier, which was the occasion of the meeting together of Trinquant, Mignon and of Menuau the King's Advocate, who was the Kinsman, and intimate Friend of Mignon and who was seiz'd with a violent Love Passion, wherein he had Grandier for his Rival, and that a Favourite Rival; It was there resolv'd to destroy him, or at least to drive him out of the Country of Loudun. A little while after, there was produc'd against him an Information before the Official of Poitiers, in the name of the Promoter; They accus'd him for having debauch'd some Women, and some Maidens; for being impious and profane; for never saying his Breviary, and for having layn with a Woman even in his own Church. His Accusers were Cherbonneau, and Bougreau, Two Pitiful Fellows of the very Scum of the People. The Official having receiv'd the Information, commission'd Lewis Chauvet, Lieutenant Civil, and Arch-priest of Saint Marcolle, and of the Country of Loudun, to inform joyntly with him.

Sect. 12.

In the mean time, Duthibaut, a rich and powerful Man, being in the Interests of the Adversaries of Grandier, spoke very disadvantageously of him in the Presence of the Marquis du Bellai, and made bloody Reproaches against him. This was reported to Grandier, who testified his Resentment in such cutting Terms, that

Duthibaut lifted up the Cane which he had in his hand, and struck him, although he was attir'd in his Priestly Habit, and ready to enter into the Church of Saint Cross, whither, he went to assist at the Service. Grandier being inrag'd at this. Affront and believing he should not have right done him so soon in that Province, as at Paris, he chose to go thither with his Complaints. But whilst he made this journey, they inform'd against him at Loudun, and there proceeded to the Hearing of inconsiderable Witnessess whom they had procur'd. Trinquant made Oath first to encourage the others, and gave Caution in the Action of the Informers. The Information being made, it was sent to the Bishop of Poitiers, near whose Person the secret Adversaries of Grandier had very powerful Friends. Besides this, he happen'd to infringe the Rights of the Bishop, in giving a Dispensation of the Banns for the Marriage of Delagarde, who dwelt in the Town of Mons. His Enemies knew so well how to aggravate this Encroachment, and to prepossess the Mind of that Bishop, that he deliver'd out against him a Warrant for the seizing of his Person, conceiv'd in these Words.

Sect. 13.

Henry Lewis Chateigner of Rochpozai by divine Mercy, Bishop of Poitiers, having seen the Accusations and Informations given to us by the Archpriest of Loudun, against Urban Grandier Priest, and Parson of Saint Peter in the Market of Loudun, by Virtue of a Commission granted by us to the aforesaid Areh-priest, and in his absence to the Prior of Chasseignes; Having also seen the Conclusions of our Promoter thereupon: We have ordain'd, and do ordain, that the said Grandier, so accusd, be brought without Tumult into the Prison of our Episcopal Palace at Poitiers, if he can be apprehended, if not, he shall be cited at his House by the chief Apparitor, Priest or Clark tonsurate, to appear within Three Days; And moreover by the chief Sergeant Royal, with the Request of the secular Arm: and to whom, and to every one of them, we give Power and Commandment to perform the same, whatsoever Oppositions or Appeals notwithstanding, concerning this Matter, and the said Grandier being heard, to take by our Promoter such Conclusions against him, as he shall see fit to be done. Given at Dissai the Twenty Second Day of October. 1629. Thus sign'd in the Original, Henry Lewis Bishop of Poitiers.

Sect. 14.

Grandier was then at Paris, when the Warrant was delive'd out against him, he had cast himself at the King's Feet, and complain'd of the Blows with the Cane, which Dubithaut had given him publickly; The King had referr'd this Affair to the Parliament, that a Process might be made and concluded against Duthibaut, his Action having appear'd very insolent, and worthy of a severe Correction; but he made use of violent Recriminations against his Adversary, he accus'd him of being a Scandalous Person, of an ill Life, and very Criminal, and produc'd for the Proof of these

Accusations, the Warrant for this Apprehension which was newly granted by the Bishop of of Poitiers, which was the Cause that the Court, before Justice was done, sent Grandier back to the Bishop, to clear himself of the Crimes laid to his Charge. He return'd to Loudun, and in a few Days came to Poitiers, to put himself into a Condition for his Defence, but could not do it; for he was no sooner Arrived, but he was arrested Prisoner by an Usher of the Court, named Chatri. Although it was the Fifteenth of November, and that the Bishops Prison was cold and dark, he remain'd however there more than two Months, and began to believe, that he would never get out of this Affair. His Enemies at least seem'd very much induc'd to think so; Duthibaut thought himself secur'd from his Prosecutions, the Issue whereof could not but be very troublesome to him; and Barot caus'd a Devolution to be executed upon his Benifice, to the Profit of Ismael Boulieau a Priest and one of his Heirs.

Sect. 15.

In the mean while, the eagerness of the Conspirators happen'd to abate, for fear of the Expences; for altho they were all very Wealthy, yet each of them excus'd themselves, as much as 'twas possible, from defraying the Charges, which could not be small, the Instruction of the Process being made at Poitiers; where the Witnesses were oblig'd to make a personal Appearance, to give their Informations, and to be confronted to the Person Accus'd. But the Animosity of Trinquant was more powerful than that of all the rest; he in the end overcame those Difficulties, and acted so, that his Associates contributed to the Expence as well as himself, and that the Prosecution was not given over.

Sect. 16.

The principal Article of the Accusation could not be made good. It was laid to Grandier's charge, That he had Debauch'd Women and Maidens; but there were no Plaintiffs produc'd; these Women and Maids were not nam'd; there was not any Witness that Swore directly to this Fact; and the greater part acknowledg'd, at last, That they never heard a word concerning many things which they found writ in the Informations. At last, it being necessary to proceed to the Judgment of the Process; there was admitted into the number of the Judges, the Advocate Richard, who was Trinquant's Kinsman; and the Bishop was beset by the secret Adversaries of Grandier, who ceas'd not to set him out in the blackest Colours, and who knew how to mix so much Probability with their Calumnies, that on the 3d of January 1630, he was Condemn'd to Fast with Bread and Water, by way of Penance, every Friday during three Months; and interdicted from Divine Offices, in the Diocess of Poitiers, for five Years; and in the Town of Loudun, for ever.

Sect. 17.

On both sides there was an Appeal from this Sentence; Grandier appeal'd to the Archbishop of Bourdeaux; and his Adversaries, in the Name of the Promoter of the Officiality, by Writ of Error, to the Parliament of Paris; to the intent only to Perplex him, and to bring him into such a Condition, as not to be able to undergo the burden of all the Affairs, with which they sought to overwhelm him. But they succeeded not as they desir'd; for he prepar'd himself, and had his Cause Pleaded before the Parliament. But it being necessary to hear yet a greater number of Witnesses, who dwelt in a Place very far off, the Court remitted the Cognisance thereof to the Presidial of Poitiers, to judge definitively. The Lieutenant Criminal of Poitiers, gave Instruction for renewing the Process, as well by the Re-examination and Confronting of the Witnesses, as by the Fulmination of a Monitory. This Instruction was not favourable to his Accusers; there were found Contradictions in the Witnesses, who would yet persist; and there were many others, who ingenuously acknowledg'd, That they had been tamper'd with: One of the Accusers desisted from the Action which-he had begun; and declar'd, with some Witnesses, who also gave over, That they had been put on, and solicited by Trinquant. At the same time, it came to the know ledge of Mechin and Boulieau Priests, That they were made to say, in their Deposition, things that they had never thought of; they were desirous to disown them by Writings under their Hands; and that of Mechin being found, we need not fear to insert it here, altho' it be long, as well as some other Writings, which shall be inserted hereafter; because we believe that this Exactness will contribute to the Satisfaction of the

Reader, and leave no cause to doubt of the truth of those things which are contain'd in this History.

Sect. 18.

"I Gervase Mechin Priest, Vicar of the Church of St. Peter, in the Market of Loudun, do certifie by this present Writing, and Sign'd with my Hand for the discharge of my Conscience, upon a certain Rumour which is caus'd to be spread abroad, That in an Information made by Giles Robert Archpriest, against Urban Grandier Priest, Parson of St. Peters; in which Information, the said Robert solicited me to depose, that I have said, That I found the said Grandier lying with Women and Maids all at length in St. Peter's Church, the Doors being shut: Also, That several times, at undue hours, both by Day and by Night, I had seen Maids and Women come to find the said Grandier in his Chamber; and that some of the said Women continued there, from one of the Clock in the Afternoon, till two or three in the Morning; and caus'd their Suppers to be brought thither by their Maid-Servants, who immediately retir'd: Also, That I had seen the said Grandier in the Church, the Doors being open; and some Women being entred there, he shut them. Not desiring that such Reports should any longer continue, I declare by these Presents, That I have never seen, nor found the said Grandier with Women, or Maids, in the Church, the Doors being shut; nor alone with them by themselves, but when he has spoken to them, they were in Company, and the Doors wide open:

And as touching the Posture, I think it sufficiently clear'd by my Confrontation, and that the said Grandier and Women were sat down a good distance one from the other: As also, I never saw Women and Maids enter into the said Grandier's Chamber, neither by Day nor Night. Indeed, 'tis true, I have heard a great many People come and go very late at Night, but I cannot say who it was; also, That there lyeth always a Brother of the said Grandier near his Chamber; and that I have neither known, that Women or Maids have caus'd their Suppers to be brought thither; neither have I depos'd, That I had never seen him say his Breviary, because that would be contrary to truth; forasmuch as that he borrow'd mine several times, which he took, and said his Hours. And in like manner, I declare, That I never saw him shut the Doors of the Church; and that in all the Discourses which I saw him have with the Women, I never beheld any thing unbeseeming, nor that he did even any ways touch them, but that they only spoke together; and that if there be found in my Deposition, any thing contrary to what is said above, it is contrary to my knowledge; and it was never Read to me, lest I should not have Sign'd. This is what I have said to give a testimony to the Truth. Made the last Day of October, 1630; Signed thus, G. Mechin."

Sect. 19.

The Presidial of Poitiers gave his Judgment the 25th of May 1631. whereby Grandier was sent away Absolv'd, for the present, of the Accusation made against him. He triumph'd and insulted over his Adversaries with so much Haughtiness, as if he had been wholly clear of this Business. In the mean time, it was necessary that he should present himself before the Tribunal of the Archbishop of Bourdeaux, to whom he had appeal'd, and that he might obtain there a Sentence of Justification. This Prelate, a little time after that this Judgment had been given at Poitiers, came to visit his Abbey of St. Jouin les Marnes, which is but three Leagues from Loudun. Grandier prepar'd himself to appear before him; and his Adversaries, who seem'd to have lost their Courage, did heartily Defend themselves. This is the Sentence of Absolution, which the Archbishop pronounc'd, after he had proceeded to a new Instruction of the Process.

Sect. 20.

"Henry d'Escoubleau de Sourdis, by the Grace of God Archbishop of Bourdeaux, Primate of Aquitain, To all Persons, to whom these present Letters shall come, Greeting. Know ye, That a Process being begun between Urban Grandier Priest and Appellant, from the Sentence given by the Most Reverend the Bishop of Poitiers, the 3d of January 1630, and from all that which ensued thereupon on the one part, and James Cherbonneau, joint Promoter of the Officiality, cited to Appear on the other part; (saving that their qualities may be prejudicial to either) our Sentence of the 30th of August last, with the Pieces there mention'd, being seen by us; the Examinations given by Giles Robert Archpriest, Gervase

Mechin, and Boulieau Priests; Our Sentence given upon a Petition, presented to us by the said Grandier the 15th of October last, at the bottom whereof is our Decree; and another Petition, which the said Grandier had presented us the 3d of this present Month; A Petition presented to us by James Caille, Porter to the Sieur de la Motte of Champdenier, the 4th of the said Month, our Decree being at the bottom thereof. Our Verbal Process of the 7th of the said Month, containing the Interrogatories put by us to the said Caille, and the Answers made by him; Our Judgment of the said Fourth Day of this Month; The Monitory deliver'd by us to our Promoter, with the Certificate of the Publication which was made in the Town of Loudun; Another Petition presented to us by the said Grandier the Seventeenth of the said Month, and our Decree thereupon, with the Determinations of our Promoter, to whom the whole has been communicated; All being view'd and consider'd, and the Advice of the Counsel taken thereupon after the Invocation of the Holy Ghost. We by our Sentence and Judgment definitive, have disanull'd, and do disanul the said Sentence; from which there is made an Appeal, and for want of other Proof made by our Promoter, have dismist, and do dismiss the said Appellant, absolv'd from the Crimes and Offences laid to his Charge, and have taken off definitively the Interdiction a Divinis, mention'd in the said Decree, Injoyning him, that he behave himself orderly and modestly in his Charge, according to the Holy Decrees, and Canonical Constitutions, without Prejudice to his Recovery of Satisfaction for Damages, and Interests, and

Restitution of the Profits of his Benefices, in such manner as he shall think good. Made by us at our Palace belonging to the Abbey of Saint Jouin les Marnes, the Twentieth of November. 1631. Signed Henry de Sourdis Archbishop of Bourdeaux, and pronounc'd by us the Register, to the said Grandier, who was then in the same Abbey the Day and Year above mention'd."

Sect. 21.

The Archbishop considering the animosity, and contrivances of the Enemies of Grandier, and having an esteem for him, for the take of his good qualities, advis'd him to change his Benefices, and to withdraw himself from a place, where so powerful a conspiracy was made against him. But he was not capable of following such wholesome advice, both Love and Hatred had too much blinded him, he hated his Enemies with too great a passion to satisfie them in that Point; But he was yet more violently possest by Love; and although this was divided towards different Objects, there was one nevertheless, which was the true Subject of his tender Affections, to which his Heart was ty'd by such strong bands, that far from being able to break them, he had not the power to remove himself any distance from her. He return'd then to Loudun, with a Branch of Laurel in his Hand, as an Ensign of his Victory.

Sect. 22.

Persons that were indifferently concern'd, were scandaliz'd at his Conduct, wherein he shew'd so little Modesty; his Enemies were enrag'd, and his own Friends disapprov'd it. He took possession of his Benefices, and scarcely gave himself Leisure to breath; so that being wholly fill'd with the Resentment of the Injury that had been done him by Duthibaut, he begun his Suit against him, and drove it so far, that he obtain'd a Decree from the Chamber of Tournelle, whither Duthibaut was sent for, and reprov'd, and was condemn'd to divers Fines and Reparations, and to pay the Charge of the Process.

Sect. 23.

Grandiers not being satisfied with the right he had done himself in this Affair, resolv'd to carry on his Revenge, as far as he could legally do it, and he began to sue his Secret Enemies for his Reparations, Damages and Interests, and for the Restitution of the Profits of his Benefices, according to the Sentence of the Archbishop of Bourdeaux. It was in vain that his principal friends would have disswaded him upon the Consideration of what had already happen'd to him, which ought to make him know what his Enemies were like to do, if he attempted every way to drive them to Extremities, and to interest their Purse, at which they would not be less sensible, than they had shew'd themselves in what concern'd their Reputation: But his Stars drew him to a Precipice; Divine Providence, whose Ways are impenetrable, would punish him for his Pride and Debauchery, and suffer, at the same time to appear upon the Theater of the World, one of the Tragical Acts, which false Zeal, or Impiety cause to be represented there from time to time; and which never fail to find in the Credulity of the People an Approbation and Applause, which the Experience of what is past, ought to hinder them from giving so lightly, and which are the evident Signs of the Weakness of Man's Understanding.

Sect. 24.

When there was to be chosen a new Confessor for the Ursuline Nuns, Grandier had been propos'd; His Enemies nois'd it abroad, that he was very desirous to be pitch'd upon; but that he was rejected because of his evil Manners, and that the Prioress had a great Dispute with one of his intimate Friends upon that Subject. But there are many Persons who writ to the contrary, and that the Nuns had caus'd him to be treated with, upon the design they had to desire him to be their Confessor, which he absolutely refus'd, although he had been very much sollicited. It is at least certain that these Maidens had dwelt Seven or Eight Years at Loudun, without his having given them any Visit; and in the Year 1634, when he and they were brought Face to Face, it appear'd that they had never seen him. Father Tranquille has also own'd it in one of his Books, that Grandier had never intermeddled in their Concerns. There is then no Likelihood that after he had so exceedingly slighted them, he should have a Design to become their Confessor, or that he ever propos'd it to them.

Sect. 25.

The Report of the Possession was a great while whisper'd about the Town, before it broke out. The Secret could not be so well kept, but that some Knowledge of what past within the Convent spread abroad; There was made the Experiment of all the Sleights of managing the Body, which they intended to make use of; There Mignon set in order the Springs of his Intreagues to have them play, when they should be in a Condition; He caus'd his Schollars to be exercis'd in feigning to fall into Convulsions, to make Contorsions and Postures of their Bodies, to the End they might gain a Habit, and he forget nothing for their Instruction, to make them able to appear true Demoniacks. 'Twas believ'd that he kept some of the simple and overcredulous Nuns in their Error, and in the Fear which they had at first, and that by Degrees he insinuated into them that which he was desirous they should at last strongly believe, and which 'twas thought they really did so; How little Resemblance soever of Truth there might be in this Imposture, He drew others into the Party, who had no Knowledge of it in the Beginning; He secur'd himself of the Fidelity of all those who were engag'd as well by Oaths, as by the Consideration of the Interest of the Glory of GOD, and the Catholick Church, persuading them, that it would draw great Advantages by this Enterprize, which would serve to confound the Hereticks, of whom the Town was very full; and be rid of a Pernicous Curate, who by his Debaucheries had dishonour'd his Character, who was also a Secret Heretick, and who drew a Numerous Company of Souls into Hell; Adding, that their Convent would not fail, to obtain by this Means an extraordinary Reputation, and that Gifts and Alms that would be bestow'd, would bring a great Plenty, which was then wanting; In a Word, be forgot nothing that he believ'd would contribute to his Designs, and when he saw that the Business was very near to the Point of Perfection which he wish'd, he began to exercise the Superior, and Two other Nuns; He call'd at first to his Exorcisms only Peter Barre, Curate of Saint James of Chinon, and Canon of Saint Meme. He was a Bigot and an Hypocrite, almost of the same Character with Mignon, but much more Melancholick and more Enthusiastick, and who practis'd a Thousand Extravagancies, that he might pass for a Saint. He came to Loudun at the Head of his Parishioners, whom he led in Procession, coming all the Way on Foot, that he might the better put a Gloss upon his Hypocrisy After that these Two pretend-Exorcists had busied themselves together very privately for Ten or Twelve Days, they believ'd this Act was in a Condition to be expos'd upon the Stage to the Eyes of the Publick and for this Effect, they resolv'd to inform the Magistrate of the Lamentable Condition of these Nuns, to whom they employ'd Granger Curate of Venier, a Man malicious and impudent, fear'd and hated of all the Priests in the Country, because being in Favour with the Bishop of

Poitiers, he many times did them ill Offices with him; He had never any Difference with Grandier; But had even receiv'd some Services of him, which did not hinder him from suffering himself to be tamper'd with by Mignon and Trinquant, and entring openly into the League with them. He went then on Monday the Eleventh of October, 1532, to find William de Cerizai de la Gueriniere Bailiff of the Loudunois, and Lewis Chauvet Lieutenant Civil, and he intreated them, on the Behalf of the Exorcists, to come to the Convent of the Ursulines to see the Two Nuns possessed by evil Spirits, representing to them that it concern'd them to be present at the Exorcisms, and to see the strange and almost incredible Effects of this Possession. He told them, that there was one who answer'd in Latin to all Questions that could be put to Her, although she had no Knowledge of the Language before this Accident. The Two Magistrates went to the Convent, either to assist at the Exorcisms, and to Authorize them, if they found themselves oblig'd, or to stop the Course of this Illusion, if they judg'd the Possession to be feign'd and counterfeited. Mignon met them attir'd with his Surplice and Tippit, He told them that the Nuns had been disturb'd for Fifteen Days with Apparitions and frightful Visions, and that after that, the Mother Superior, and Two other Nuns had been visibly possest for Eight or Ten Days by evil Spirits, but that they had been driven out of their Bodies, as well by the Ministry of him. as of Barre, and some other Religious Carmelites; But that on Saturday Night the Sixteenth of the Month, the Mother Superior nam'd Jane Belsiel, the

Daughter of the late Baron of Cose, of the Country of Xaintonge, and a lay Sister, the Daughter of Maignoux, had been tormented afresh, and that they were possest again by the same Spirits; That they had discover'd in their exorcising; that this was done by a new Pact or Covenant, the Symbol or Mark whereof were Roses, as the Token of the First had been Three black Thornes. That the evil Spirits had not been willing to name themselves during the First Possession, but that he who then possest the Mother Prioress call'd himself the Enemy of GOD, and said, his Name was Astaroth, and that he who possest the Lay Sister, nam'd himself Sabulun. At last he told them that the possess'd were now taking their Rest, and he desir'd them to deferr the Visit to another Hour of the Day. These Two Magistrate; were ready to go out, when a Nun came to give them Notice, that the Persons possess'd were again tormented; They went up with Mignon and Granger into an upper Chamber, furnish'd with Seven little Beds, in one of which lay the Lay Sister, and the Prioress in another. This last was encompass'd with some Carmelites, with some of the Nuns of the Convent, with Mathurin Rosseau Priest and Canon of Saint Cross, and Manouri the Chirurgion. The Superior had no sooner discover'd the Two Magistrates, but she had violent Commotions, and perform'd strange Actions; She made a Noise which was like to that of a Pig; She sunk down into the Bed, and contracted her self into the Postures and Grimaces of a Person who is out of his Wits; A Carmelite Friar was at her right Hand, and Mignon at her left, the last of these put his Two Fingers into her

Mouth and presupposing that the was possess'd, us'd many Conjurations, and spake to the Devil, who answer'd him after this Manner, in their First Dialogue. Mignon demanded, Propter quam Causam ingressus es in Corpus hujus Virginis? For what Reason hast thou enter'd into the Body of this Virgin? Answ. Causa Animositatis; Upon the Account of Animosity. Q. Per quod Pactum? By what Pact? A. Per Flores, By Flowers. Q. Quales? What Flowers? A. Rosas. Roses. Q. Quis misit? Who sent them? A. Urbanus. Urban. She pronounc'd not this Word before she had stammer'd many times, as if she had done it by constraint. Q. Dic Cognomen. Tell his Surname. A. Grandier. This was again a Word which she pronounc'd not, till she had been very much urg'd to Answer. Q. Dic qualitatem; Mention his Quality. A. Sacerdos, A Priest. Q. Cujus Ecclesiæ? of what Church? A. Sancti Petri, Of Saint Peters. She utter'd these last Words very boldly. Q. Quæ Persona attulit Flores? What Person brought the Flowers? A. Diabolica, a Diabolical Person. She came to her Senses after this last Answer, She pray'd to GOD, and she cryed to eat a little Bread which was brought her; she put it from her however a little after, saying she was not able to swallow it because it was too dry. There was brought to her Liquid Sweatmeats of which she eat but very little, because she was frequently perplex'd by the Return of her Convulsions. The Bailiff and Lieutenant who stood near her, and observ'd with good Attention that which past, seeing that they gave no more any Sign of a Possession, withdrew towards the Window; Mignou came near them and said, that in the

Action which was presented, there was something like the History of Peter Gaufredi, who was put to Death by Virtue of a Decree of the Parliament of Aix in Province; to whom there was no Answer made, but the Lieutenant Civil told him, that it would have been proper to urge the Prioress upon this Cause of Animosity, whereof she had spoke in her Answers, upon this he excus'd himself, that he was not allow'd to make any Questions of Curiosity. The Lay Sister had also several Convulsions, and the motions of her Body seem'd very extraordinary. They were desirous to propose some Questions to her, but she cry'd out Twice, To the other, to the other; which was interpreted, as if she had been willing to say, that 'twas only the Superior, who was sufficiently instructed to answer. The Judges retir'd, and understood the same Questions had been already put divers times to the Nuns, especially in the Presence of Paul Grouard Judge of the Provostship at Loudun, and of Trinquant the King's Attorney, of which, and all other things they had seen and heard, they drew up a Verbal Process, and sign'd it.

Sect. 26.

The Noise which this Possession began to make, produc'd different Opinions; the Devout Souls who regarded with respect and veneration, the Ministers of the Church, and who were inclin'd to receive blind-fold, and without inquiry all that was presented to them on their part, could not perswade themselves that Barre, Mignon, the Carmelites, Ursulines, Priests, Friars and

Nuns, could possibly be the Authors of so wicked a Contrivance, or invent so devilish an Imposture. But the Worldlings not judging so charitably, were more inclin'd to suspect the whole; they could not apprehend how these Devils, who happen'd to go out at one Door, did as quickly re-enter at another, to the confusion of the Ministers of him, by whose Authority they had been dispossest They were astonish'd, that the Devils of the Superior spake Latin, rather than that of the Lay Sister; and that she spake not better than a Scholar of the second Form. They made reflections upon this, that Mignon had not been willing to interrogate her upon the cause of the Animosity, of which he himself had spoken, and they concluded that it was because the Devil was at the end of his Lesson; that he had not as yet learnt any further, and that he was oblig'd to play the same part before all sorts of Spectators, seeing he had spoke nothing before the Bayliff, but what he had already said before the Judge of the Provostship; they were not ignorant, that some time before, there had been a meeting of all the most violent Enemies of Grandier, at the Village of Puidardane, in one of the Trinquant's Houses, and there found a great deal of probability, that what was acted there, had a Relation to the Possession. They could not also relish that Mignon had so readily explain'd himself upon the conformity which he saw in his Affair with that of Gaufredy the Priest executed at Aix. And in fine, they had rather that other Friers than Carmelites had been call'd to their Exorcisms, because the Quarrels of these good Fathers with Grandier, had been known to all the World, by the Sermons which he had made against a priviledged Altar, of which they so much boasted, and by the contempt which he publickly shew'd of their Preachers.

Sect. 27.

The next Day after, being the Twelfth of October, the Bayliff, and the Lieutenant Civil accompanied with the Canon Roussau, and follow'd by their Register, return'd to the Convent of the Ursulines, upon the Knowledge that they had, that they did continue the Exorcisms. They call'd Mignon aside, and remonstrated to him, that this Affair would be henceforward of such importance, that it was necessary that they, the Magistrates, should be acquainted when they would proceed in it; they added, that it was convenient that he should forbear to Exorcise, and that other Exorcists, should be call'd by those of the Magistracy, to avoid the suspitions of Suggestion, which his quality, of being Confessor, might justly give, by reason of the Mortal hatred which had been between him, or his near Kindred, and Grandier, who had been nam'd by the Superior as the Author of the Pact and Magick which was now in Question. Mignon answer'd them, that neither he, nor the Nuns, would be against their being present at the Exorcisings, and declar'd to them that Barre had exorcis'd that Day, but he did not promise not to Exocrise any more for the future, although since that time he had always abstain'd from exorcising in Publick. Barre drawing near, told the Magistrates, that in this exorcising, there past very surprising things; That he had learnt from the Superior, That there were in her Body Seven Devils, whose Names he had taken in writing; That Astaroth was the first in order; That Grandier had given the Pact, between him and the Devils, under the Symbol of Roses, to one named Jane Pivart, who had put them into the Hands of a Maiden, who had brought them to the Convent, over the Walls of the Garden; That the Prioress had said, that this happen'd to her on Saturday Night, Hora Secunda Nocturna, at two of the Clock in the Morning, which were the very Words she us'd. That she would not Name the Maiden, but had nam'd Pivart; That he demanded of her who that Pivart was? And that she answer'd him. est pauper Magus, 'tis a poor Magician; That he had urg'd her upon this Word, Magus, Magician; and that she repli'd Magicianus and Civis, Magician and Citizen. After this Discourse, the Magistrates went up into the Chamber of the possessed, which they found fill'd with a great Number of inquisitive Persons; she made not any Wry-Face, nor did any Action of a Person possest, neither during the Mass which Mignon celebrated, nor before nor after the Elevation of the Sacrament; They Sung also with the other Nuns; the Lay-sister only being sat down by the help of those who were nearest to her, had a great trembling in her Arms and Hands. This is all that was observ'd, and thought worthy to be inserted into the Verbal Process of the Morning Work of that Day.

Sect. 28.

The Design of the Judges being to take an exact Account of this Affair, return'd to the Convent about Three or Four of the Clock in the Afternoon, with Ireneus of Saint Marte, the Sieur Deshumeaux; They found the Chamber again fill'd with People of all conditions; the Superior had at first great Convulsions in their presence; she thrust out her Tongue, she Foam'd and Froth'd at the Mouth, well nigh as if she had been really in a Fit of Madness, or was tormented by an Evil Spirit. Barre demanded of the Devil, when he would go out? Those that were near, heard this answer, Cras mane, to Morrow Morning. The Exorcist insisted, and ask'd him why he would not go out of her then? The Answer was Pactum, a Contract, or it is a Contract. The word Sacerdos, Priest, was afterwards pronounc'd, then that of Finis, or Finit, an end, or does end; for this good Nun, or the Devil spoke between their Teeth, and 'twas not easie to understand her; Prayers were made, and Exorcisms, and Adjurations, but she answer'd nothing. The Pix was put upon her Head, and this Action was accompanied with Prayers and Litanies, which had no effect; only some People observ'd, she was tormented with more Violence, when the Names of certain Saints were pronounc'd, as Saint Augustine, Saint Jerom, Saint Anthony, and Saint Mary Magdalene. Barre commanded her at that time, (as he did very often since) to say that she gave her Heart and Soul to GOD; she did it freely, and without constraint: But when he bid her say, that she gave her Body, she made resistance, and seem'd not to Obey, but by force; as if she were willing to say, the Devil possest her Body, but not her Soul. After she had made this last Answer, she recover'd her natural condition; her countenance was also Pleasant and Calm, as if she had not undergone any extraordinary Agitation; and looking upon Barre, with a smiling Countenance, she told him, That there was now no more of Satan in her. She was ask'd whether she rememb'red the Questions which had been put to her, and her Answers? she replied no. Afterwards she took some Food, and told the Company, that the first Pact had been given her about Ten a Clock at Night; That she was then in Bed, and that there were several Nuns in her Chamber; she felt that something took one of her Hands, and after having put into it Three Black Thorns, they clos'd it; That this being done, without her having seen any person, she was troubled, and seiz'd with a great Terror, which made her call the Nuns who were in her Chamber; That they came near her, and found the Three Thorns in her Hand. As she continued to speak, the Lay-Sister had some Convulsions, the particulars whereof the Judges could not take notice, because this happen'd whilst they went nigh the Superior, and were attentive to her Discourse. This Day's work concluded with an Adventure pleasant enough; whilst Barre made his Prayers and Exorcisms, there happen'd a great Noise amongst the Company; and some said that they saw a Cat come down the Chimney; This Cat was carefully search'd for, throughout the Chamber; it threw it self upon the Tester of the Bed; it was catch'd upon the Superiors Bed, where Barre had made many Signs of the

Cross; upon it, and added several adjurations, but at last it was known to be one of the Cats of the Convent, and no Magician, or Demon.

Sect. 29.

The Company being ready to withdraw, the Exorcist said that it was requisite to burn the Roses, where the Second Pact had been put; and in effect he took a great Nosegay of White Musk Roses, already wither'd, and cast them into the Fire; there happen'd no Sign upon this occasion, and the Roses caus'd no ill smell in burning. Nevertheless, they promised the Company that next Day they should see wonderful Events, That the Devil should go out; That he should speak more plainly than he had hitherto; and That they would urge him to give such convincing and manifest Signs of his going out; that no Body should be able to doubt of the Truth of this Possession. Rene Herve the Lieutenant Criminal, said that he ought to ask her concerning the Name Pivart; Barre answer'd in Latine, and hoc dicet, and puellam nominabit, she shall tell it, and Name the Maid, meaning to speak of her, who had brought the Roses.

Sect. 30.

Grandier, who at first made a Mock at these Exorcisms, and the Testimony of these pretended Devils, seeing that this Affair was push'd on so far, presented a Petition to the Bayliff the same Day, being the Twelfth of Octocter, by which he remonstrated to him, That

Mignon had exorcis'd these Nuns in his presence; That they had nam'd him as the Author of their Possession; That it was an Imposture and a perfect Calumny suggested against his Honour, by a Man who rais'd another false Accusation against him, of which he had clear'd himself; That he requested him to sequester these Nuns, who pretended to be possest, and cause them to be examined separately; That if he found any appearance of Possession, he would be pleas'd to nominate some Ecclesiastical Persons, of a requisite Ability and Honesty, not suspected by him the Petitioner, as Mignon and his Adherents were, to exorcise them if there were occasion, and to make his Verbal Process of that which should pass at the Exorcisms, to the end, that he the Petitioner might be able afterwards to provide as he should see cause. The Bayliff gave Grandier an Act of his Issues and Conclusions, according to his desire, and told him; that 'twas Barre who did exorcise the Day before, by the Orders of the Bishop of Poictiers, as he had boasted in his presence; adding, that he declar'd this to him, to the end that he might provide so as he thought fit; by which Grandier understood that he should be referr'd to his Bishop. Sect. 31. The next Day, October the Thirteenth, the Bayliff, Lieutenant Civil, the Lieutenant Criminal, the King's Attorney, the Lieutenant of the Provostship, and Deshumeaux, follow'd by the Clerks of the Two Jurisdictions, went to the Convent at Eight of the Clock in the Morning; they past the first Gate which they found open, Mignon open'd the second, and introduc'd them into the Parlour; he told them that the Nuns were preparing themselves for the Communion, and entreated them to retire to a House, which was on the other side of the Street, whence he would cause them to be call'd within less than an Hour. They went out after they had given him notice of the Petition presented by Grandier to the Bayliff the Day before. The Hour being come, they entred all into the Chappel of the Convent, and Barre coming to the Gate with Mignon, told them, that he came from exorcising the two possessed Persons, who had been delivered from the unclean Spirits by their Ministry; that they had toil'd at the Exorcisms since Seven a Clock in the Morning; That there had pass'd great wonders, of which they would draw up an Act; but that they had not judg'd fit to admit other Persons there than the Exorcists. The Bayliff remonstrated to them, that this Procedure was not reasonable; That it render'd them suspected of Imposture and Suggestion in the things which were said and done the foregoing Days, by the variation that was found in them, and that the Superior having publickly accus'd Grandier of Magick; they ought not to do any thing clandestinly, since that Accusation, but in the Face of Justice and the Publick. That they had taken upon them a great deal of boldness to pray so many People, and of such Quality, to wait the space of an Hour, and in the mean while to proceed in the Exorcisms in private. That they would make the Verbal Process, as they had already done in other things, which past in their presence. Barre answer'd, that the end they aim'd at, was the expulsion of the Devils; That their Design had succeeded; And that they shou'd see a great good turn to happen upon it, because he had expresly commanded the evil Spirits to produce within Eight Days some great effect, capable of hind'ring for the future any one's doubting the Truth of the Possession, and deliverance of the Nuns. The Magistrates drew up a Verbal Process of this Discourse, and of all that had proceeded in it; but the Lieutenant Criminal only would not Sign it.

Sect. 32.

Although the Impostures of the Enemies of Grandier were not very ingeniously contriv'd, he could not but dread their Malice, their Impudence, and their Credit. He saw combin'd against him the Lieutenant Criminal, the Advocate, and the King's Attorney, Mignon, and his Brother the Sieur de la Coulee, President of the General Assessors, Granger, Curate of Venier, Duthibaut and Barot. But that which did terrifie him most, was this; That he had understood, that they had engag'd on their side Rene Memin Sieur de Silly, Major of the Town, a Man who had very much Credit, as well for his Riches, as the many offices he possest, and above all for his Friends, amongst whom might be reckon'd Cardinal Richelieu, who had not forgot many singular kindnesses which heretofore he had receiv'd of him in the Country, when he was but a Curate or Prior, and which had continued even since his Elevation, and principally at the time of his first Disgrace. All these considerations oblig'd Grandier not to neglect this Affair; and to this effect, believing that he was tacitly referr'd by the Bailiff of Loudun, to the Bishop of Poictiers, he went to find him at Dissai, whither he was accompanied by a Priest of Loudun, nam'd John Buron. The Steward of the Bishop who was call'd du Pui, having told him that the Bishop was indispos'd, he addrest himself to his Almoner, and pray'd him to let him understand, that he was come to present him the Verbal Processes, which the Officers of Loudun had made of all things which had past in the Convent of the Ursulines; and to complain of the impostures and calumnies which were disperst against him. The Almoner returning told, on the behalf of the Bishop, in the presence of du Pui, Buron, and Sieur de la Brosse, that he was to Address himself before the Judges Royal, and that he should be very glad that he had Justice done him in this Affair. Grandier having been able to do nothing more with the Bishop, return'd to Loudun, and applied himself again to the Bailiff. He acquainted him with that which befel him in his Journey to Dissai, reiterated his Complaints of the calumnies which were industriously promoted against him, and besought him to acquaint the Kings Justices with the Truth of this business, protesting that he would make application at Court to obtain a Commission, to bring an Information against Mignon and his Complices, and demanding to be put under the protection of the King, and safeguard of Justice, seeing that his Honour and Life were attempted. The Bailiff gave him an Act of his Protestations, with prohibitions to all forts of Persons to speak ill of him or to hurt him, this Order was of the Twenty Eighth of October, 1632.

Sect. 33.

Mignon seeing himself accus'd in his turn for having Plotted a Contrivance to destroy Grandier, came to make his Declaration to the Bailiff, without allowing his Jurisdiction; That Grandier and he being Priests of the Diocess of Poctiers, he ought not to address himself to other Judges than their Bishop to accuse him of the most horrible of all the Calumnies that Hell hath ever produc'd, and that he was ready to render himself to the Prison of the Officiality, to make known to all the World, that he did not shun the Light of Justice: He added, that he had protested his innocence the Day before, by Swearing on the Holy Sacrament of the Altar, in the presence of the Justices themselves, that he had never thought of the Calumny for which he was complain'd of, that he had given Grandier notice to put himself on his part, in a condition of defence; and to forbear in the mean time to accuse him of being a Calumniator; of which Words and Protestations the Bailiff decreed him an Act, which he caus'd to be signified to his Adversary.

Sect. 34.

Since the Thirteenth of October, that Barre had boasted of having expell'd the Devils out of the Two Nuns; they past some time without any talk of the Possession; Grandier however inclin'd not to believe that the business would stop there, nor that there had a Design to let him be quiet; he imagin'd that these Maids took time to study their part, and to exercise themselves in the presence of the Director of the Work, in order to act their parts the better, when it should be time to represent the other Acts of this Comedy. He fail'd not in his conjecture; for Rene Mannouri the Chirurgeon was sent the Twenty Second of November, to Gaspard Joubert a Physician, to pray him to come to the Convent of the Ursulines, and to get himself accompanied with the other Physicians of Loudun, in order to visit two Nuns who were again tormented by evil Spirits? Joubert being a Frank Man, and an Enemy of Imposture, and unwilling to go upon this occasion, but under the standard of Justice, went speedily to find the Bailiff, to know, if it was by his order, that Monnouri had call'd him? The Bailiff answered that he had not, and sent for Mannouri to know of him himself, by whose order he had spoke to Joubert; Mannouri declar'd, that the Maid belonging to the Convent, came to his House, and told him that the possessed had never been so ill treated as they were then; and that the Nuns pray'd him to get all the Physicians of Loudun, and some Chirurgeons, to come to the Convent. Upon which, the Bailiff sent for Grandier to tell him, that as he was nam'd the Author of the bewitching of the Nuns, he thought himself oblig'd to give him notice, that Barre was retun'd from Chinon the Day before, to renew the Exorcisms, and that the Report went about, that the Superior, and the Sister Clair, were a new tormented with Evil-Spirits, as they had been before. Grandier reply'd, that it was a continuation of the Conspiracies which had been made against him, which he had complain'd of at Court, and would again complain; That in the mean while, he besought him to resort always to the Convent with the other Officers to assist at the Exorcisms, and to call thither the Physicians; and that if they saw any Appearance of Possession, he would be pleas'd to sequester the Nuns, and to have them interrogated by other Exorcists, than Mignon and Barre, against whom he had very just Causes of Suspition. The Bailiff sent for the Kings Attorney, who gave his conclusions; Whereupon the Clerk was sent to the Convent, to know of Mignon and Barre if the Superior was again possest; and in case they answer'd affirmatively, he was order'd to tell them they were forbidden to proceed clandestinely in the Exorcisms, and that they were enjoyn'd to advertise the Bailiff, to the end that he might be there with the Physicians whom he would call, and the Officers whom he should think proper to accompany him, and all upon the Penalties thereunto belonging, without prejudice to the right of Grandier, upon the request made by him, for the sequestration of the possessed, and nomination of unsuspected Exorcists. Mignon and Barre having heard the reading of this Order, declar'd, without allowing the Jurisdiction of the Bailiff, that they were again call'd by the Nuns, to assist them in the continuation of a strange Disease, which they suppos'd to be a Possession of the Evil Spirits; that they had exorcis'd, even to the present Day, by Virtue of a Commission from the Bishop of Poictiers, the Date whereof was not yet expir'd, which Bishop they had nevertheless judg'd requisite to inform with the State of the Business, to the intent that he might come himself, or send such Exorcists as he should think good to act by his Orders, and to judge judicially of the present Possession, which had been treated as an imposture and illusion, to the great comtempt of the Glory of GOD, and the Catholick Religion; although the Maids who had been tormented, during the second Possession, had been visited by many Doctors of Physic, and by Chirurgeons and Apothecaries, who had all alike given their attestations; and also a great many Persons of Honour and Piety had seen the Wonders of GOD. In sum, that they should not hinder the Bailiff and other Officers, accompanied with Physicians, from coming to the Nuns, whilst they waited for the Bishop's answer, which they hop'd to receive the next Day, and that they consented that the Gates should be open'd, if it would please the Ladies to open them. They repeated once again, that they did not acknowledge the Bailiff for their Judge, and that they did not suppose that he could hinder them from executing the Commands of the Bishop of Poictiers, as well in the matter of exorcising, as all other acts which depended on his Ecclesiastical Jurisdictions. In fine, they protested, that if these Maids should be violently Tormented, they should proceed to exorcising for their relief; and that the Bailiff and the Officers, and Physicians might assist there, if it seem'd good to them, to see if the Possession were an imposture, or a truth. The Bailiff having receiv'd this Answer, deferr'd till the Day following in the Morning, to make his Visit, hoping that the Bishop would come, or at least that he would send other Ecclesiasticks who were not suspected. As soon as the Morning was come, he repair'd to the Convent, where he waited in vain, till Noon; after which, to do right upon another Petition presented to him, by Grandier, He order'd that Prohibitions should be made to Barre and all others, to put Questions to the Superior and other Nuns, tending to blacken the Petitioner or any other person, whosoever it was, upon the Penalties that should fall thereon. This Order being signified to Barre, and to one of the Nuns, for all the rest, Barre continu'd to Answer, that the Bailiff could not hinder him from executing the Orders of the Bishop; and that he declar'd, that he would exorcise henceforwards by the advice of the Ecclesiasticks, without calling Lay-persons thither, but only as far as he should think it necessary, for the greater Glory of GOD; That he would complain of the great violences, which he had seen in the Morning, and of the obstacle that was put to the Continuance of the Exorcisms, the Bailiff having not been willing to suffer, that he should reiterate to the Evil Spirit, the command to speak the Truth, upon a Question that had been propos'd to one of the possessed, when she was brought into the Choir of the Church; That he declar'd nevertheless, that he would execute that which he had said, till the coming of the Bishop or his Orders; Adding, that the Nuns desir'd that he would continue to execute his Commission for their Relief, and that 'twas sufficient that the Order of the Bailiff had been notified unto them.

Sect. 34.

The Day was almost gone, and the Bishop not arriv'd, nor was there any Probability that he would give himself the Cognizance of an Affair, with which he seem'd to look on as a trifling Matter. This gave Grandier Occasion to Present at Night another Petition to the Bailiff, who sent for all the Officers of the Bailiwick, and those belonging to the Law to communicate it to them. The last of which declin'd the taking Cognizance of it; The Advocate, because he was sensibly provok'd and offended with the Scandalous Discourse which the Petitioner made in his Presence against Mignon, whose near Kinsman he was; And the Attorney, because he was Cousin-German to the same Mignon by his Wife, who was the Daughter of Trinquant, whose Office he had lately taken Possession of; and because he had several Quarrels with Grandier for the last Six Months, and that he had obtain'd of the Bishop of Poictiers a Dispensation not to acknowledge him for his Parson, Each of them declaring that they humanely believ'd that the Nuns were really possess'd by the Devils, being convinc'd by the Testimony of the Physicians from other Towns who had seen them, and by that of divers Ecclesiasticks, Seculars and Regulars, and yet without having a Thought that Grandier was the Author of this Fatal Accident. Their Declarations being writ and sign'd, the Judges order'd that the Superior and Lay Sister should be Sequestred and put into a Citizens House, That each of them should have a Nun to keep her Company; That they should be assisted as well by their Exorcists as by Women of Honesty and Quality and by Physicians and other Persons whom they them selves would appoint to have the Charge of them; Forbidding all others, without Permission, to come near them. The Register was sent to the Convent with an Order to declare this Sentence to the Nuns. The Superior having heard it read, answer'd as well for her self as for all the Society, That she did not acknowledge the Jurisdiction of the Bailiff; That there was a Commission of the Bishop of Poictiers, dated the Eighteenth of November, importing such Orders as he desir'd should be held in the Present Affair, and the she was ready to put a Copy of it into his Hand, to the End that he might not plead Ignorance; As for the Sequestration, that she did oppose it, because 'twas contrary to the Vow of perpetual Confinement, for which she could not be dispenc'd with but by the Bishop. This Opposition having been made in the Presence of the Lady de Charnazai, Aunt by the Mothers Side to Two Nuns, and in that of the Chirurgion Mannouri, Brother-in-Law to another, each of them Joyn'd together and protested against the Proceeding, if the Bailiff would go on further; and also to take it upon themselves in their proper and private Names. The Act was sign'd, and carried by the Register to the Bailiff, who order'd that the Partys should provide themselves for a Sequestration, and that he would come to the Convent next morning being the Twenty fourth of November, to assist at the Exorcisms. He went thither at the Hour appointed, and having sent for Daniel Roger Vincent de Faux, Gaspard Jouburt, and Matthew Fanton Physicians, he told them that he would take their Oaths when they made their Report, and commanded them in the mean while that they would attentively consider the Two Nuns who should be shew'd to them, and to examine if the causes of their Disease were Natural or Supernatural; They were plac'd near the Altar, which was separated by a Grate from the Choir, where the Nuns did usually Sing, and over against which the Superior was a little after laid upon a Couch; She had great Convulsions whilst Barre said Mass, her Arms and Hands were distorted, her Fingers were half shut, her Cheeks seem'd to be much swoll'n, and only the white of her Eyes was to be seen; The Friars and Nuns stood about her, and assisted her, and there was a great Number of Spectators in the Choir and near the Altar. Mass being ended, Barre came nigh her to give her the Communion, and to exorcise her, and holding the Sacrament in his Hand, he spake to her in these Words, Adora Deum tuum, Creatorem tuum. Adore thy God, thy Creator; she being urg'd answer'd, Adoro te, I adore thee. Quem adoras? Whom dost thou adore? said the Exorcist several times, Jesus Christus, reply'd she; making Motions as if she had suffer'd Violence. Daniel Drouin, Assessor of the Provostship, could not for bear saying aloud, Here's a Devil who is a bad Latinist. Barre changing the Phrase, demanded of the possess'd, Quis est iste quem adoras? Who is he whom thou adorest? he hop'd that she would say again Jesus Christus, but she answer'd Jesu Christe; Then there was heard a great Noise of the Assistants who cry'd out this is ill Latine. Barre maintain'd boldly that she said

Adoro te Jesu Christe, I adore thee, O Jesus Christ. There was afterwards put to her some Questions concerning our Saviour, to which she made this answer, Jesus Christus est substantia Patris, Jesus Christ is the Substance of the Father; Look you here is a Devil who is a great Divine, said the Exorcist. Next after, he demanded the Name of the Devil, to whom it was answer'd, after great Urgency and violent Convulsions, that e was call'd Asmodee; He enquir'd also what were the Number of the Devils who were in the Body of the Possessed, she answer'd Sex, Six. The Bailiff requir'd of Barre, that he should ask Asmodee how many Companions he had, which was done, and the Nun answer'd Quinque, Five; But when he was adjur'd, upon the Request of the said Bailiff to tell in Greek, that which she had said in Latin, she made no Answer, though the Adjurations were often repeated, and she also presently return'd to her natural State. The Exorcist ask'd her again, by the Order of the Bailiff, if she remembred what had past during her Convulsions, No, said she, I do not Remember any thing; At least reply'd the Bailiff, you must needs remember the things which past at the Beginning of your Agitations, seeing that the Ritual enjoyns the Exorcists to demand of the possessed what are the Inclinations of your Bodies and Minds in the beginning of them; she answer'd, that she had a Desire to Blaspheme; The same Day there was produc'd another young Nun, who twice pronounc'd the Name of Grandier, bursting out into a Laughter, then turning towards the Company, she said, All you do is nothing to the Purpose. Barre drew near her to give her the

Communion, but he believ'd that he ought not, because she ceased not to laugh. Afterwards she retir'd to make Room for the Lay Sister who was called Sister Clair. As soon as she came into the Choir she made a kind of sighing, and when they had laid her upon a Couch, she said laughing, Grandier, Grandier you must buy it in the Market. Barre being come near to exorcise her, she made a Show as if she would spit in his Face, and the often held up her Nose in token of Derision; She made wanton Motions, before all the Spectators, and several times pronounc'd an obscene beastly Word. The Exorcists having adjur'd her to tell the Name of the Devil who possess'd her, she nam'd at first Grandier; and when he urg'd her further, she nam'd at last the Devil Elomi, but she would not tell the Number that she had in her Body; He demanded of her also in Latine, Quo pacto ingressus est Dæmon? By what Pact is the Devil entred? She reply'd Dupplex, Double, which made it known that this Devil was no better a Latinist than the other; During the Convulsions which she had, she was prick'd in the Arm by a Pin which pinn'd her Sleeve; It did not at all appear that the Devil had made her insensible of bodily Pains, for she cry'd out, take away this Pin, it pricks me. When she was recover'd out of her Convulsions, she said to the Assessor of the Provostship, that she remembred all that was past, and that Barre had done her much Harm. So this was the Scene of the Morning's Work of this Day; but there were several things that happen'd at the Actions of the Evening, which pleas'd neither the Exorcists nor the Nuns.

Sect. 35.

The Bailiff follow'd by his Clerk, and accompanied with divers Judges, and a considerable Number of other Persons being entred at Three or Four of the Clock in the Afternoon, into the Chamber of the Superior, said to Barre that 'twas requisite to separate her from the Sister Claire, to the Intent that all their Motions might be more distinctly observ'd, their Eyes not being drawn aside by Objects differing and distant one from the other, which was done. They began also presently the Exorcisms, and the Superior likewise to be tormented again with great Convulsions, almost like those in the Morning, saving that her Feet seem'd to be more bow'd, which had not been seen before. The Exorcist, after many Adjurations, made her say her Prayers, and demanded of her again the Number and Names of the Devils which possess'd her, she answer'd, after many Instances oftentimes repeated, that one of them was nam'd Achaos. The Bailiff requir'd that this Question should be propos'd to her, if she were possess'd Ex pacto Magi aut ex pura Voluntate Dei? By the Pact of the Magician, or by the pure Will of GOD? Her answer was, Non est Voluntas Dei? It is not the Will of GOD. Barre to break off this way of Qestioning, demanded of her by his own Authority, Who was the Magician, and when she had answer'd Urbanus, he urg'd her, saying, What Urban? Estne Urbanus Papa? Is it Urban the Pope? She reply'd, Grandier. The Bailiff propos'd that they would demand of her, Cujus esset ille Magus? Of what Country the Magician was? A. Cenomanensis, Of Mans. Q. Cujus Diocesis? Of what Diocess? A. Pictaviensis, Of Poictiers. She was again urg'd, and adjur'd by the Order of the Bailiff, to say in Latine these last things which she had express'd in French, when she had nam'd one of the Devils, concerning whom she endeavour'd to speak Twice or Thrice, but could only say Si, Si, or else Ti Ti, and then her Convulsions ceas'd, and she continued without being tormented or disquieted a considerable space of time; during which Barre had this horrid Discourse with her, I will that you be tormented for the Glory of GOD, and that you give your. Body to the Devil to be tormented, as our Lord gave his to the Jews. He had scarcely finish'd these Words, but the Nun fell into her usual Convulsions. The Bailiff open'd his mouth to propound Questions, but the Exorcist made haste to prevent him; and demanded, by his own Authority, of the Devil, Quare ingressus es in Corpus hujus Puellæ? Wherefore hast thou enter'd into the Body of this Maiden? A. Propter Præsentiam tuam, Because of thy Presence. The Bailiff interrupted him, and desir'd that he would interrogate her upon that which was propos'd by him and the other Officers, promising, that if she would answer justly to the Three or Four Questions which should be put to her, they would believe the Possession and Sign it. They offer'd to obey him, but the Convulsions ceas'd at that very time, and for as much as it was late, every one retir'd.

Sect. 36.

The next Morning being the Twenty Fifth of November, the Bailiff with the greater Part of Officers of the Two Courts, and the Register, being return'd to the Convent, the Superior was brought to the Choir of the Church, and the Curtains of the Grate having been drawn, Barre began according to his Custom with the Celebration of the Mass. The possessed had, during the Service, great Convulsions like those of the Day before, in one of which she cried out, being neither exorcis'd, nor interrogated, Grandier, Grandier, a naughty Priest. Mass being ended, the Exorcist entred into the Choir with the Pix in his Hand, and protesting that his Action was pure, and full of Integrity, without Passion, or evil Design, he plac'd it upon his Head, and pray'd to GOD with a great Appearance of Zeal and Fervency, That he would confound him, if he had made use of any evil Means, Suggestion, or Perswasion to the Nuns in all this Action. After which, the Prior of the Carmelites put himself forwards, and made the same Protestations and Imprecations, having also the Pix upon his Head, and added, as well in his own Name, as in the Name of all the Carmelites present and absent, that the Curses of Dathan and Abiram might fall upon them, if they had sinn'd or committed any Fault in this Affair. 'Tis by these Ways that the Exorcists endeavour'd to extinguish the ill Opinion, which the Behaviour of the Nuns had caus'd to be conceiv'd of them. Immediately after, Barre drew near to the Superior to give her the Communion, but she fell into Convulsions, the Motions whereof were extraordinary violent, even to that Degree, that she endeavour'd to pluck the Pix out of his Hands; However he overcame this Difficulty, and gave her the Communion She had scarcely receiv'd the Sacrament into her Mouth, but she put out her Tongue, and made a Shew as if she would throw it out; the Exorcist thrust it back with his Fingers, and forbid the Devil to cause her to Vomit it; and because the possessed declar'd, that this Wafer did one while stick to the Roof of her Mouth, another while to her Throat, he made her drink some Water thrice, after which, he interrogated the Devil as he had done in the foregoing Exorcisms. Q. Per quod Pactum ingressus es in Corpus hujus Puellæ? By what Pact hast thou enter'd into the Body of this Maiden? A. Aqua, by Water. The Bailiff had then near him a Scotehman named Stracan, who was Principal of the College of Loudun, He requir'd that the Devil should say Aqua, in the Scots Language, for the convincing of all the Assistants, that there was not any Suggestion by any one whatsoever. Barre reply'd, that he would cause him to say it, if GOD would permit it, and at the same time he commanded him, and repeated it several times, but the Nun answer'd, Nimia Curiosuas, 'Tis too great a Curiosity; and after she had repeated it Twice or Thrice, she said Deus non volo; some cry'd out that this was ill Syntax; the Devil was adjur'd on the part of GOD to speak congruously, but these Words Deus non volo, were again repeated, by which she would have said GOD will not; The Exorcist finding himself confounded, said, that in Effect there seem'd that there was in this too great a Curiosity; The Question is pertinent and reasonable reply'd the Lieutenant Civil, and you may find by the Ritual which you have in your Hand, that the Faculty of speaking in strange and unknown Languages is an undoubted Mark of a Possession, and that that of telling the things that are done a great Way off is another. The Exorcist reply'd, that the Devil knew this Language very well, but he would not speak it; But if you will, added he, that I command him to tell presently your Sins, he shall do it; Desiring to let them know by this Discourse, that the Devil he was dealing with, knew well enough hidden things. This will not trouble me, said the Lieutenant. Upon which Barre turn'd towards the Superior, as if he would have interrogated her; but the Bailiff having told him, that this was not fit to be done, he forbore, and said, that he never meant to do it.

Sect. 37.

In the mean time, the Assistants being very eager to know if the Devil understood strange Languages, the Bayliff upon their importunities propos'd the Hebrew Tongue as a dead Language, and the most ancient of all Languages, which the Devil ought to know better than any other, which being follow'd by a General Applause, the Exorcist commanded the possessed to say in the Hebrew Tongue the word Aqua, Water, she answer'd not; but some understood that she pronounc'd very low these Words, Ah! je renie, Curse on't: It was affirm'd by a Carmelite, who was a little way from her, that she did say Zaquaq, and that it was an Hebrew Word, which signifies, Effudi aquam, I have pour'd out Water; although they who were nearest to her unanimously attested that she said, Ah! je renie, which caus'd the Subprior of the Carmelites to reprove publickly the Friar. The possessed had again several convulsions, in one of which she rais'd her self above the Couch, her Head was also presently supported by a Nun, and her Body by those that stood nearest to her, by whom it was affirm'd, that she rais'd her self so high, as even to carry her Hand near the Beam of the Cieling, without touching the Bed, but with one Foot, which was seen but by a very few Persons. After these Convulsions, which had been long and violent, she seem'd no more concern'd that she was before, nor even her Colour was not more lively. Afterwards, and at the very time that the Spectators were ready to be gone, she pronounc'd twice, of her own accord, two Latine Words, which signified, unjust Judgments.

Sect. 38.

Grandier having discover'd that besides the Exorcisms that were made in the presence of the Bayliff and Lieutenant Civil, there were others yet made in the presence of the Lieutenant Criminal, who made Verbal Processes thereof, he presented him with a Petition, remonstrating that he had been a Witness, and that he had depos'd in an Accusation, which was falsly contriv'd against him the Petitioner, who had receiv'd upon this occasion (and many others) Marks of his ill will; that there were yet differences to be clear'd between them;

that one of the Persons pretended to be possess'd, was his Cousin German, and had been his Domestick; that all these considerations and others to be produc'd in time and place, ought to withhold him from medling in those things which concern'd him the Petitioner; and nevertheless, that he besought him he would not do, say, or write any thing in this Affair. This Petition having been signified to the Lieutenant Criminal, in the Convent of the Ursulines where he then was, he gave an Act to the Petitioner of his words and declarations; and declared, that when he was accus'd in a Court of Justice, he would do what should be sit; ordering in the mean time, that the present Petition should be sent to the Register to be ingross'd.

Sect. 37.

The Bayliff and Lieutenant Civil return'd to the Convent the same Day, between Three and Four of the Clock in the Afternoon, Barre having walk'd Two or Three turns with them in the Court, said to the Lieutenant Civil, that he very much wonder'd at this, that he supported Grandier, after having inform'd against him, by the Orders of the Bishop of Poictiers; the Lieutenant reply'd, that he should be yet altogether ready to do it, if there was occasion; but that for the present matter, he had no other aim but to know the truth. This answer being not well relish'd by him who began this Discourse, he took the Bayliff aside, and to engage him to a Party, to which he seem'd not more favourable than the Lieutenant, he represented to him, that being descended of many Persons of Quality, some whereof were possessed of very considerable Ecclesiastical Dignities; and he appearing at the Head of all the Officers of a Town, ought to shew less repugnance in believing the Possession of the Nuns, which tended to cause GOD to be glorified, and to raise the Advantages of the Church and Religion. The Bayliff answer'd him coldly, and in a few words, that he would do always that which he was bound to do in justice. When they were come up into the Chamber, where was a great Assembly, the Superiour seeing Barre, and the Pix in his Hand, she had very great Convulsions, as if the Devil had fallen in a rage at the Sight of this Object. The Exorcist demanded yet once more of the Devil, Per quod Pactum ingressus esset in Corpus hujus puellæ? By what Pact he was entred into the Body of this Damsel? The Nun, who ought to understand this Lesson well, answer'd as before, Aqua, by Water. Q. Quis Finis Pacti? What was the intent of the Pact? A. Impuritas, Impurity. The Bayliff requir'd that they would make her say in Greek, Finis Pacti Impuritas, which was propos'd to her by the Exorcist; but she freed her self from the Matter as she us'd to do, with a Nimia Curiositas, it is too great a Curiosity. He begun again, and demanded of her of his own Motion, who had brought the Pact, Q. Quis attulit pactum? And after her Answer, Quale nomen Magi? What is the Name of the Magician? A. Urbanus, Urban. Q. Quis Urbanus? estne Urbanus Papa? What Urban is it, Pope Urban? A. Grandier. Q. Cujus Qualitatis? Of what quality is be? A. Curatus, meaning the Curate. The Bayliff desir'd that they would ask her, Sub quo Episcopo ille Grandier, tonsuram accepisset? Under what Bishop had Grandier receiv'd his tonsure? A. Nescio, I know not, reply'd she; Barre said in effect, this was a thing which the Devil might be ignorant of. He put to her, yet another Question, which the Bayliff had also propos'd, Sub quo Episcopo, Cenomanensi natus esset ille Grandier? Under what Bishop of Man's was that Grandier born? She repeated Cenomanensi, of Man's. But whatsoever instances could be made to her, She answer'd not to the Question, nor could tell the Name of the Bishop. It was not so in those Questions which the Exorcist had put to her of his own Head, viz. Q. Quis attulit aquam pacti? Who is it that brought the Water of the Pact? A. Magus, the Magician, Q. Qua hora? at what Hour? A. Septima, at Seven a Clock. Q. An maiutina? At Seven in the Morning? A. Sero, in the Evening. Q. Quomodo intravit? How came he in? A. Janua, at the Door. Q. Quis Vidit? Who saw it? A. Tres, Three. Barre confirming this testimony of the Devil, assur'd them, that being at Supper with the Superior in her Chamber the Sunday after she had been delivered from the second possession, Mignon her Confessor, and one other Nun who was indispos'd, supping there also, she had shew'd them at Seven in the Evening, her Arms, wet with some Drops of Water; without seeing any Person who put them on; that he forthwith wash'd her Arm with Holy Water, and said some Prayers, during which, the Prayer-Book of the Superior was twice pull'd out of her Hands, and cast at her Feet, and that there was given her a Box on the Ear. Mignon also made a long Speech to confirm that which was said, and concluded with great Oaths, and horrible Imprecations, in the presence of the Sacrament, which he adjur'd to confound and destroy him, if he did not speak the truth. When he had given over speaking, the Exorcist ask'd the possessed, whether she understood well these Latine Words, Sub qua Episcopo natus essen? She swore that she understood neither the words, nor the Latine. He said them to the Assembly that was ready to depart, that next Day he would expel the Devil; and that he exhorted them all to Confession, and the Communion, to be rendred worthy of the contemplation of this Miracle.

Sect. 39.

That which past at this last Exorcism being publish'd through all the Town, Grandier went to present, the next Morning, November the Twentieth, a large Petition to the Bailiff, wherein he declar'd, that the Nuns maliciously, and by suggestion, continued to name him in their Convulsions, as the Author of their pretended possession; That he had never seen these pretended possessed, and That he never had any Communication with them, no more than with their pretended Devils; That to justify the suggestion, whereof he complain'd, it was absolutely necessary to sequester them; that it was not just, that Mignon and Barre, his Mortal Enemies should govern them, and pass whole Days and Nights with them; That this procedure render'd the suggestion visible and palpable; That the Honour of GOD was concern'd, and that of him the

Petitioner, who held, whatever they thought of him, the first rank amongst the Ecclesiasticks of Loudun. For which considerations he besought him to command, that the pretended possessed should be sequestred and separated one from the other; That they should be govern'd by Persons of the Church not suspected by the Petitioner, and assisted by Physicians; and that all should be perform'd, whatsoever Oppositions or Appeals notwithstanding, and without prejudice to them, because of the Importance of the Affair; And that in Case he would not be pleas'd to order a Sequestration, he, the Petitioner, protested that he would complain, as being denied Justice. The Bayliff writ at the bottom of his Petition, that Right should be done him that very Day.

Sect. 39.

Grandier was scarce gone from the Bayliff's House, when the Physicians of the Town, who assisted at one of the Exorcisms, came in to make their Report, which was inserted in the Verbal Process. It contain'd, That they had seen the Convulsive Motions in the Person of the Mother Superior, but that one single Visit was not sufficient to discover the Causes of these Motions, which might be Natural, as well as Supernatural; That they desir'd to see them, and examine them more particularly, that they might be able to judge with Certainty and a good Conscience; That for this Effect, they requir'd that it might be permit, ted them to abide yet near the Nuns some Days and Nights, without separating themselves, and to treat them in the Presence of other Nuns and some of the Magistrates. That they should not receive Food nor Physick, if 'twas necessary, but from their Hands; That no Body should either touch them, or speak to them but aloud; And that then they promis'd to report faithfully, and truly, that which they observ'd relating to the Cause of their Convulsions.

Sect. 40.

After this Report was written and sign'd, time pressing, the Bayliff repair'd forthwith to the Convent, where he found in the Second Court the Lieutenant Civil, and the Assessor, Cesvet and Gautier Counsellors, with the Lieutenant and Assessor of the Provostship: They caus'd Barre to have Notice of their being come, by whom they were introduc'd into the Chappel, a great Croud of People going before and following them. This Exorcist now chang'd his Note, and commanded the Devil to acknowledge and confess the Reality of the Body of our Saviour in the Sacrament. The Superior had great Convulsions before she came to this Confession; she rais'd her self upon her Couch, as she had already done another time, being held by the Head and Body. In fine, she receiv'd the Communion after some Struggles, like those of the former Days, and after that, she had some Rest. We must not omit here, that which pass'd during the Celebration of the Mass: The Roman Catholicks were all upon their Knees out of Respect to the Sacrament, the Bayliff perceiv'd that a young Man nam'd Dessentiers had his Hat upon his Head, he commanded him to uncover, or be gone. The Superior cried out at that Instant that there were Huguenots there; The Exorcist ask'd her how many there were; She answer'd Two, whence some concluded that this Devil did not know how to reckon, or that he knew not the Huguenots; for besides Dessentiers, there was Abraham Gautier a Counsellor, with his Brother, and Four of his Sisters, Rene Fourneau an Assessor, and Peter Angevin an Attorney. It was observ'd that Barre the Day before had demanded of the Possessed if she understood Latine; and that she swore she did not. He ask'd her the same again, and she reply'd as before; he urg'd her yet to Swear upon the Pix; at First she was at a Stand, saying, My Father, you make me take great Oaths, I fear that G O D will punish me; Daughter, said he, you ought to swear for the Glory of G O D: And after she had sworn, he told her, that 'twas nois'd abroad however, that she expounded the Catechism to her Schollars, which she deny'd, acknowledging, nevertheless, that she did explain the Pater noster and Creed. When she fell again into Convulsions, he ask'd the Devil in French, Who had introduc'd him into the Body of the Superior? The Answer was, that 'twas Urban Grandier; And that this Grandier was the Parson of Saint Peters in the Market Place. The Bailiff order'd the Exorcist to ask her, where this pretended Magician was at that time? The Question was in the Words of the Ritual, and he was oblig'd to obey and do it; The possessed reply'd, that he was in the Castle-Hall. This will be found false, said the Bayliff aloud, because before my coming hither I order'd him to go to a certain House, where he will be assuredly found, being willing to take the Advantage of this Proof to come to the Knowledge of the Truth without a Sequestration, which was a difficult Course to take with Nuns; He affirm'd still, that if Grandier went that Day to the Castle, as he might do, at least he was sure, that 'twas a long time since he was there, for the Proof whereof, and to make it known to all the Assistants, that the Devil was badly serv'd by his Spies, he order'd Barre to nominate some of the Friars who were there present to repair to the Castle, and to accompany thither one of the Magistrates and the Clerk; The Exorcist nam'd the Prior of the Carmelites, and the Bayliff nam'd Charles Chauvet Assessor of the Bayliwick, Israel Bouleau Priest, and Peter Thibaut the Register Deputy, who thereupon went to execute their Commission.

Sect. 41.

The Superior was struck with so great an Astonishment by this Procedure of the Bayliff, that she continued mute, and fell no more into her Convulsions, although they continued yet some time to exorcise her; They had Recourse to the singing of Hymns, at the end of which her Silence ended not, for it lasted more than half an Hour; after which Barre being a little recover'd out of his Surprize, propos'd the bringing of the Sister Clair into the Choir, saying, that one Devil would excite the other; But the Bayliff represented that that might cause Trouble and Confusion, and that some might in the mean while suggest something to the Superior concerning the Matter in Question, and that 'twere fit, at least, to wait the Return of those that were gone; but how pertinent soever this Reason was, his Desire was not comply'd with. It was necessary to be rid of the Bayliff at any rate, and of the other Magistrates who were of his Opinion, or to find some Occasion to put an Illusion upon them. Sister Clair came in notwithstanding the Oposition of the Bayliff, and the other Officers, who not being able to endure this foul Play, retir'd, expressing the Resentment which they had. The Persons which had been sent to the Castle, found them yet in the Court of the Convent, and they related to them, that they had seen the Lady d'Amagnac, who went to follow her Husband the Governour of the Town, whom they carried into the Country in a Litter, by reason of some Indisposition; That she told them that 'twas near Three Hours since Grandier came to the Castle to bid Adieu to the Governour; but that he went away at that Instant, and that she had not seen him since; That afterwards having obtain'd Leave to seek for him in the Castle, they went in the great Hall, in all the Chambers, and every where else without finding him; That from thence they came down into the place of Saint Crosse and to Charles Maw at's House, where the Bayliff inform'd the Assessor that he might find him, as having order'd him to go and stay there the rest of the Day, when he came to present his Petition; That they found him in that House, in the Company of Father Veret Confessor of the Nuns of Gaine, of Mathurin Rousseau, and of Nicolas Benoit Canons, and one Coutis a Physician, from whose Mouth they understood that 'twas above then Two Hours that they had been together. The Magistrates went away after they heard this Report, and the Prior of the Carmelites went into the Choir where the Superior remain'd; She had again some Convulsions, during which one of the Carmelite Friars ask'd her again, where Grandier was at that time, she answer'd, that he was walking with the Bayliff in the Church of Saint Crosse, but they, who had suggested to her this Answer, were deceiv'd in their Conjecture, for de Canaye, Sieur de Granfonds, and John Cesvet Counsellor, being gone to know whether the Devil had guess'd better than at the First time, they went into the Church of Saint Crosse, where finding not the Bayliff, they went up to the Palace and there found him, holding a Court; he assur'd them that he came directly thither, when he went out of the Convent, and that he had not at all seen Grandier. The Exorcist not knowing how to prevent such troublesome Experiments as had been put upon them that Day, resolv'd at last to make the Nuns say, that they would no longer have the Exorcisms perform'd, either in the Presence of the Bayliff, or of the other Officers who usually accompanied him. Grandier having had Notice of this Resolution, presented again another Petition to the Bayliff the Day following, the Twenty Seventh of November, remonstrating, that the pretended Possession had been contriv'd and suggested with Design, only to blast his Reputation, and to render him odious and unprofitable to the Church of G O D; That his Enemies had employ'd all their Credit, and all Sorts of Artifices to make it believ'd real, but that having not been able to succeed, they had call'd together from all Parts, Persons engag'd and at their Devotion, to make use of their Testimonies; That these Practices were very prejudicial to the Public, to Religion, and to him the Petitioner, whose Name was considerable for his Character and Dignity, and that he was nevertheless horribly blacken'd, unjustly reproach'd and defam'd; That it being impossible to clear this Affair, and attain to the Knowledge of the Truth by such Practices, he continued to request the Sequestration of the pretended Possessed, and that they might be taken out of the Hands of Mignon, Barre, and Granger, and their Adherents, and put into the Hands of the Ecclesiasticks approv'd by the most Reverend Bishop of Poictiers, and of Physicians, and other Persons, whom it should please the Bayliff to nominate, to the Intent that the Innocence of him, the Petitioner, might be known and manifested; Desiring that it might be order'd, that the Sequestration should be perform'd, whatsoever Opposition or Appeals notwithstanding, and without Prejudice thereof. There was again writ at the Bottom of the Petition, that Right should be done him in due time, The Request appear'd to be equitable and just, but it seem'd very difficult to attempt the Sequestration of the Nuns, to the Prejudice of their Opposition, which was grounded upon their being dependent on the Ecclesiastical Jurisdiction; and they fear'd that the Bishop of Poictiers and the Clergy would be offended, and cause the Procedure to be disanull'd: Therefore they were contented to Assemble the Inhabitants of the Town, to consider of what might be done for the publick good: The result of this Assembly was, That they should write to the Attorney General, and the Bishop of Poictiers, and that they should send the Verbal Process which had been made; and that they should beseech them to stop by their Authority and Prudence, the course of these dangerous Intrigues. The Attorney General answer'd, that the Matter in question being purely Ecclesiastical, the Parliament ought not to take cognizance of it; and the Bishop made no answer at all.

Sect. 42.

But that Prelate continued not so silent upon the Requests which were made to him, by the Enemies of Grandier, the Authors and Favourers of the Pessession. The ill success the Exorcisms had the Twenty Sixth of November, having oblig'd them to use more precaution, they judg'd it requisite to obtain of the Bishop a new Commission, by which he should nominate some Churchmen to assist on his part at the Exorcisms. Barre took a Journey forthwith to Poictiers, and the Bishop nam'd Basit Dean of the Canons of Champigni, and Demerans, Dean of the Canons of Thouars, each of them being the Kinsmen of the Secret Enemies of Grandier, whom they had chosen and nam'd. This is the Copy of the Commission:

Sect. 43.

Henry Lewis le Chateigner, of Rochepozai, by Divine Mercy, Bishop of Poictiers, to the Deans of the Jurisdiction of Saint Peter of Thouars, and Champigni upon Vede, greeting; We Command you by these presents, to repair to the Town of Loudun, to the Convent of the Nuns of Saint Ursula, to assist as the Exorcisms which shall be made by the Sieur Barre, of the Nuns of the said Monastery, tormented by evil Spirits, to which Barre we have given that Commission, And to the end also a Verbal Process may be made of all that shall pass, and for this purpose to take such a Clerk as shall seem good to you. Given and made at Poictiers, the Twenty Eighth of November. 1632. signed, Henry Lewis, Bishop of Poictiers and lower, by the Command of the said Lord. Michelet.

Sect. 46.

These two new Commissioners, without more ado, went immediately to Loudun, and being instructed and prepar'd, as they were before their nomination, they begun from the first of December to assist at the Exorcisms, and to make their Verbal Process of what past there; Marescot, one of the Queen's Almoners, assisted there also. This Princess had heard of the Possession of the Ursuline Nuns; but no body being able to inform her, but confusedly, she desir'd it might be made clear, and order'd her Almoner to make a journey to Loudun, and to take an exact account of all the Circumstances of this Matter, to give her a faithful Relation. He arriv'd at Loudun the last Day of November, and went to the Convent the next Day in the Morning, to see what past in the presence of the two Deans delegated by the Bishop. The Bailiff, and the Lieutenant Civil, whose Verbal Process had been publish'd, and sent into many Places, fear'd lest he should be prepossess'd, or abus'd, and that he might make a Report to the Court, which might cause a doubt of the Truth of those things contain'd in the Verbal Process; Wherefore they repair'd thither also, notwithstanding the Protestations which had been made not to receive them; They were accompanied by their Assessor, the Lieutenant of the Provostship, and one of the Registers Deputy; they knock'd a long time, before they would open to them: At last, there came a Nun to the Gate, to tell them that they must not come in, and that they were suspected, having publish'd abroad, that the Possession was but a Fiction and Imposture. The Bailiff without staying to contend with this young Nun, order'd her to cause Barre to come, who appear'd sometime after, arrayed in his Priestly Habits. The Bailiff complain'd in the presence of Marescot, that the Gate was not open'd to him and the other Officers with him, which was contrary even to the Orders of the Bishop of Poictiers. Barre declar'd, that for his part he hindered not their coming in. We are come, repli'd the Bailiff, to that intent, and also to entreat you to put Two or Three Questions to the pretended Devil, which shall be propos'd, and shall be conformable to what is prescrib'd in the Ritual; you will not doubtless refuse, (added he) to make this proof, in the presence of the Queen's Almoner, who is sent from Her, seeing that it will be a most effectual means to dissipate all suspition of Suggestion and Imposture. I will do it, if I please, reply'd the Exorcist, in an impudent Manner; 'tis your Duty to do it, said the Bailiff, at least, if you proceed with sincerity, seeing that this would be rather to abuse G O D, than to glorifie him by a false Miracle; and rather injure Religion, than to authorise its Truth by Cheats and Illusions. Barre answer'd, that he was a Man of Probity, that they knew to what his Office oblig'd him, and that he should do his Duty; but as for them, they ought to remember, that the last time they assisted at the Exorcisms, they went away in a Passion. The Magistrates, after many repeated instances having obtain'd nothing, expresly forbid him to put any Question which might tend to defame any one, of whatsoever quality he was, upon pain of being treated as a Seditious Person, and a Disturber of the publick Peace. He reply'd to him again, That he did not acknowledge their Jurisdiction. Whereupon they retir'd.

Sect. 47.

The Possession, doubtless, would have gain'd a new Reputation, by the Direction of the two Deans, who were entirely at the Devotion of the Enemies of Grandier, if the report of the coming of the Archbishop of Bourdeaux, more efficacious than all the Exorcisms, had not broke the Measures which had been taken. He had Power to make the Devils disappear, to raise the courage of the person accus'd, and to restore to the Nuns Peace and Tranquillity, which they had the Gift to acquire, and to loose, as often as it was judg'd expedient for the end which had been propos'd to them. In effect, the Archbishop was no sooner arriv'd at Saint Jouin, but he sent his Physician to Loudun, with an

Order to see the Persons pretended to be possessed, and to consider well, and examine all their Grimaces, Distortions, and Convulsions; and recommended him to Mignon, by a Letter, to the end that this Canon should not fail to let him have an exact knowledge of the condition they were in. Mignon brought him to the Convent, and let him see the Superior, and Sister Claire; but he told him, that they had been miraculously deliver'd from the evil Spirits. He had no trouble to perswade him that they were not then possessed; for the Physician found them peaceable, quiet, and compos'd, as if they never had any disturbance; and after his return to Saint Jouin, it was not known that any new Accidents happen'd to them. Grandier attended sometime to judge by the Steps that were made, if there were reason to hope that the Possession were at an end; or whether it was not to be fear'd, that the Devils would return to Loudun, when the Archbishop should be gone. But at last this fear having prevail'd upon him and his Friends, he presented his Petition to that Prelate, the Twenty Seventh of December, and remonstrated, That his Enemies having endeavour'd to oppress him by a false and calumnious Accusation, and having not been able to succeed, because he had been sent back absolv'd, as well by his Lordship's equitable Judgment, as by the Sentence of the Presidial of Poictiers, in the Quality of Judges delegated by the Court, they had for Three Months last past suppos'd, and publish'd every where, that he had sent evil Spirits into the Bodies of the Nuns of Saint Ursula of Loudun, to whom he had never spoke. That besides, John Mignon, their Confessor was his Mortal

Enemy, and one of the Authors of the first Accusation which had been rais'd against him, had not forborn to exorcise them secretly; That having associated to him Peter Barre, Priest of the Diocese of Thouars, and some other Ecclesiastick Seculars and Regulars, they boasted of having Three or Four times, driven away the pretended Devils, who were as often return'd by new Pacts, which they suggested to be made between the Devils and him the Petitioner; That he had made known to Mignon and Barre, that they were suspected by him; the one by reason of the Differences that were between them, and the other, because of his strange Proceedings, and his Friendship with the former: But that they had not forborn to assist the Nuns, and to be near them Day and Night with their Adherents; That he address himself to the Judges of the Place, to be secur'd from the Fury of the People, whom they excited against him; and also his Lord the Bishop of Poictiers, who had caus'd his Almoner to tell him, that he desir'd not to be concern'd in this business; That to the prejudice of the Declaration, which he had made to Barre, he had got by surprize, from the Bishop, a new Power, to exorcise in the Presence of the Deans of the Canons of Thouars and Champigni, who are near Kinsmen of his profest Enemies. That during Three several pretended Possessions, Mignon and Barre had made it their business to put Questions manifestly tending to defame him, and to raise a sedition against him; that he had reason to fear, that these Devils whom his coming had put to flight, would return as soon as he was gone; and that the innocence of him the Petitioner might be overwhelm'd, by the strange Artifices of so many Enemies, cruelly bent against him, if this Matter were left in the sameconfusion, as it had been till then, for want of a lawful Authority to decide it. He requested him to consider all these Reasons, and that he would be pleas'd to forbid Barre, Mignon, and their Adherents, as well Seculars as Regulars, in case of a new Possession, to exorcise for the time to come, and to govern the Persons pretended to be possess'd; appointing such other Persons, Ecclesiasticks and Laicks, whom he should think fit, to see them dieted, physick'd, and exorcis'd, if it were needful, and that all should be done in the presence of the Magistrate; And finally, that he would be pleas'd to Order the Persons pretending to be possess'd, to be sequestred, to prevent all evil suspitions, and to make the Truth evident. Here follows the Ordinance, which the Archbishop writ at the bottom of the Petition.

Sect. 48.

Having seen the present Petition, and heard our Promoter upon the same, we have referr'd the Petitioner to our Promoter at Poictiers, to do him Right. And in the mean while we have commanded the Sieur Barre, Father l'Escaye Jesuit, residing at Poictiers, and Father Gau of the Oratory, residing at Thouars, to take upon them the Exorcisms, if there should be need, according to the Order we have given them to this end; forbidding all others to intermeddle in the said Exorcisms, upon the Penalties of the Law. This is also the Order mention'd in that Ordinance. The Order sent by the Archbishop of Bourdeaux, to the Bailiff of Loudun, to be observ'd at the Exorcisms of the Ursulin Nuns, in case of a new Possession. FIrst, assoon as the Sieur Barre shall have notice hereof, he shall take with hi Father l'Escaye, Jesuit of Poictiers, and Father Gau of the Oratory of Thouars; and all Three shall in their turns, and in the presence of Two others, perform the Office of the Exorcism, in case that it be needful; they shall separate the possessed from the Company of the Society, putting her into such a borrow'd House, as they shall judge proper for this purpose, without leaving any of her Acquaintance with her, except one of the Nuns, who had never before that time been possess'd. They shall cause her to be visited by two or three of the ablest Catholic Physicians of the Province; Who, after their having consider'd some days, or purg'd her, if they think it fit, shall make their Report. After the report of the Physicians, they shall endeavour by Menaces and Disciplines, if they judge it requisite, or other natural means to discover the truth, and whether the Possession be not grounded either on humours, or on her Willfulness; after these things, if they see some supernatural Signs, as her answering the thoughts of the Three Exorcists, which they shall tell their Companions secretly, and that she declares many things that were done in a far distant place, or where there is no suspition, that she could know it at the time she is requir'd to tell it: Or, that in many and different Languages, she makes a Discourse of Eight or Ten words congruous and coherent; and that being bound

Hand and Foot, and laid upon a Quilt on the ground, where they shall suffer her to lie without any one coming near her, she shall raise her self up from the around, some considerable time. In this case, they shall proceed to the Exorcisms, Fastings and Prayers, being previously observ'd; And in case that they come to the Exorcisms, they shall do all their endeavour to make the Devil give some visible, and not suspicious Sign of his going out; and in executing this present Order, any other Priests, if they are not call'd by the common consent of the Three Commissaries, and not suspected, shall not intermeddle, upon Pain of Excommunication, speak to, nor touch in any manner of Fashion the possessed. And in case there are more at the same time, the same order shall be observ'd. And to the intent that some Libertines may not speak ill of the care the Church takes in such an occurrence to know the Truth of the Possessions, and of the charitable Succours that its Ministers bring, the Judges, the Bailiff and Lieutenant Criminal only, and no others, are desir'd to assist at the execution of the present Order; and to sign the Verbal Process, which shall be made by the Persons nominated, who shall take for their Register, the Prior of the Abby of Saint Jouin. And forasmuch as there will be occasion for great Expences, as well for the removal of the Nuns, as for calling in Physicians for the charge of Diet, for Exorcists, and for Women to be appointed to attend the Sick; We have order'd (considering the Poverty of the Convent) that the expence shall be defray'd by us; and for this Purpose, we have forthwith Commanded the Sieur Barre, to order the Farmer of our. Abby of Saint

Jouin, to furnish them with such Sums of Money as they shall have need of. And if the above nam'd Father l'Escaye, and Father Gau, are not at Poictiers and at Thouars, or for some reason they cannot be mer with, the Superiors of the Convents shall supply their default, by furnishing others of an equal merit, if possible.

Sect. 47.

As soon as this Order was publick, the Possession intirely ceas'd, all the Rumours vanish'd, Barre retir'd to Chinon, the Two Deans return'd to their Chapter, and the Nuns continued in quiet within their Convent; the Devils shewing more regard to the Cross alone, which the Archbishop had made at the top of his Writing, than the infinite number of the Signs of the Cross which the Exorcists had made over those Persons in the time of their agitations. The difference of the Procedure of this Prelate, and of that of the Bishop of Poictiers, produc'd also very differing sentiments in the minds of honest, well-meaning People; the justice, impartiality and charity of the first, gain'd their esteem; But the insensibleness, or Connivance of the latter (to say nothing more) left him blemish'd with a Stain, which nothing was able to obliterate. In the mean time, Grandier being taught by two dreadful Experiments, fear'd that there were new Snares laid for him; and considering that the Bailiff had but one Copy of this Order, which was sent him in a Letter, by the Archbishop; and that the Original was in the Hands of Barre; he remonstrated to the Judge, that these Papers might be lost, or at least supprest in time, it care were not taken to prevent it; and besought him, to put the Copy and Letter (which he had receiv'd) into the Registry, with the Petition by which the Order was obtain'd, to the end, that recourse might be had to them if there should be occasion. The Bailiff granted his request, and the said Writings were put into the Registry the Twenty First of March, 1633.

THE HISTORY OF THE 𝕯𝖊𝖛𝖎𝖑𝖘 𝖔𝖋 𝕷𝖔𝖚𝖉𝖚𝖓:

Or, an Account of the
Possession of the Ursuline Nuns.
AND THE
Condemnation and Punishment of
URBAN GRANDIER,
a Parson of the same Town.

BOOK II.

Sect. I.

THE prudent Orders which the Archbishop of Bourdeaux had left, were very powerful in keeping the Nuns, the Exorcists, and even the Devils themselves in silence; but they hindred not the People from speaking and declaiming against all those who had been concern'd in, or favour'd so detestable a supposition. There were only some Bigots, who entirely and blindly submitted to the Monks and Churchmen, that withstood the proofs of the falshood of the pretended Possession. They took away the Boarders that were in the Convent of the Ursulines; they forbore to send thither to School the young Maids of the Town; and shew'd them all sorts of Marks of Contempt and Aversion; their very kindred were asham'd to have any commerce with them again, and the greatest part forsook them: This disposition of minds towards them, cast them into despair. They blam'd Mignon, and reproach'd him, that instead of all the advantages spiritual and temporal that he had made them hope for, they saw themselves overwhelm'd with Misery and Infamy. The Canon fretted, by his own displeasure needed no Provocations to excite his Malice and Rage: He spent Days and Nights in devising which way he might re-establish his own Reputation, and that of the Nuns, and revenge the Affronts he had receiv'd. The Enterprize was great, and sufficient to quell a Spirit less obstinate and less passionate. He had already experimented the difficulties, and there was a probability that he should never bring it to pass, if something, which he could not foresee, had not happen'd, and offer'd a new occasion, favourable for the execution of his Design.

Sect. 2.

A resolution had been taken, in the King's Council, to demolish all the Castles and Fortresses which were in the Heart of France, and to preserve only those of the Frontiers. Cardinal Richelieu, who was the Author of this Design, was not willing to let the Castle of the Town of Loudun stand; for the demolishing whereof he had particular Reasons, and which he had very well pursued, by causing one part of the Right and

Jurisdiction of Loudun, to be transferr'd, and given to his Town of Richelieu although he succeeded not in the Project he had form'd, to oblige the better sort of the Inhabitants to go and People his own Town, those who had a Mind to retire, to change their Habitations, having chose rather to go seek for places of protection and safeguard any where else. The Commission to raze this Fortress, was given to Lauberdemont. He was one of those Men who were absolutely devoted to the Cardinal, and whom he employ'd, when he had a Mind to exterminate, ruin, and she Blood unjustly, by observing, nevertheless, the Forms of Justice. He had been already made many times Commissary on these Bloody Occasions, and had the Honour to be often so afterwards: He came to Loudun to acquit himself of the Employment which had been given him. His principal conversation was presently with Memin de Silly, a Creature also of the Cardinal; Mignon and all his Friends apply'd themselves to Memin; he presented them to Laubardemont, by whom they were very kindly receiv'd, and who averr'd, that he would be concern'd for the affront which had been done to all the party, and to the Nuns, whose Superior was his Kinswoman. They consulted to find out some means, by which they might engage the Cardinal to concur with their Designs, by some interest which might touch him in particular, and they fail'd not; For what pretences will not treachery, hatred and revenge make use of? And what are they not capable to invent or discover?

Sect. 3.

There was at that time, about the Queen-Mother, a Woman nam'd Hammon, who pleas'd that Princess upon an Occasion, in which she had the Honour to talk to her; she was Born at Loudun, amongst the ordinary People, and there she had spent the greater part of her Life; Grandier who had been her Parson, and who knew all the ingenious Women in his Parish, was particularly acquainted with her. There had been publish'd under her Name, a Bloody Satyr against the Ministers, but above all, against the Cardinal, wherein many Particularities of his Life and Ministry were laid open, for which he shew'd much displeasure, and a very deep resentment. The Conspirators judg'd it convenient to attribute this Piece to Grandier, and to give out, that he kept a constant Correspondence, by Letters, with the said Hammon, of whom he must needs learn what was contain'd in that Satyr. There was so much the more probability in this accusation, that the Satyr had been publish'd during the disgrace of the Cardinal, who formerly, when he was but Prior of Coussai, had little piques against Grandier, who pretending himself the first of the Ecclesiasticks of Loudun, would no ways yield in any thing to the Prior of Coussai. This contrivance was approv'd by Laubardemont as very excellent, and likely to produce in the Mind of the Cardinal an eager desire for revenge, to which he was naturally inclin'd. They brought after this, the Commissary, to see the Grimaces, Postures and Convulsions of the Nuns, who had, by this time, acquir'd new Degrees of perfection in their management; by the practice of which they were found very dextrous and expert in the Art of Counterfeiting Devils. Laubardemont at least seem'd exceedingly satisfied, and promis'd to Second their endeavours as soon as he was at Paris; whither he return'd as soon as the Castle was entirely demolish'd.

Sect. 4.

At his departure, he left at Loudun the Devils, which his presence had recall'd thither, though they had been disperst by the presence of the Archbishop of Bourdeaux. They return'd then, as into a House swept and garnish'd, fit to receive many others, who fail'd not to accompany them thither. The Superior and Sister Clair, had not the Honour only to receive these guests; They took possession of Five other Nuns, besides Six which were beset, and two bewitch'd. They took also a turn to the Town of Chinon, where they lodg'd themselves as it were in the House of a Friend and Acquaintance, with Two very Devout secular Maids, whose Confessor Barre was, as Mignon was of those at Loudun, possessed, beset, or bewitch'd. There was written afterwards by these Priests, or by their Friends, a Book, intituled, The Demonomania of Loudun, wherein are contain'd, all the Names of the Devils, and of all the Maids who were Tormented, whose Pains and Sufferings being therein describ'd, without doubt, excited an extraordinary compassion in the Hearts of all good Persons who read it, and gave credit to all that was there related.

Sect. 5.

Whilst the Devils were thus employ'd, to the great Astonishment of all People who believ'd that they would never presume to return, and who could not comprehend or divine upon what Ground they had that Confidence, Laubardemont, who was at Paris, made such good use of his Credit, and Application in their Favour, that he receiv'd an Order to go back to Loudun, to be the Arbitrator of their Practises, and preside at all their Commerce. He arriv'd there the Sixth of December 1633. at eight of the Clock in the Evening, and came to the House of Paul Aubin Sieur de Bourneuf, and Son in Law to Memin. His coming was so secret, because of the Hour and Situation of the Place, which was in the Suburb, that Grandier and his Friends had no Knowledge of it; Memin, Herve and Menuau being quickly come to him, he boasted of his Cunning in the Prepossessing the Cardinal, who was highly provok'd, and had put into his Hands the Care of his Revenge; and afterwards gave them Proofs of the Diligence he had us'd, by shewing them his Commission dated but the last Day of November, and the Contents whereof were as follows:

Sect. 6

That the Sieur Laubardemont, Counsellor of the King in his Council of State and Privy Council, shall go to Loudun and other Places as there shall be Occasion, to inform, with Diligence, against Grandier upon all the Facts of which he has been heretofore accus'd, and others which shall be a new laid to his Charge Concerning the Possession of the Ursuline Nuns of Loudun, and other Persons who are said to be possess'd and tormented by Devils, by the Sorcery of the said Grandier, and of all that which has past since the Beginning, as well of their Exorcisms, as otherwise, upon the Fact of the said Possession; To make Report by the Verbal Processes and other Acts of the Commissaries delegated thereunto; To assist at the Exorcisms that shall be made; And of all, to make a Verbal Process, and otherwise to proceed as shall be fitting for the Proof and absolute veryfing the said Facts; And upon the whole, to decreee, instruct, make, and cause to be made Process against the said Grandier, and all others whom they. Shall find complices in the said Case, even to a definite Sentence exclusively, notwithstanding any Opposition, Appeal or Recusation whatsoever; for which, and without Prejudice to the same, it shall not be delay'd, even considering the Quality of the Crimes, without having Regard to the Appeal which may be demanded by the said Grandier; His Majesty commanding all the Governours, Lieutenant Generals of the Province, and all the Bailiffs, Seneshals, and c. And other Officers of the Town, and Persons whom it may Concern for the

Execution hereof, to give all Assistance, and Aid, and Imprisonment, if there be cause, and that they shall be requir'd.

Sect. 7.

He shew'd also Two Ordinances of the King Signed Louis, and lower, Philippeaux, dated the same last Day of November, 1633. Ordaining the said Laubardemont to cause the said Grandier and his Complices to be imprison'd, with the like Command to all the Marshalls, Provosts, and c. and other Officers and Persons, to assist the Execution of the said Ordinance, and to obey, for the Doing thereof, all the Orders that should be given by the said Lauberdemont; And to the Governours and Lieutenant Generals, to give all Assistance which shuld be requir'd of them.

Sect. 8.

This large and extraordinary Power which was given to Laubardemont, very pleasingly surpriz'd the Company which came to hear it read; but when it was publish'd, 'twas not less surprizing, although after a very different Manner, to all the honest People who beheld this Affair with a just and disinterested Eye. They could not sufficiently wonder that he had again been allow'd to inform upon all the Facts of which Grandier had been heretofore accus'd, and upon those which should be laid to him again, as the Commission imported. The Astonishment however increas'd yet, when they saw with what Violence they us'd the Authority they had in their Hands; for they began, contrary to all the Rules of Justice, with the Imprisonment of Grandier, before they had made any Information against him, to the End, that this Blow might be consider'd as coming from the Hand of the King; or rather as Anathema darted by the Cardinal, and which was sufficient to dishearten all the Friends of Grandier, encourage the Witnesses whom they would produce against him, and give the Nuns more Liberty and Confidence to act the Parts which were appointed them. For this Purpose, William Aubin Sieur de la Grange, Brother of Bourneuf, and Lieutenant of the Provost, was sent for by Laubardemont, who imparted to him his Commission and the Ordinances of his Majesty, by Virtue of which, he order'd him that next Morning betimes he should seize the Person of Grandier. As this Officer did not believe himself oblig'd to be altogether of the Opinion of Memin, the Father-in-Law of his Brother, he caus'd Grandier to be secretly inform'd with the Orders he had receiv'd. Grandier, who did not think himself guilty, return'd Thanks to Grange for his Generosity, and sent him Word, that confiding in his Innocence, and the Mercy of GOD, he resolv'd not to go aside: So he rose next Morning before Day, according to his Custom, and went with his Breviary in his Hand to the Church of Saint Crosse, to assist at Matins. As soon as he was out of the House, la Grange seiz'd on him, and arrested him Prisoner in the Presence of Memin and a great Number of his other Enemies, who were desirous to feed their Eyes with this Spectacle, and to watch the Proceedings of Grange, of whose

Intention they were not assur'd. At the same instant, the Seal Royal was set upon his Chambers and Presses, and all other Places of his House, and upon his Moveables; and John Pouquet Archer of the Guards to his Majesty, and the Archers of the Provost of Loudun and Chinon, were commanded to conduct him to the Castle of Angers. There he remain'd above Four Months in Prison, where Michelon Commandant of the Place, order'd him to be put. He shew'd, during that time, much Resignation and Constancy, writing often Prayers and Meditations, the Manuscript whereof, which was Twelve Sheets in Quarto was produc'd at his Tryal, but very unserviceably; as also the Advantageous Testimony which was given of him by Peter Bacher Canon, who was his Confessor, and who gave him the Communion during his Confinement at Angers.

Sect. 9

Laubardemont deferr'd not long to search the House of the Prisoner, and to make an Inventory of his Books, Papers and Moveables; He found nothing sufficient to hurt him, but a Treatise against Celibacy, writ with his own Hand, and Two Sheets of French Verses, which were never publish'd, but which his Judges treated as lascivous and immodest, without declaring that they were writ, and much less compos'd by him. They were not contented to seize these Pieces, they carried away all the Papers, Evidences, Sentences of Absolution, which the Person accus'd might have made use of in his Defence, notwithstanding the Complaints and

Oppositions of Jane Estievre his Mother, then Seventy Years of Age. As they did: not proceed continually and without Intermission in making, this Inventory, it was not finish'd till the last Day of January, 1634. and in the Mean time they fail'd not to begin an Information on the Second of the precedent Month. Peter Fournier, an Advocate, perform'd the Office of the King's Attorney; The Mother of Grandier seem'd much afflicted, because he was the Son-in-Law of Richard a Proctor, against whom she had complain'd, for that he went at Midnight into a House to perswade Two Women to depose falsely against her Son; But, Fournier requir'd very quickly after to be discharg'd of his Commission, in the Execution whereof One may very probably conclude, that he found his Conscience touch'd, because through all the Course of his Life, before and since that time, he was always accounted a Man of Honour and Integrity.

Sect. 10.

This First Information was not so soon finish'd, but that there was another made the Nineteenth of the same Month; and the Thirtieth they began to draw up in writing the Depositions of the Nuns. The Friends and Counsell of Grandier's Mother did their utmost to oppose the Torrent of so strange and violent a Procedure: She presented, by their Advice, the Seventeenth of December, a Petition to the Commissary, wherein she appeal'd from him, because he was the Kinsman of the Superior of the Nuns, That he lodg'd at the House of one of her Son's Enemies; That he had made him a Prisoner before any Information of Decree was made against him; That he had made the Lieutenant of the Provost one of the Assistants, who was one of Grandier's Mortal Enemies, when they seiz'd upon his Person; That he had depriv'd him of all Means to defend himself, by seizing on all his Papers, and by causing him to be carried out of Loudun. But far from allowing of so just Reasons for an Appeal. This is the Order which Laubardemont writ at the Bottom of the Petition. That considering his Commission, and not being inform'd from any other Part of any just and true Cause to Supercede, he should proceed to the Execution of the said Commission, notwithstanding and without Regard to the said Petition, and without Prejudice to the Petitioner to address her self, to his Majesty, if it shall seem good to her so to do. They urg'd him to declare concerning the Truth or Falshhood, the allowing or disallowing of the Facts contain'd in the Petition; but he would do nothing, and never answer'd but in General Terms.

Sect. II.

Without the Clause which impower'd this Commissary to proceed notwithstanding any Opposition, Appeal, or Recusation, it is certain, all his Proceedings would have been disannull'd. For besides the Causes of Appeal before produc'd, there were every Day new Ones presented which were very lawful. Mignon, Memin, and Menuau, Moussaut, and Herve were always at his Elbow, and he made no Difficulty to hear the Witnesses in their Presence. There were however some who stuck not to depose for the Discharge of the Person accus'd, but their Depositions were not taken in Writing, and they were sent away with many Threats, to the End that those who were examin'd next, should not follow their Examples. They publish'd also a Monitory, gloss'd with many Additions, done by by several Hands, and stuff'd with infamous Facts, the Reading whereof one could not hear without Horrour. The Name of Grandier was mention'd therein, and the Crimes, the Knowledge whereof they sought for, were so foul and abominable, that the Ears of all good Men were scandaliz'd. Mounier, the Priest who had had a Suit against him, and who had been a Witness in the First Affair, of which Mention has been made before, was chose to make this Publication, as if they had a Mind to make use of Persons suspected, and that they gloried in trespassing upon all the Forms of Justice, and Bounds of Equity.

Sect. 12.

Tho these Ways of Proceeding were so extraordinary that there was some Hope that they should not continue, Grandier's Mother would not stand idle, or neglect any thing which might contribute to the Defence of her Son. Therefore the caus'd an Act to be given to Laubardemont the Third of January, 1634. wherein she declar'd, that she Appeal'd from his Order of the Twelth of December, 1633. and would take upon her to question it; Whereupon he order'd the same Day.

Sect. 13.

That without any Regard to her Appeals, Proceedings should be made as well by him, as by the King's Attorney, nam'd in the said Commission; and that the Publication of the Monitory obtain'd by the Attorney of the King should be continued, with Prohibitions to all Persons to terrifie the Witnesses, and in Case of Contravention, the Attorney was permitted to make Information. The Bishop of Poictiers fail'd not on his Part to concurr with this Proceeding, and without regarding the Order left by the Arch-bishop, his Superior, he sent another far less proper to attain the Knowledge of the Truth. Grandier's Mother Appeal'd from this new Order, to the King, by a Writ of Error, and gave a Copy of that Order of the Archbishop to the Bishop of Laubardemont, to the end, that they should not plead Ignorance. Grandier's Brother presented likewise Two Petitions, the Ninth and Tenth and January, the one to have a Copy of the Monitory which had been publish'd, the other to the Intent that it might be carried to the Registry, and that there should be made by the Petitioner a Verbal Process cum Figura; It was answer'd, That there was no Room at Present to allow of these Petitions. They Appeal'd from this Order, the Act of Appeal was signified the same Tenth Day of January, The Twelfth of the said Month they gave Notice that they took upon them the Defence, which having produc'd no Effect with the Commissary, Grandier's Mother presented another Petition the Seventeenth of the same Month, containing new Causes of Appeal, which were no more allow'd of than the First; for 'twas order'd, That having consider'd that the Causes of Appeal were not pertinent or fit to be allow'd, he would proceed further, saving to her the Petitioner to address her self to the King, as she should think good.

Sect. 14.

When she had receiv'd Notice of this Order, she also the next Day after signified an Act of Appeal by Lambert and Bertrànd; Ushers, and at the same time a Relief of Appeal was sued out by Commission, in the Chancery of the Parliament of Paris, the Fourteenth of the foregoing Month; But the Commissary tore the Acts, the King's Attorney requiring it, as Null, and done by an Attempt to the prejudice of the Power given him by his Majesty, ordaining as heretofore that they should go on without any Intermission, and proceed to the Instruction of the said Process, and for these Ends, the Publication of the Monitory shall be continued by me. -- Rene le Mounier, and others shall be requir'd by the King's Attorney, who together with the said le Mounier, the Register, and others are by him discharged of the Assignations given them to appear in the said Court, with Prohibitions to the said Bertrand and all other Ushers and Sergeants, to serve any Writs, whither by Virtue of the said Relief or Appeal, or otherwise upon Pain of Exemplary Punishment; This strange Order, dated the Twenty first of January, having been signified to the Party, she Appeal'd from it, as from the other, and the Act of Appeal was signified the Twenty Seventh of the same Month to Giles Pouquet, to be put into the Hands of Laubardemont.

Sect. 15.

The course of all these proceedings, in which they were busily imploy'd, delay'd for a while, that of the Possession. They did not however omit to Exorcise from time to time, according to the new Order of the Bishop, but Laubardemont having not leisure to assist at the Exorcisms, they did not pursue them with the same Vigour, nor had they the same reputation they gain'd since. Besides, there remain'd yet in the Mind of the Conspirators some fear, that the Parliament would take some Cognizance of this Affair; and for this reason they judg'd it convenient to suspend it for a time, to the end, they may know better what Measures they ought to take in it. In the mean while, they sought all fort of ways to authorise themselves on the Execution of the Designs they had projected. They besought the Bishop of Poictiers to come himself, or to send some considerable Ecclesiastick, to act in his Name. That Prelate forthwith sent a new Commission to the same Demorans, Dean of the Canons of Thouars, and Bachellor in Divinity, of the Faculty of Paris, to assist in the Quality of his Vicegerent, at the instruction of the Process of Grandier, notwithstanding he was the Kinsman and Friend of his chief Enemies, and that they had not fail'd to inform the Bishop of it. The Second of Feburary, Laubardemont brought the Vicegerent to Angers, with the King's Attorney, and James Nizai, Clerk of the

Commission; and he began the Fourth of the same Month, and continued every Day, till the Eleventh, to examin Grandier. It is not to be found in the Extract of the Proofs which were in the Process, that he had ever contradicted himself, nor that he had own'd any thing, whence they could draw an advantage against him, except that he confest ingenuously, that he was the Author of the Manuscript, against the Celibacy of Priests, which had been found in his Closet.

Sect. 16.

The Confessions and Denials of the Person accus'd upon the Fact which were propos'd, being sign'd by him, Laubardemont return'd to Paris, where he resided all the rest of the Month of Feburary, and part of that of March, without acquainting his Friends at Loudun, when he would return; which having cast them into an extraordinary trouble, oblig'd them to send to him Granger, Curate of Venier, to intreat him instantly to return to their assistance, and to propose to him on their parts, the conditions on which they recall'd him. That Curate had no great trouble to conclude the Bargain, because his Commission did admirably agree with the Humour and violent Inclinations of Laubardemont. But for prevention of all the inconveniencies which happen'd in the former Journey, and which might yet arise upon Account of the Parliament; he obtain'd the last Day of May, a Decree of the Council of State, which was not less strange than the Commission which he had already obtain'd. This Decree imported, That without having regard to the Appeal intended to be brought into Parliament, and to the Proceedings made in pursuance, which His Majesty has annull'd, It is order'd that the Sieur Laubardemont, shall continue the Process begun by him against Grandier, notwithstanding, all the Oppositions, Appeals, or Recusations made, or to be made, and without Prejudice to the same. The King, as far as it shall be requisite, having committed to him anew, the Cognizance thereof, and interdicted the same to the Parliament of Paris, and all other Judges, with Prohibitions to the Parties to meddle therein, upon the Penalty of Five Hundred Livres Forfeiture.

Sect. 17.

Being Arm'd with such a Decree, which render'd him the supreme Arbitrator in this Matter, Laubardemont went to Loudun with Grandier, the Ninth of April, to the great satisfaction of all the Cabal. He dispatch'd away forthwith the Archers to Angers, to take Grandier, and bring him back to Loudun; and in the mean time he caus'd an extraordinary Prison to be prepar'd for him, in a House which belong'd to Mignon, and which was inhabited by a Sergeant, nam'd Bontems, who had been Trinquants Clerk, and Witness against Grandier in the first Accusation that had been rais'd against him; so that the Person pretended to be possest, had notice of almost all he did and said. Mignon caus'd some Windows of the Chamber appointed to be his Prison, to be wall'd up, which was in the upper Story; he caus'd the Windows which remain'd open, to be sccur'd with strong and thick Grates, and the Chimney to be cross'd with thick Bars of Iron, to the end that the Devils might not come to pluck the pretended Magician out of his Chains, who being come from Angers, was conducted into his Chamber; where finding himself almost depriv'd of the Light of Day, and lodg'd upon Straw, he writ this Letter to his Mother. Dear Mother,

Sect. 18.

I Have receiv'd yours, and all that you have sent me, except the Serge Stockings. I bear my Affliction with patience, and bewail yours more than my own; I am much incommoded, having no Bed; endeavour to get my own brought me, for if the body does not repose, the Spirit will fail; send me also a Breviary, a Bible, and a Saint Thomas for my consolation; and for the rest do not afflict your self, I hope GOD will manifest my innocence; Commend me, to my Brother and Sister, and to all our good Friends. This is from your very dutiful Son, To serve you, Grandier.

Sect. 19.

When they had thus advanc'd the judicial Proceedings, and the pretended Magician was shut up again, they apply'd themselves to the work of the Possession, and to give it an Air of truth, which it had not had, to that time; for this purpose they judg'd it sit to sequester the Possessed, because that Refusal, which had been made in the former Possessions, had seem'd unjust and suspected, and entirely dispos'd the Publick to doubt that they were real and true. Next, they separated the Possessed into three Companies: Sister Claire, and Catherine de la Presentation, were put into the House of Maurat a Canon; The Superior Louisa de Jesus, and Anne de Saint Agnes in the House of Sieur de la Ville Advocate, and Counsel to Nuns, and Elizabeth de la Croix, Monique of Saint Marthe, Jeanne du Saint Esprit, and Serasique Archer, were put into another House: They were govern'd by Memin's Sister, the Wife of Nicolas Moussaut, who always continued near the Superior, when they exorcis'd her, and whisper'd into her Ear, what she had learn'd of Bontems Wife concerning Grandier; and who went and came continually, and so publickly, that almost every Body perceiv'd it.

Sect. 20.

Grandier besought the Judges, that it would please them to order a real and effectual Sequestration, instead of one feign'd and in appearance, such as was that which they pretended to have made, and was but a pure illusion, seeing that 'twas necessary that the Nuns should be lodg'd apart, to stop their talking together, taking Measures, and encouraging them to perform an Exercise, which possibly was more painful than they did imagine; That they should be govern'd by persons unsuspected, whether Churchmen, Physicians, or Women; That they should continue some Months, without having any Communication, either with his

Enemies, or the favonrers of the Possession; And that then, he doubted not, but that some one would be found, who being press'd by the remorse of her Conscience, and deliver'd from the presence of her Tyrants, would confess the Truth, and make it publickly known. But it was to shun a like disgrace, that the Exorcist had shifted off the Demands of a sequestration, and that they agreed not to it then, but because they had a full liberty to it after what manner they pleas'd, as they did effectually, by lodging the Nuns at their choice, and by Companies, and by giving more confident and obstinate Persons, for companions to those, who, they believ'd, had a more tender Conscience, or had less Resolution; which was not properly a Sequestration, but a way, by which they seem'd to cast a Mist before the Eyes of the Publick. Having had no regard to the demand of Grandier, they continued to leave the Nuns to be order'd by the Sister and Wife of his Enemies, by whose intermedling, Mignon and the Exorcists suggested all they had a Mind to. They let them remain in the House where they had sequestred them, to the Number they had been put there; And as a compleat irregularity and injustice, instead of calling in the more Famous Physicians of the great neighbouring Towns, such as Poictiers, Angers, Thouars, or Saumur, they chose out of the petty Towns, all kind of People, without merit or reputation, excepting Daniel Roger, a Physician of Loudun, who was in Truth, in some esteem, but whose Sentiment alone could not prevail over that of a set of Pretenders, who had neither Learning nor Practice; one of which was DuBourg of

Fontevraut, who never had either a Degree or Diploma, and who had been oblig'd, for this Reason, to retire from Saumur. Another was of the Town of Chinon, where he had no Employment, being a Melancholick-man, and over run with Black Choller, who had also favour'd the pretended Possession at Chinon; which was known afterwards, to be a Cheat, and of which the Authors and Actors were punish'd, as may be seen in the sequel of this History; Another who was of Thouars, had past his younger Days at Londun, in the Shop of a Tradesman, whose Journey-Man he was, and afterwards turn'd Physician, and was not a little Proud to be employ'd in a business of so high an importance; Another of the same Town, and one of the Town of Miribaut, were of no greater Reputation, but the only merit they had, was that they were Kinsmen to the Enemies of Grandier.

Sect. 21.

The Choice which was made of an Apothecary and a Chirurgeon, was neither more equitable, nor more plausible. The Apothecary named Peter Adam, was Mignen's Cousin German, and had been a Witness in the First Accusation against Grandier. And because his Testimony touch'd the Honour of a Gentlewoman of Loudun, he had been condemn'd by a Decree of the Parliament of the Tenth of March, 1633. to undergo an honourable Amand; Nevertheless, they relied on him for the preparation of Medicines; no body either saw, or knew, whether he us'd those which were prescrib'd by the Physicians, or whether he doubled not the Dose; if instead of gentle and easie Purgatives, he did not administer violent Remedies, and proper to make the Nuns fall into Convulsions and Traunces. The Chirurgion who was Mannouri, Memin's Nephew, and Brother-in-Law of one of the Nuns, had already in that quality, made an opposition to the Sequestration above mention'd, and the choice they made was generally disapprov'd. The Mother and Brother of Grandier, made in vain, several Remonstrances to the Commissary upon the Subject, but they could not so much as obtain Copies of the Petitions which had been presented to him; he promis'd however, that he would cause them to be enter'd in his Registry, but never perform'd it. Grandier also made his complaints to the unjust choice of these Physicians, to the Judges who were delegated to judge his Process; he besought them to place about the Persons pretended to be Possess'd, People of Capacity and Experience, and Apothecaries who should not give Crocus Metallorum, instead of Crocus Martis, as 'twas known that Adam had done; but the Judges being sent to confirm the Proceedings of Laubardemont, and not to correct them, they had no regard to those Petitions.

Sect. 22.

The Ninth of April, and the following Days, they made several Acts for the calling and employing Physicians, and Apothecary and Chirurgeon; And the Twelfth, the Commissary made an interlocutory Sentence, by which he order'd, That all, and every of the Witnesses heard in the said Charges and Informations, and others, as it shall seem good to the Kings Attorney to produce, should come in, and those that were not heard, and to hear their Deposition read; and if it be needful, to be confronted with the said accused Person, who to this purpose shall be continued a close Prisoner. The next Day they began the Confrontations, which were continued divers times the Days following. There was propos'd upon this Subject in the Cafe of Grandier, the Example of that which happen'd to Saint Athanasius, as an excellent means to attain the Knowledge of truth by Confrontation. This Saint having been accus'd in the Council of Tyre, by an impudent Woman, who had never seen him; when this Woman, enter'd into the Assembly, to make her Accusation in publick, a Priest named Timothy, rose up, shew'd himself to her, and spake to her, as if he had been Athanasius; she believ'd him so, and manifested thereby to all the Assembly, both her own Crime and his Innocence, which she had attacqued. If Laubardemont had been willing to make the same Trial, and presented to the Nuns at the same time Three or Four Priests with Grandier, a like cloth'd, and near of the same Stature, and Hair, whom they had never seen before, 'Tis certain, that if by chance, Grandier had been mark'd out by some one of them, there would have been others who would not have been able to distinguish him, and who by their mistake, would have made the Truth appear. But the Design of that Commissary, was to conceal the Truth, and not to discover it, and for this effect, after he had finish'd these Proceedings, having a little more leisure than he had, when he was thus employ'd, he order'd the Exorcisms to begin again. The Bishop of Poictiers having rejected Father l'Escayz, and Father Gau, nam'd by the Archbishop his Superior, had sent Two others in their place, who were his Chaplain, and Father Lactance a Franciscan. This choice of the former was highly condemn'd, because he had been of the Number of the Judges who had given the first sentence against Grandier, which the Archbishop of Bourdeaux had invalidated. They were lodg'd in the House of Nicolas Moussaut, and some time after, some of the Nuns were lodg'd there also, to the great astonishment of all unconcern'd Persons. Memin, Menuau, and Herve, went every Day into this House, to visit the Exorcists, and Discourse with them in private. These last began to perform their Charge, the Fifteenth of April. Lactance seeing that the Superior understood Latine very little, order'd her to speak in French, although he often put to her Questions in Latine. There were some Persons who objected to him, that she ought to answer her in the same Language, and that the Devil ought not to be ignorant of any; To which this Father answer'd, sometimes, That the Pact had been so made, and at other times, That there were some Devils more ignorant than the very Peasants. A little while after, there was observ'd to come a Recruit of Exorcists, who were Four Capucin Friars, named Father Luke, Father Tranquille, Father Potais, and Father Elizee, besides two Carmelites, who had intruded themselves there from the beginning of the Possession, and had been tolerated by the Bishop of Poictiers, to wit, Father Peter, of Saint Thomas, and

Father Peter of Saint Mathurin. They joyn'd themselves with the Capucins, who had been sent with great expectation, and for particular Ends, concerted amongst the principal Monks of France, of whom the famous Father Joseph was the Head. The chief design was to establish that Proposition, which is found in the Book of Father Tranquille, That the Devil duly exorcis'd, is constrain'd to speak the Truth; and there-by they pretended to prove undeniably the bodily Presence of Jesus Christ in the Sacrament, and all other Tenets of the Roman Church; but they hoped above all, that this would give them an opportunity to bring in a kind of Inquisition; and that it would be a certain means to make all the Churchmen, the Wealth, the Honour, and the Lives of private Persons, and chiefly the Hereticks, to depend upon the Ecclesiasticks. Father Joseph went also to Loudun Incognito, to examin himself this pretended Possession, to the end, that if he found that it had a sufficient Air and Appearance of Truth he might put himself at the Head of the Exorcists, to assume the greater part of the glory of having dispossest the Devils, and acquire a high reputation of Piety and Sanctity. But this subtil Monk, had no Mind to engage in this Matter: he knew well, that it would not become a Man of his Importance, and that he ought to leave it in the Hands of his Inferiors, who would content themselves with the esteem of Bigots, and mean People, and not be concern'd though they were expos'd to the derision of the better sort, and Men of Wit.

Sect. 23.

The Persons possessed, were allotted by Classes to each of the Exorcists, and they exorcis'd them in four several Places, which were in the Churches of Saint Crosse, of the Convent of the Ursulines, of Saint Peter du Martrai, of the Priory, and of Notre Dame du Chateau. There past little in the Exorcisms of the Fifteenth and Sixteenth of April. Laubardemont omitted to put Interrogatories to Grandier, from the Seventeenth of the same Month, upon the Cases arising from the Verbal Process which he had made. The Physicians, Apothecary and the Chirurgeon began also to make their Reports of what they had seen, and the Observations that were made upon the Condition of the Possessed, and upon their Feats of Activity. They drew up Twenty Six Articles during the time of their Commission; the Sum whereof was, That the things which they had seen, were supernatural, and surpassing as well the knowledge, as the Rules of Physick. In the mean time, that which happen'd the Twenty Third of the same Month of April, seem'd not very Miraculous, Lactance exorcising the Superior, demanded of her in Latine, bad enough, In what shape the Devil had enter'd in her? Of a Cat, reply'd she, a Dog, a Stag, and a Goat; Quoties? that is to say, How often? continued the Exorcist. I have not well observ'd the Day said she, because she believ'd that Quoties was the same thing as Quando, When? The next Day being the Twenty Fourth, the same Nun, returning from the Exorcism, staid near the House of the Widow Barot, and said, she could not go on, further, because she had seen the Hand of Grandier through the Window of his Chamber; but this Window was so small, that scarce any Light could come in there, and this Action did only excite the Laughter of some of those that were there Present.

Sect. 24.

The Twenty Sixth it was order'd that Grandier should be visited, upon Occasion, that the Superior had declar'd, that his Body was marked with Marks of the Devil, and that he was insensible in all Places where the Marks were. This unhappy Man was treated so inhumanely upon that Occasion, that the very Thought of the Anguish which they made him suffer, is enough to make one tremble; They sent for Mannouri the Chirurgion, one of his Enemies, and the most unmerciful of them all: When he was come into the Chamber, they stripped Grandier stark naked, blinded his Eyes, shav'd him every where, and Mannouri began to search him. When he would perswade them that the Parts of his Body which had been mark'd by the Devil were insensible, he turn'd that End of the Probe which was round, and he guided it in such Manner, that not being able to enter into the the Flesh, nor to make much Impression, it was push'd back into the Palm of his Hand; The Patient did not then cry out, because he felt no pair; but when the Barbarous Chirurgeon would make them see that the other Parts of his Body were very sensible, he turn'd the Probe at the other End, which was very sharp pointed, and thrust it to the very

Bone; and then abundance of People, who were at the Bottom of the Prison without, heard Complaints so bitter, and Crys so piercing, that they mov'd them to the Heart; But Laubardemont, who was present at this Action, did not seem to be touch'd with any Sense of Pity; The Superior, who was content the first time to say that the Magician had Five Marks of the Devil upon his Body, without specifying them, nor the Places where they were, did not fail the next Day, the Twenty Seventh of the Month, to nominate the Places, where those, who had seen him all naked, had observ'd Two of these Spots. As for the Three others, the Physicians could not see them, because, says the Extract of of the Proofs, and c. they were too hard to be distinguish'd. But if the Devil, who had possess'd her, had no great knowledge of the things which were somewhat secret, or conceal'd so near him, at least that he had not been inform'd of by the Reports of Men, he knew not much more of what past further off; For the Thirtieth of the same Month, the Exorcist having demanded of him, Why he had not been willing to answer the Saturday before, It was, said he by the Mouth of the Nun, because I was imploy'd, that day in conducting to Hell the Soul of le Proust Attorney of the Parliament of Paris. The Curious did not fail to make an Exact Inquiry, if there had been an Attorney of this Name in the Parliament; They caus'd the Registers of the Dead to be examin'd, to know whether at that time, some Person of the same Name, of what quality soever, was dead at Paris. But neither the one, nor the other of these things were found true, nor has it been seen in any of the Books which have been writ in Favour of the Possession; that they have dar'd to alledge this Particular, amongst the Miraculous Knowledge which has been attributed to the Superior.

Sect. 25.

They Exorciz'd again in the Church of the Carmelites, where the Exorcist demanded of one of the Persons possess'd, Where were the Magick Books of Grandier: She answer'd that they would find them in the Lodgings of a certain Gentlewoman whom she nam'd, and who was the Person that caus'd Adam the Apothecary to undergo an honourable Amand. At that Instant, Laubardemont, Herve, Menuau, Moussant, and many others, went into the House of this Gentlewoman; They view'd the Chambers and Closets; They open'd the Coffers, search'd in all the most secret Places, and having not found any Magical Book, the Exorcist, at their Return, reproach'd the Devil, that he had deceiv'd the Court, and he adjur'd him again to speak the Truth; He answer'd, that a Neece of this Gentlewoman had taken away those Books; They ran presently to this Neece's House, but they found that she was in a Church at her Devotions, and that it was impossible that she should be gone to her Kinswoman's House in the time mention'd by the Devil; so that they could not carry the Revenge of Adam so far as he had wish'd, and had been promis'd him in Requital of his Services, and he was fain to content himself with this Affront which he had put upon his Enemy.

Sect. 26.

Grandier had a Brother, an Advocate in the Parliament, and who had also an Office of Counsellour in the Bailiwick of Loudun; They judg'd it requisite to hinder his solliciting the Parliament to take Cognizance of the Affair of his Brother, as being already concern'd by the Appeals, and by the Petition which had been presented to them; Therefore the Superior accus'd this Man also of Magick. He had no sooner Advice of this Accusation, but he gave a Petition to the Court, to have a Satisfaction for this Calumny, declaring that they had accus'd him, only to deprive his Brother of all the Means he had of Assistance. But Duthibaut, who was at Paris, caus'd him to be Arrested Prisoner, by Virtue of an Order of Laubardemont; and to be brought into the House of one of the Favourers of the Possession, from whence he did not get out till after the Death of Grandier, at the urgent Sollicitation of his Friends.

Sect. 27

In the Beginning of May, one of the Devils of the Superior had promis'd to raise her up Two Foot high; Lactance call'd upon him often to perform his Promise, which he did not however, because the Nun having been willing to dazzle the Eyes of the People, by trying one time to do something near it, There was one of the Spectators who lifted up the Bottom of her Garment, and made all the others see that she touch'd the Ground with the End of one of her Feet. The Devil Eazas had also promis'd to raise up la Nogeret Three Foot from the Ground; and another Devil nam'd Cerberus, to lift up his Nun Two Foot; But neather the one nor the other were Devils of their Word. The Devil Beherit pretended to have done his Part so well, as to retrieve the Honour of his Companions by establishing his own Reputation; He vaunted, for this purpose, to take off Laubardemont's Cap from off his Head, and to keep it hanging in the Air, during the Space of a Miserere. The time which he had appointed being come, Lactance adjur'd him in all the requisite Forms to shew this Marvel before the Eyes of the Spectators; This Exorcist us'd Flatteries, Complaints, and Threatnings, but when he perceived that he obtain'd nothing, he knew well that some Accident was fallen out, which had given Vent to his Mine, or had put some of the Springs of the Machine that was to play, out of Order. And, in Truth, he was not deceiv'd, for some Suspicious People considering that it was late, that they were about to light their Flambeaux, that that time was very proper to perform some Illusion, and that Laubardemont was plac'd in a Chair distant enough from the Company, and just under one of the Arches of the Church, they ran out to go up and place themselves upon the Arch, where they found the Man who was appointed to act his Part, and who was constrain'd to give over his Work of Darkness, and to carry away his little Hook, and the Hair or Thread to which it was fasten'd. He was to let slip his Hook through a little Hole made on Purpose, above and overagainst the Place design'd for Laubardemont, who was to take the Hair, and fasten it to a little Loop sewed to his Cap, making a Shew to make it right, and some time after this Hair was to be drawn up into the Air, and should have carried up the Cap with it; Then the Exorcist should have caus'd the Miserere to be sung, during which the Cap should have been continued hanging in the Air, and not have fallen down till the Musick had been ended. But this Honour was not reserv'd for Beherit, who remain'd under the same Confusion with his Companions.

Sect. 28.

They well perceiv'd that so many Attempts failing, would bring the Possession into Contempt. A great Number of Gentlemen and other Persons yet of a better Quality, who came to Loudun with an Expectation that they should see there daily some new Miracle, began to be disgusted with what they had seen, and to return into their several Countries, whither they brought no News able to Augment the Belief of that diabolical Intrigue. Father Tranquille complains in his Book in these Terms, Many, says he, being come to see the Miracles at Loudun, if presently the Devils give them not such Signs as they require, they go away discontented, and have increas'd the Number of Unbelievers; Wherefore 'twas resolv'd to produce some great Exploit to revive their languishing Curiosity, and renew their Belief, that was upon the point of expiring. Lactance promis'd that of Seven Devils which possess'd the Superior, three of them should go out of her the Twentieth of May without Fail. These Three were Asmodee, Gresil of the

Thrones, and Aman of the Powers. They were to give her, at their going out, Three Wounds on the left side, and make as many holes in her Shift, Bodice, and Gown. The greatest of the Three Wounds, were to be a Pin's Length, which was shew'd to those who assisted at the Exorcism, where he made this kind of Proclamation; The Place where the Wound should be made was likewise mark'd. They assur'd also the Commandeur de la Porte, who was then at Loudun, that the possessed should have her Hands tyed behind her Back, when the Wounds should be made. The Day appointed being come, and the Church of Saint Crosse being fill'd with the inquisitive Persons, who had a Mind to observe whether the Devils would keep their Word once in their Lives, they caus'd presently some Physicians of the neighbouring Towns, who were there present, to view the Sides, the Bodice, the Shift, and the Gown of the Nun. Their Report was; that they sound not any Wound upon her Side, any Cut in her Garments, nor any sharp Instrument in the Plaits of her Cloaths. After this diligent Search, Father Lactance put Questions to her for the Space of two Hours almost always in French, and the Answers were made in the same Language; and when he proceeded to Commands and Adjurations, there was a Physician of Saumur named Duncan, a Scotch-man, who was Principal of the University of the Protestants, and Professor in Philosophy, who said, that they were promis'd that the Nun should have her Hands tyed. The Exorcist acknowledg'd, that it was sit to bind her to remove all Suspicion of Deceit and Fraud. In the mean time he declar'd, that there were many Persons in the Company, who had never seen the Convulsions whereinto the possessed us'd to fall, and that 'twas requisite for the Satisfaction of such, that they should Exorcise this Nun before she was bound. Then he began the Exorcisms and Adjurations, and at the same time she made a Contorsion of her Body which seem'd very frightfuul, her Hands and her Feet were a-like turn'd outward, and after that the Palms of her Hands, and the Soles of her Feet, were joyn'd very close one to the other; all her Limbs return'd to their former Condition, and then she rose up. The Exorcist gave her no Intermission, for she was scarce recover'd out of that first Convulsion, but he repeated to her his Adjurations, and this was done at that time, that she lay upon her Face on the Ground, and that they saw her right Thigh drawn outwards, then being bow'd down upon her Arm and right Side, she continued in this Condition some little time, and at last they heard her groan; and when she drew her hand out of her Bosom, they perceiv'd the tops of her Fingers stain'd with Blood. The Physicians who had heard her Groans, search'd quickly after the Cause, both with their Eyes and Hands, in her Cloaths and upon her Body; They found her Gown pierced in two places, and her Bodice and Shift in three places, the Holes being in Length a Fingers Breadth; They found also the Skin pierc'd in three places beneath her left Breast. The wounds were so slight, that they scarce past through the Skin; that in the Middle was of the Length of a Barly Corn, the Two others were not so large, nor so deep; In the mean while there issued out Blood at all Three, with which her Shift was stain'd. Laubardemont was in some Confusion at the Performance of this Trick, by Reason of the Number and Quality of the Spectators, and esepecially of the Commandeur de la Port, who had Assurance given him that the Nun should be bound, and he could not forbear, to say, That this was not fair. However he would not suffer the Physicians who attested the Fact, to joyn to their Attestations the judgment which he made of the sufficient and Instrumental Causes of those Three Wounds. But Duncan was no soonor at Saumur, but he publish'd a Writing, containing Observations which were made upon this pretended Miracle, which are in Brief, 'That the Devils of Loudun being cunning and fraudulent, had not attempted to make any other Sign, but that which was the easiest of all those they had promis'd, and where they could more readily, with a little Slight, deceive the Eyes of the People; That the Cloaths of the Superior had not been search'd, because they presuppos'd that her Hands should be tyed, when the Wounds were to be made in her Flesh: That instead thereof, she had her Hands at Liberty, and hid from the Assistants when she was wounded; That the Wounds were not found to be exactly made in the Place where she her self had design'd; That they were not so large as they were promis'd; That they seem'd to have been made by the Incision of a little Penknife, or by the pricking of a Launcet; That the Incisions were much greater in the Garments than in the Skin, which made it appear that they were made from without; inwards, and not from within outwards. That the Cloaths were not examin'd after the Wounds had been made, because it 'twould have been expedient to strip the Nun to her Smock to do it exactly, which Decency would not suffer; Moreover that she might have thrown amongst the Croud of People, without being perceiv'd, the Instrument she us'd, which must be very small. That if the Devils were then gone out, they had not been compell'd by the Force of the Exorcism, seeing that the Exorcist had not given them any Command; That there were not made in her Gown three Cuts as well as in the Shift and Stays, though they were promis'd all alike, because one of the Incisions was made where none of her Garment lay, it being open before.' Laubardemont was extreamly provok'd by the boldness of the Author of this Writing, who overthrew the Miracle by such pertinent Reasons, and solid Proofs: He vow'd to be reveng'd of Duncan, and to prosecute him to the utmost, and the Printer who had sold his Books; but the Marshal de Breze, who promis'd them his Protection, laid the Storm which threatned them, and which otherwise could not but have been very violent and dangerous.

Sect. 28.

'Grandier, on his part, made almost the same Observations upon this Action; to which he added further, That if the Superior had not Groan'd, the Physicians would not have open'd her Cloaths, and that they would have suffer'd her to be bound, not imagining that the Wounds had been already made; and that then the Exorcist would have commanded Three other Devils to go out, and to give the Signs they had promis'd; That the Superior would have made the strangest contorsions she had been able, and would have had a long Convulsion, at the end whereof she would have been deliver'd, and the Wounds found upon her Body. But that this groaning had betray'd her, and had broke, by GOD's Permission, all the Measures concerted by Men and Devils; For what Cause think you (said he) in his Exceptions and Absolvatory Conclusions, that they chose for a Sign, Wounds resembling those which are made with a sharp Instrument, since the Devils are accustom'd to make Wounds like to those by burning? Is it not because 'twas more easie for the Superior to hide an Instrument, and to wound her self slightly, than to hide Fire, and to make a Wound by burning? Why think you they chose the leftside, rather than the Forehead or Nose? unless that she could not hurt her Forehead or Nose, without exposing the Action to the Eyes of all the Company. Wherefore should they chuse the left side rather than the right? Were it not that it was more easie for the Righthand, which the Superior us'd, to extend it on the left side, than to bend it on the right? Wherefore did she turn her self upon her Arm and left side? Were it not to the end, that this Posture, in which she continued a very long time, might make easie to her the means of concealing from the Eyes of the Spectators, the Instrument wherewith she wounded her self? whence think you, proceeded the Groans which she gave, in spite of all her constancy? If it was not from the Sence of the Hurt she did to herself, the most couragious being not able to refrain from trembling, when the Chirurgeon lets them Blood? Why did the ends of her Fingers appear bloody? unless because they held the Instrument which made the Wounds. Who perceives not, that this Instrument, having been very small, 'twas impossible to prevent, that the Fingers which were employ'd, should not become Red with the Blood which was caus'd to issue out? In brief, whence was it, that these Wounds were so slight, that they scarce were Skin deep, seeing that the Devils are us'd to break and tear in pieces the Possessed, when they go out of them? unless for this, that the Superior did not hate her self enough, to make Deep and Dangerous Wounds.'

Sect. 29.

Though this pretended Miracle, studied with much Care, and manag'd with much Skill, had not however, succeeded very well, the Commissary, who supprest universally, whatsoever made against the Possession, and who gave Authority to all that might confirm it, forbore not to make his Verbal Process of the Expulsion of three Devils, Asmodee, Gresil, and Aman, by three Wounds, made beneath the Region of the Heart of the Sister Jeanne des Anges, and they were not afraid to produce the Verbal Process, amongst the Papers which they made use of against Grandier. Lactance seeking to dissipate the suspicions which he knew to be rais'd in the Minds of the Beholders of this illusion, demanded the next Day of Balaam, one of the Four Devils who continued in the Body of the Superior, why Asmodee and his two Companions were gone, whilst the Face and Hands of the Superior were hid from the Eyes of the People? 'Tis, said he, to retain a great many in unbelief. After this manner this Devil, who was in good intelligence and agreement with Father Tranquille, endeavour'd to make good the Father's reasons. 'They have cause (said this Father, complaining of those that were dissatisfied) to be offended at the small civility and courtesy of these Devils, who have not had a respect for their Merits, and the Quality of their Persons; but if the greatest part of these had examin'd their own Consciences, possibly they would find that the cause of their dissatisfaction proceeded from thence; and that they ought rather to be reveng'd of themselves by a good Penance, and not to bring prying Eyes and a vicious Conscience, to return incredulous.' Thus these crafty Exorcists do always find reasons to confound the Gainsayers, or rather evasions to dazle the simple and the bigots; for if the Parts they acted happen'd to succeed, they were Miracles, wherein shone the Power which the Church gives to its Ministers; and if the Success was not favourable, 'twas the incredulity of the Spectators, which was the Cause; If the Devil obey'd, he was constrain'd by the Power of Exorcisms; and if he were not obedient, 'twas permitted him to use them so, for a just Punishment from GOD, against the Unbelievers, to continue them in unbelief.

Sect. 31.

IT was reported, that Six lusty and strong Men, could not restrain the Possessed from making their Contorsions. Duncan perhaps, with a little to much confidence, depending upon the Protection of the Marshal de Breze, attempted to try an Experiment, to the great Displeasure of the Father Recollet; for having laid hold on the Right-Hand of the Superior, with one of his, she endeavour'd to make him loose his hold, as soon as Lactance had order'd the Devil to make her Contorsions; but she could not perform them, but with her Legs, and her Left-Arm; she was in vain conjur'd to do them with her Right-Arm, as with her Left; I cannot, said she at last, for he holds me; let go her Arm, said the Exorcist, to Duncan, for how can Contorsions be made, if you hold her? If it is a Devil, reply'd Duncan, with a loud Voice, he ought to be stronger than I; As good a Philosopher as you are, this is ill Logick, reply'd Lactance, with eagerness, for a Devil out of a Body, is stronger than you; but being in a feeble Body, such as she is, tis not necessary that he should be as strong as you, for his natural Actions are proportion'd to the force of the Body that he possesseth. 'This good Father (says Duncan, in the Book where he has left this History, remembers not that he has Read in the Gospel, that the Demoniacks broke the Cords and Chains wherewith they were bound, and that the Ritual puts amongst the Marks of Possession, Vires supra ætatis and conditionis naturam ostendere, To exert strength beyond the nature of the Age or Quality of the Party possessed. Duncan added, that next Day he did the same thing to the Sister Agnes, and that he was pray'd not to hold her Hand too fast, because the Superior had complain'd that he had hurt her, by holding her too strongly; and that these things were done in the presence of the Commandeur de la Porte, Lauberdemont, and a great many Persons of Quality.' He reported further, that the first time that he saw the Nun, his arrival caus'd a little disgrace to the Devil Gresil, because the Exorcist having adjur'd him to tell his Name he was twice deceiv'd, calling him the first time Benoit, and half an Hour after Texier, which were the Names of the two other Physicians of Saumur, after which he would not conjectrue more, although at the Third time he might have been able to find out the true Name, because the Nun had at other times heard these Physicians spoken of, especially during the Sickness of her Mother, of which she died, or at least there was one of them sent for, to visit her, but their Countenances were alike unknown to her.

Sect.. 32.

There past nothing remarkable, from the Twentieth of May, till the Thirteenth of June, which was Famous for the vomiting a Quill of a Feather, of a Fingers length, which the Superior cast up, for only the Devils that possest her, were fertil in Miracles, and obey'd from time to time, the Voice of the Exorcists; the others were Malicious, Rebellions, and Disobedient, who took care to do nothing extraordinary, for the Glory of GOD, and for that of the Church and its Ministers. The Commissary made a very exact Verbal Process of this last Miracle, and of another Vomiting of a Silk Button, which the same Nun did Vomit the Eighth of July following. But what Verbal Process might he not have made of that which Saint Augustine reports? That there were several People, who after their having swallow'd several Things, and kept them some time in their Bowels, fetch'd up those they had a mind to, and drew them as out of a Pouch. This Marvel was yet greater than that of the Superior, and for all that, those that wrought them, were not possess'd with Devils.

Sect. 33.

The Bishop of Poictiers, came to Loudun, the Sixteenth of the same Month of June; 'twas told him directly, by Father Tranquille, 'That the Devils, who had sojourn'd there for some time, could not be driven out but by a Blow of the Scepter; and that the Crosier was not sufficient to break the Head of this Dragon, who had cast his Poison against innocent Souls.' For the Bishop never had a Mind to be concern'd in Person in this Affair, if it had not been supported by the Royal Authority, and that of the Cardinal; but with such Warrantees he made no difficulty to enter into the List. He told those who came to salute him at his arrival, That he was not come to take Cognizance of the Truth of the Possession, but to make it believ'd by those who were yet doubtful, and to discover the Schools of Magick, as well for Men as Women. It was well understood what that meant, That he came to begin an establishment of a kind of Inquisition which had been before projected. He himself did not exorcise, 'twas the Father Recollect that exorcis'd in his presence; and he permitted that the Exorcist should presuppose, as evident, that Grandier was a Magician, although this was the thing in question. Infringo, said he to the Devil, Omne Pactum, sive a Domino tuo Lucifero, sive a Magistro tuo Grandiero, I dissolve every Pact, whether from thy Lord Lucifer, or from thy Master Grandier. Then they began to publish among the People, that they ought to believe the Possession, seeing that the King, the Cardinal, and the Bishop, did credit it, and that one could not suspect it, without rendering himself guilty of High-Treason against GOD and Man, and without exposing himself in the Quality of a Complice of Grandier, to the strokes of the terrible Justice of Laubardemont. And indeed, if there were any one yet who durst hesitate and suspend his Judgment, he was presently treated as one damn'd, and worse than a Heretick; and most of the other Catholicks, would no more communicate with him, than with one excommunicated. Memin and all the Cabal publish'd boldly every where, that he must be a Devil, who could make any doubt of the Possession. 'To words, some added Writings; 'Tis this which mades us say, with assurance, (says Father Tranquille, in one of his Books) that this Enterprize is the Work of GOD, seeing that 'tis the work of the King. And writing against the Case of Grandier, and some other Pieces made by the Incredulous, he says, That their Libels did offend the

Two Powers, the Regal, and Episcopal. He says further, That if there be a Person in the World, who has seen clearly into this business, and whose Judgment ought to be follow'd; it is the King, who believes the Possession, and who makes not this Affair his own, to render himself a Complice of a Cheat. 'Tis the most Eminent, my Lord the Cardinal, the first Person of State, who believes the Possession; and not only believes it, but next to his Majesty, the Enterprize of this Affair is owing to his Piety and to his Zeal, as the Letters which he has writ to Monsieur Laubardemont sufficiently testifie; at the reading whereof, one cannot but admire his goodness, as well as the greatness of his Soul, to see that he who moves the World, and shakes Monarchies by his Wise Counsels, undertakes, with the Care of a Father, the comforting these Nuns; and with the Zeal of a Prelate, the complaint of the Church, offended by this Sorcery. The Author of the Demonomany of Loudun, proves also the Possession, by this Argument, the King and Monsieur the Cardinal do Authorise it; it cannot than be doubted.' So that no one durst open his Mouth to tell his Sentiment, and some already began to feel the Yoke of this kind of Inquisition, which the Exorcists had design'd to establish.

Sect. 34.

Amongst many particular things which were done before the Bishop, this deserves to be related in the same Words wherein they are set down in a Manuscript Relation, which has been accounted faithful, and very exact by all Persons that liv'd at that time; it seems to have been writ by a good Roman Catholick, throughly convinc'd of the Truth of the Possession, and of the Power of the Exorcists over the Devils, as well as of the Integrity of these last; and is as follows: 'Friday the Twenty Second of June, 1634. being the Vigil of Saint John, at Three of the Clock in the Afternoon, Monsieur de Poicters, and Monsieur de Laubardemont, being in the Church of Saint Crosse at Loudun, to continue the Exorcisms of the Ursuline Nuns, by the Order of the said Sieur Laubardemont Commissary; Urban Grandier, Priest and Parson, accus'd, and nam'd Magician, by the said possessed Nuns, to whom were produc'd by the said Commissary, Four Pacts, reported at several times, in the foregoing Exorcisms, by the said Possessed, which the Devils who possess'd them, said were made with the said Grandier, for many ends; but one in particular, made by Leviathan, on Saturday, the Seventeenth of the present Month; compos'd of the Flesh and Heart of an Infant, taken at one of their Sabats (or Witches nocturnal Assemblies) held at Orleans, in 1631. and of the Ashes of a Consecrated Wafer, and of the Blood and the-- of the said Grandier, by which Leviathan said, he had entred the Body of the Sister Jeanne des Anges, Superior of the said Nuns; and had possess'd her with his Associates, Behemot, Isaacarum, and Balaam, and this the Eighth of December, 1632. The other compos'd of the Seeds of Oranges and Pomegranades, given by Asmodee, then possessing the Sister Agnes, Thursday the Twenty Second of the present Month, made between the said Grandier, Asmodee, and a

Number of other Devils, to hinder the performance of the Promises of Beherit, who had promis'd for a Sign of his going out, to lift the Cap of the Commissary two Pikes high, the Space of a Miserere. All which Pacts shew'd to the said Grandier, he said, without being any way astonish'd, but with a constant and generous resolution, that he knew not in any sort, what belong'd to those Pacts; nor had ever made them; and knew not an Art capable of such things, nor ever had communication with the Devils; and was absolutely ignorant of that which they alledged. Where of there was made a Verbal Process which he sign'd. This done, there were brought all the said possessed Nuns, to the Number of Eleven or Twelve, comprizing the three Secular Maids also possess'd, into the Choir of the Church, accompanied by a great many Friars, Carmelites, Capucins, and Recollects, Three Physicians, and a Chirurgeon; which Nuns, at their entrance, us'd some wanton Expressions, calling the said Grandier their Master, testifying to him their Joy to see him. Then Father Lactance, Gabriel a Recollect, and one of the Exorcists, exhorted all the Assistants to lift up their Hearts to GOD with an extraordinary fervour, to make acts of Contrition, for the Offences committed against that adorable Majesty; and to beseech him, that so many Sins might not put a stop to the designs which his Providence had for his Glory, on that occasion; and for an outward Mark of their inward contrition, to say the Confiteor, in order to to receive the Benediction of Monsieur the Bishop of Poictiers; which being perform'd, he continued to say, the Matter in question was of so great weight, and so important to the Truths of the Roman Catholick Church, that this only consideration, ought to serve for a Motive to excite their Devotion; and that otherwise, the Affliction of these poor Nuns were so strange, after their having been so long, that Charity oblig'd all those who have right to labour their Deliverance, and the expulsion of the Devils, to employ the power of their Character for so worthy a Subject, by the Exorcisms which the Church prescribes her Pastors; and directing his Speech to Grandier, he told him, that being of this Number, by the Holy Unction of Priesthood, he ought to contribute his power and Zeal, if it pleas'd Monsieur the Bishop, to permit him, and to commute his suspension, by his Authority; which Monsieur the Bishop having granted, the Father Recollect presented a Stole to the said Grandier; who turning himself towards the said Bishop, ask'd him, if he allow'd him to take it, to whom having answer'd Yes, he put the said Stole on his Neck, and then the Father Recollect gave him a Ritual, which he desir'd leave of the said Bishop to take as before, and receiv'd his Benediction; prostrating himself at his Feet to Kiss them. Whereupon the Veni Creator Spiritus having been Sung, he arose and directed his Speech to the Bishop of Poictiers, and said to him, my Lord, whom must I exorcise? To which it being answer'd him, by the said Bishop, These Maids. He went on and said, What Maids? To which he was answer'd, These possessed Maids; So that (said he) my Lord, I am then oblig'd to believe the Possession; the Church believes it, I believe it then also, although I think that a Magician cannot cause a Christian to be possess'd, without his consent. Then some cry'd out, that he was a Heretick to advance this Belief, that that was an unquestionable Truth, receiv'd unanimously by all the Church, and approv'd by the Sorbon. Whereupon he answer'd, that he had never grounded his Faith upon it, that 'twas only his Opinion; that in every case he submitted to the Judgment of the Body, of which he was but a Member; and that no Person was ever accounted a Heretick, for having had Doubts, but for obstinately persevering in them; and that what he had propos'd to the said Lord Bishop, was to be assur'd by his Mouth, that he should not abuse the Authority of the Church. And being brought by the Father Recollect to the Sister Catharine, as the most ignorant of all, and least suspected to understand Latine, he began the Exorcism in the form prescrib'd by the Ritual, but could not continue long, because all the other Possessed began to be tormented by the Devils, and made strange and horrible Cries; and amongst the other, the Sister Claire advanc'd towards him, reproaching him for his blindness and obstinacy, so fully, that in that contention, he left the other possessed which he had undertook, and directed his Discourse to the Sister Claire. But 'tis to be observ'd, that before the Exorcism began, he told her, speaking in Latine, as he had almost always done, explaining himself a little after in French, That as for her, she understood Latine, and that he would ask her Questions in Greek, it being one of the Marks requir'd, to justify an undoubted Possession, and that the Devils understood all forts of Languages; To whom the Devil reply'd, by the Mouth of the Possessed, Ah! how cunning art thou? Thou knowest well, that this is one of the Conditions of the Pact, made between thee first and us, not to answer at all in Greek. To which he answer'd, O fine Illusion, O excellent Evasion! And then 'twas told him, that he was permitted to exorcise in Greek, provided that he writ down first, what he would say. The said Possessed offer'd however, to answer him in what Language he would, but there was no room for that; for all the Possessed began again their Cries and outrages, with Imprecations not to be equal'd, and mighty strange Convulsions, persisting to accuse the said Grandier of Magick, and of the Sorcery which infested them; offering to break his Neck, if 'twas permitted them, and striving all manner of ways to abuse him, which was hind'red by the Protection of the Church, and by the Priests and Friars there present, taking extraordinary pains to restrain the Fury wherewith they were all agitated. He in the mean time, continued without any trouble or emotion, beholding stedfastly the said Possessed, protesting his Innocence, and praying G O D to be his Protector; and addressing himself to Monsieur the Bishop, and to Monsieur de Laubardemont, he told them, that he implor'd the Authority Ecclesiastical and Royal, whereof they were Ministers, to command these Devils to break his Neck, or at least to make a visible Mark in his Forehead, in case that he was the Author of the Crimes of which he was accus'd, to the end, that thereby the Glory of G O D might be manifested, the Authority of the Church exalted, and he himself confounded; Provided nevertheless, that these Maids might not touch him with their Hands, which they would not at all permit, as well not to be the cause of the Mischief which might befall him, as not to expose the Authority of the Church to the Wiles of the Devils, who might have contracted some Pact upon this Subject with the said Grandier. Then the Exorcists, to the Number of Eight, having enjoyn'd the Devils silence, and to cease the Disorder's they made, they order'd Fire to be brought in a Chafindish, into which were thrown all the Pacts, one after another, and then the former Assaults redoubled with Convulsions so horrible, Cries so hideous, and Postures so frightful, that that Assembly might pass for a Sabat of Witches, were it not for the Holyness of the Place, and the Quality of the Persons present, of whom the least concern'd, at least to outward Appearance, was the said Grandier, although he had more Cause than any other, the Devils continuing their Accusations, naming to him the Places, the Hours and Days of their Communications with him; his first Sorceries, his Scandals, his Insensibility, his Renunciations made of his Faith and of GOD; To which he reply'd, with a bold Assurance, that he gave the Lye to those Calumnies, so much the more unjust, as they were far remote from his Profession; That he renounc'd Satan and all the Devils; that he knew them not, and fear'd them yet less; that in spite of them he was a Christian, and a person consecrated with Holy Orders; That he trusted in GOD, and in Jesus Christ, although a great Sinner as to the Rest; but however, that he had never given Way to these Abominations, and that they could not give a pertinent and Authentic

Testimony against him. And here 'tis impossible by any Discourse to express that which sell under the Senses; The Eyes and Ears receiv'd the impression of so many Furies, that there was never any thing seen like them, and at least, without being accustom'd to such horrid Spectacles as those are who sacrifice to Devils. There was no courage which could defend it self from the Astonishment and Horrour, that this Action produced. Grandier amidst all this, continued always the same; that is to say, insensible of many Prodigies, singing the Hymns of the Church, with the rest of the People, being fearless, as it he had a Legion of Angels for his Guard. And truly one of these Devils cry'd out, that Beelzebub was then between him and Father Tranquille a Capucin; and upon what he had said, addressing his Speech to the Devil, Obmutescas, Be silent, the said Devil began to swear, that that was the Watch-Word between them; but they were forc'd to tell all, because GOD was incomparably stronger than all Hell. So that all were ready to fall upon him, offering to Tear him in Pieces, to shew his Marks, and to strangle him, though he were their Master. Whereupon he took occasion to tell them, that he was neither their Master, nor their Servant; and that 'twas an incredible thing, that even in the same confession, they should declare him their Master, and offer to strangle him. And then the Maids having thrown their Slippers at his Head, he said, see how the Devils accuse themselves. At last this Violence and Outrages increast to such a Degree, that without the succour and hind'rance of Persons who were in the Choir, the Author of this Spectacle would have infallibly ended his Life; and all they could do for him, was to get him out of the Church, and to save him from the fury which threatned him. So that he was brought back to his Prison, at Six of the Clock in the Evening, and the rest of the Day was employ'd to recover the Spirits of these poor Maids out of the Possession of the Devils.'

Sect. 35.

Those who writ for Grandier, after this Storm said, that these Maids who appear'd so insolent, that they neither had a respect for the Place, nor the Persons who were there assembled, and so enrag'd against this Poor Man, that they seem'd to have a mind to tear him in Pieces, without the aid of the Guardian of the Capucins and other Exorcists, whose intention was not to leave him then for a Prey to their rage, but to reserve him for more terrible Punishments, the horror and quality whereof, would not suffer the Truth of the Possession to be doubted of, and whereby they pretended to gain to themselves the reputation of an extraordinary Sanctity, and miraculous Power. 'Twas observ'd further, that the more prudent Persons were much astonish'd to see, that whilst they were exorcis'd by Grandier, they answer'd only by a torrent of Injuries and of spitings which they vomited against him, and especially that the Superior made use of so bad an evasion for not answering in Greek; saying, That there was a Pact between him and her, which debarr'd her from answering in that Language. As for the Four Pacts, of which there has been mention made, 'twas promis'd solemnly, that one of the Four should fall from the Top of the Roof of the Church to the Bottom, although the Relation has mention'd nothing of it, no more than of the precedent Fact; but they were much surpriz'd to see it fall from under the Hood of the Superior. 'Twas also observ'd that Grandier had expresly requir'd, That this pretended Pact of Silence should be broke. That may be done (said he) for GOD has given Power to his Church over the Devils, and in Truth you boast of having broken several others which were not of any consequence. But they took care not to deprive themselves of the only means they had to except these Devils from a proof which they were not able to undergo. The Author of the Demonomania of Loudun has been bold enough to write, that Grandier durst not venture to interrogate the Nuns in Greek; but although the foregoing Relation was writ by a Man so persuaded of the Possession, that for want of other Proofs in his favour, he makes use of the accused Person, which one cannot too much admire, and which could not come from the Testimony of a good Conscience. This Relation is however, sufficient to confute this Lye, for it expresly maintains, That when Grandier endeavour'd to interrogate in Greek, the Possessed interrupted him by confused and dreadful Noises, which were all the Marks of Possession that they gave in that Circumstance, which had not been so great, nor would have frighted so much the Author of the Relation, if they had not produc'd at one time the Possessed in so great a Number; and if they had not intermingled and confounded so many Cries and Voices together, and made so many Postures and different

Contorsions, that they gave doubtless to this action, the air of a Diabolical and Infernal confusion, which surpriz'd those that were struck by these outward appearances, who could not imagine that the perversness of humane Nature alone, was able to produce effects so horrible, and so extravagant, that they confounded Religion, Piety and Reason.

Sect. 36.

The last Day of the same Month of June, one of the Possessed, who was exorcis'd in the Church of Notre Dame du Chateau, was impudent enough to say, that Grandier had sent to a great many Damsels, to make them conceive with Monsters; a Thing which modesty suffers not to be nam'd, and which she then boldly call'd by the right Name; the Exorcist presupposing that the Devil had spoke the Truth, and without objecting to her that the pretended Magician was too well guarded to be able to attempt any thing like it; nor that one could apprehend what advantage he could receive by it, especially in his present condition, he was contented to ask her, why the effect did not succeed? To whom the Maid reply'd, with abundance of immodest, filthy, and unbeseeming Words, which made not any coherent Discourse; and by unheard of Blasphemies, which founded shameful to Chast Ears, and made People tremble who had the least Piety. Neither could they contain the indignation which all these Horrors had excited; and they began to speak of it openly, when they saw affix'd to all the Corners of the Town, and heard publish'd through all Publick Places, the following Order.

Sect. 37.

'TIS expresly forbid, to all Persons of whatsoever Quality or Condition they be, to defame, or otherwise to undertake to speak against the Nuns and other Persons of Loudun, afflicted with evil Spirits; their Exorcists, or those that assist them, whether in Places where they are exorcis'd, or elsewhere, in any fashion or manner whatsoever, upon the Penalty of Ten Thousand Livres fine, and other greater Sums, and Corporal Punishment, if the Case deserves it. And to the end that none pretend ignorance, this present Order shall be read or publish'd this Day, in the Parish Churches of this City, and affix'd as well to the Gates of the same, as in all other Places where it stall be requisite, Given at Loudun the Second of July, 1634.

Sect. 38.

That Order absolutely stopt the Mouths of all those that had a Mind to defend the Innocence of Grandier. For to maintain that the Nuns where not possessed, was a Black and unpardonable reproach, against which, the justice of Laubardemont was arm'd with all severity, and which he pretended to punish rigorously, whilst there was no way to attain to the justification of Grandier, but by making out that Truth, and by convicting the Possession of Imposture. The Cabal believing themselves out of Danger, by the precautions they had taken, acted with more liberty, and with what carrier they pleas'd, in assurance, that now no one durst be so bold as to take upon him to dare only to Murmur in Private. Wherefore Astaroth, and two other of his Companions, or if you will, Elizabeth Blanchard, and two other Secular Maids, who had listed her self in the Regiment of the Possessed, did not fear to take a turn in the Country, with the Exorcist Father Peter a reformed Carmelite, and his Brother Ecoute; in spite of the scandal they must needs know it would cause in those who wond'red that the Devils who possess'd these Maids, had not hind'red these good fathers, from having so great a familiarity with them; but they knew not that as the Jesuits gave a Play-day to their Schollars every Thursday, the Exorcists had a sufficient power to give one every Tuesday to the Devils, of whom without doubt they were the Masters.

Sect. 39.

'Tis to be presum'd, that next Day, the Third of July, the Devil of Sister Claire was also gone into the Country, and that he had left this Miserable Creature to her self; seeing that with Tears in her Eyes, she declar'd publickly in the Church of Chateau, whither they had brought her to Exorcise her, that all that she had said for Fifteen Days, were but meer Calumnies and Impostures; That she had done nothing but by the Order of the Recollect, Mignon and the Carmelites; and if they sequester'd her, 'twould be found that all these things were but feign'd and malicious. She made again the same Declarations two days after, which was the Seventh of the Month; and she proceeded so far this last time, that she went out of the Church where they exorcis'd her, and would have run away, but Demorans ran after her and stopt her. The Sister Agnes embolden'd by this Example, said many times the same Things, with Tears in her Eyes, intreating those who assisted at the Exorcisms, that they would take her out of that horrible captivity, under the weight whereof she groan'd. She refus'd one Day to Communicate, assuring her Exorcist, with a serious Air, that she did not find her self in a condition to do it. He did not omit to make her believe that 'twas her Devil that caus'd that repugnance, and gave her the Communion in spite of her, notwithstanding the impiety that appear'd in this Action, and whatsoever consequences the Enemies of the Church might draw from it. These two Miserable Maids seeing no hope of Succour, said at last, that they prepar'd themselves to be extraordinarily ill treated at Home, for having reveal'd so important a Secret, but that they were tormented by their Consciences, and forc'd to speak for their Discharge; and to give Glory to GOD and the Truth, whatsoever might happen to them. La Nogeret protested also one Day, that she had accus'd an innocent Person, and that she begg'd Pardon of GOD; and turning herself one while towards the Bishop, another while towards Laubardemont, she declar'd, that she thought her self bound to make this Confession, for the discharge of her Conscience. This last did nothing but laugh, and the Bishop and the

Exorcists maintain'd, that the Devils made use of this Artifice to keep the People in unbelief. 'Twas necessary to render Grandier a Magician, whatsoever it cost, and whatsoever Authentick and convincing Proofs which daily appear'd in favour of his Innocence; for they had the Secret to know, that the Devil lied, when he spake to his Discharge; and that he said the Truth when he accus'd him; the Church imparting to her worthy Ministers, her infallible lights, to discern the Truth from a Lie, in the contradictory propositions of the Devils; and these communicating them to the People, by means of the Authority of Laubardemont, whom no body had the Power or goodness to contradict.

Sect. 40.

A young Man who was at the Exorcisms the Eighth of July, having said in Latine, that there was in the Body of Agnes, three Devils serving Grandier, Tres Damones Servientes Grandiero; say Mago, Magician, replies a Magistrate, and not Grandiero, Grandier; this was a Name they resolv'd to extinguish, and to be swallow'd up by that Magician, or at least, which should be reserv'd for one of the Devils. Wherefore the Demonomania of Loudun, relating the Names of the Eight which possessed Sister Claire, said, that the Third was call'd Sans Fin, or else Grandier de Dominationibus: But People were persuaded, that this Name, as it had Relation to Grandier, was likely in a short time to be extinguish'd with his Blood, when they understood that they had nam'd Commissaries to try him. The World was already so well acquainted with the Method of Cardinal Richelieu, by very many sad Examples, such as had been the Execution of the Marshal de Marillac, and many others, that since they saw Commissaries nam'd to take notice of an accusation of a Crime, although it was not Capital, they were assur'd that the Cardinal was resolv'd that the accused Person should perish by the Hands of a Hang man, and that the Commissaries who were always his Creatures, would not fail to execute the Bloody Orders for which they were sent.

Sect. 41.

These Commissaries, to make and perfect the Process of Grandier, were, in consequence of a former Commission, already come to Loudun, where they had assisted at the Exorcisms, by the Subdelegation of Laubardemont, the one in one Church, and the other in another; but they would produce at the Process, only the Verbal Processes of the Eighth and Ninth of July, as made since their last Commission, which was made the same Eighth Day of July, whereby it is signified, That the King appoints the Sieur de Laubardemont, the Sieurs Roatin, Richard and Chevalier, Counsellors of the Presidial Court of Poictiers; Humain, Lieutenant Criminal to the Presidial of Orleans; Cottereau President; Pequineau special Lieutenant; and Burges, Counsellor to the Presidial of Tours; Texier, Lieutenant General to the Royal Tribunal of St. Maixant; Dreux, Lieutenant General; de la Barre, Special Lieutenant to the Tribunal Royal of Chinon; la Picherie, Lieutenant

Particular to the Royal Tribunal of Chatelleraud; and Rivrain, Lieutenant General to the Royal Tribunal of Beaufort. For altogether, or Ten of them in the Absence, Sickness, or lawful hindrance of the others, to make and perfect the Process of Grandier and his Complices, even to a definitive Sentence, and Execution of the same inclusively, whatsoever Oppositions or Appeals notwithstanding, All according to the Form prescribed by Edicts and Orders; And further appoints and ordains to the Offices of Advocate, and Attorney of the King, the Sieurs Constant Counseller and Advocate of the King of the Presidial Court of Poictiers, and James Deniau, Counsellor at la Fleche, in that Quality, to use conjointly, or one of the two in the place of the other, all diligence and needful expedition. By Virtue of which Commission, all those who were there named, except Constant, the King's Advocate at Poictiers, who forbore medling in it, made the Process against Grandier, and condemn'd him to be burnt alive. But it was not put into the Hands of the Commissaries, as soon as it had been deliver'd; in the mean time there had happen'd, and did happen still, surprizing things at Chinon, as well as Loudun.

Sect. 42.

Barre, to whom the Function of Exorcist was exceedingly acceptable, seeing himself, for convenience, excluded from exorcising at Loudun, instructed and fitted so well in secret, two of his Votaries of Chinon, that he ventur'd at length, to produce them in Publick, as being possessed; One was call'd Catharine, and the other Jeanne, he began, the Thirtieth of May, 1634, to exorcise them in the Church of Saint James, of which he was the Curate. The Lieutenant General of the place made Verbal Processes of that which past at these Exorcisms, and for as much as by the Example of those of Loudun, they accus'd Grandier of their being bewitch'd, they fail'd not to produce also, their Verbal Processes against him, to which there was much regard shewn, as also to other Pieces of this nature, whereas they gave none to those of the Bailiff of Loudun, the Leiutenant Civil, and the other Judges, where the Truth was so clearly represented, and where might have been found more than convincing proofs of the Falshood of the Accusation, and of that of the Possession, which they perceiv'd so well, that to destroy them, they had recourse to new Artificers, by rend'ring these Magistrates suspected. For they caus'd the Bailiff to be accus'd of Magick, by the Persons Possess'd at Chinon; whose Probity so well known to all the World, could not shelter him from this attempt; and there were some People credulous enough to believe so ridiculous a Calumny, which was not contriv'd till after the Cabal of the Confederates of the Possession had fail'd in another attempt; which they would have put upon him in this manner. A Beggar-Woman having knock'd at his Gate, put a Letter into the Hands of one of his Servants, which she said she receiv'd of a Man who rode through the Street on Horse-back, ordering her to carry it to him: The Bailiff having receiv'd that Letter, and open'd it, he saw that there was a Proposition made him, to assist in a Design for Grandier's escape, which they promis'd to execute infallibly, if he would well instruct them where the place of his Prison was, giving him notice that they waited for his answer, at the White-Horse-Inn in Chinon. As the Name, the Seal, and Writing were unknown to him, he mistrusted the Snare that was laid for him; and in Order to escape it, he sent the Letter to Laubardemont; causing him to understand, that he thought himself bound in Duty to take that course, to the end, that whether feignedly, or otherwise, it happen'd, that some violence should be offer'd to the House where Grandier was Prisoner, he might not be accus'd or suspected of being the Author of such an Enterprize. Sometime after, judging that he had nothing more to fear in that intrigue, he earnestly desir'd to have the Letter again, and offer'd to give his Receipt for it; and upon the refusal that was made him, he entreated at least a Copy of it, compar'd with the Original, to make a strict enquiry after those who were the Authors, and to prosecute them at Law. Laubardemont was deaf to his requests, and thereby secur'd his Friends from a diligent search, which would not have been for their reputation, although he should even have made use of his Authority, which seem'd without bounds to shelter them from the rigour of Justice.

Sect. 43.

They gave not thus over their Designs upon him, they endeavour'd to affront him to the utmost; for one of his near Kinswomen was accus'd of Magick, by Elizabeth

Blanchard, a secular Maid, Possessed, who was lodg'd in the House of the Widdow Barot Sister of Mignon's Brother-in-law, and allied almost to all the Cabal. This possessed Person said one Day, in the presence of the Judges Commissaries, Roatin, Richard, and Chevalier, that that Gentlewoman was a Witch; and that one of her intimate Friends had brought from her a Pact, compos'd almost as the others, whereof mention has been made before; but they found that that Accusation had caus'd so much scandal and murmuring in Loudun, where the Bailiff was much belov'd, that they thought best to oblige the Devil to unsay it again next Day, and to order him also to be silent; concerning other Officers of the Town, whom he had resolv'd to accuse of keeping a School of Magick, as he had already dar'd to speak the precedent Day to the Bishop of Poictiers in his Ear, and the Bishop had reveal'd it, before they had determin'd to stifle this Project, or at least to suspend it till after the Death of Grandier.

Sect. 44.

In the mean time the Bailiff was so odious to the Authors of the Possession, that they could not refrain from discovering their hatred and mischievous intentions against him, in the Person of his Wife; who going into a Church where they exorcis'd, and where the Bishop was present; one of the Possessed Whisper'd to him, that that Lady was a Magician. Afterwards she repeated it aloud, speaking it to her self, you have brought a Pact into this Church, said she to her impudently. The Bailiffs Wife, who wanted not Presence of Mind nor Courage, addrest instantly her Prayers to G O D with a loud Voice, and made divers Imprecations against the Devils, and against the Magicians; and in conclusion, she call'd upon the Exorcist to confound immediately, either her, or the pretended Possessed; and to make appear the Truth or the Falshood of that Accusation, by causing the Devil to produce the Pact, according as they had the Power of the Church, and had boasted to have caus'd many others to be produc'd. Whereupon the Exorcists Conjur'd the Devils, and order'd them to Obey, and repeated to them their Commands and Conjurations so long, and at so many several times, that they spent two whole Hours in it; till the Night came upon them, which put them out of Perplexity, compelling the Company to depart.

Sect. 45.

The last Commission before mention'd, appear'd by the Publication which was made, and by the regist'ring of it; after which the Judges Commissaries being assembled the Twenty Sixth of July, at the Convent of the Carmelites, they appointed there the Sessions, and the next Day, the Twenty Seventh, they nam'd for Reporters Houmain, Lieutenant Criminal of Orleans, and Texier Lieutenant General Saint Maixant. The first was lodg'd at Duthibaut's House, and every one of the others lodg'd with the Enemies of Grandier. The Twenty Eighth they order'd that a Copy of their Commission should be signified to him, and the Order was executed the same Day. He writ to his Mother at the same time, the following Letter. Mother,

Sect. 46.

THE Kings deputed Attorney has given me your Letter, by which you inform me, that they have found my Papers in my Chamber, and have retain'd such as might serve for my justification, to put them into my hands, but they have not given me them; If I should have them, I am not in a condition to draw up Writings. As for the Memorials I cannot say any thing, but what I have said at the Process, which consists in two Articles. To the first, they examin'd me upon the Facts of my first accusation, to which I have given satisfaction, and alledged that I am fully justified, which must be made appear by producing my Four Sentences of Absolution, viz. Two of the Presidial of Poictiers, and two others of my Lord Archbishop of Bourdeaux. That if my Lords the Commissaries doubt of the Equity of the same, they may, by their Authority, procure the Process which is in the Registry of the Court of Parliament, with my Case, which serves to discovor the Evil Practices that were then us'd against me. The Second Article is touching Magick and the Affliction of the Nuns, upon which I have nothing to say but a very evident Truth, which is, that I am wholy innocent, and wrongfully accus'd; for which I have made my complaint to Justice; Which must be made appear by producing the Verbal Processes of Monsieur the Bailiff, wherein are inserted all the Petitions that I have presented, as well to the Judges

Royal, as to my Lord the Archbishop; whereof I gave once a fair Copy to my Lord de Laubardemont, that the King's Attorney has told me that he had also produc'd them. Be pleased to cause a Petition to be drawn up by our Attorney, who shall take such counsel as he shall think good. My Answers contain my Defences and Reasons: I have exhibited nothing that I do not justifie by my Writings and Witnesses, if my said Lords give me leave. For the rest, I rely upon the Povidence of GOD, the Testimony of my Conscience, and the equity of my Judges; for the inlightning of whom I make continual Prayers to GOD, and for the conservation of my good Mother; to whom I pray GOD to restore me shortly, to render her better than I have ever done, the Services of her Son, and Servant, Grandier. And by a Postscript. Forasmuch as I know nothing here of that which is past abroad in the World, if there has happen'd any thing in those Public Acts which may be useful, you may employ them as the Counsel shall thikn fit. They have read to me the Comssimion of the King, with the Names of my Lords the Judges deputed to judge the Process definitively; and they have given me the List of their Names, which I send you.

Sect. 47.

Whatsoever was the Opinion that he had of his Judges, those amongst the disinterested Persons, who had some Commerce with them, knew well that his destruction was resolv'd on, with which they were not then so sensibly touch'd, as they had been, if they had not had a

Mind employ'd in attending all the consequences of that Affair, which seem'd to threaten every particular Person with a like usage in his turn, by the Establishment of that Proposition, That the Devil duly exorcis'd, is compell'd to speak the Truth. The Judges Commissaries shewing by all their proceedings, that they had Order to Authorize this Maxim. This Reflection concern'd the most insensible Persons, and oblig'd them to put themselves into a condition to prevent the effects of so dangerous a Doctrine; At last all the Inhabitants being assembled upon the ringing of the Bell of the Town-House, resolv'd to address themselves directly to the King, to whom they writ the following Letter: SIR,

Sect. 48.

THE Officers and Inhabitants of your Town of Loudun, do find themselves at last oblig'd to have recourse to your Majesty, most Humbly remonstrating, that the Exorcisms, that are made in the said Town of Loudun, on the Nuns of Saint Ursula, and some secular Maids, who are said to be possess'd with evil Spirits, a Thing is committed very prejudicial to the Public, and to the quiet of your faithful Subjects, in as much as the Exorcists abusing their Ministry, and the Authority of the Church, propose Questions in the Exorcisms, which tend to the defamation of the best Families of the said Town, and Monsieur Laubardemont, Counsellor, deputed by your Majesty, has heretofore given so much credit to the Sayings and Answers of these Devils, That upon a false indication by them made, he had been in the House of a Gentlewoman with a great noise and number of People, to make a search for imaginary Books of Magick. As also other Gentlewomen had been stopt in the Church, and the Doors shut to make an enquiry for certain pretended Magical Pacts, likewise imaginary. Since then, this mischief has gone so far, that at this time, they make such consideration of the Denunciations, Testimonies and Indications of the said Devils, that there has been Printed a Pamphlet, and publish'd in the said Town, by which they would establish this Belief in the Minds of the Judges, 'That the Devils duly exorcis'd speak the Truth, that one may upon their Deposition pass a reasonable Judgment; and that next to the Truths of the Faith, and Demonstrations of Sciences, there is not a greater certainty than that which comes from them; and that when they believe the words of the Devil duly exorcis'd, they take his words not as the Father of Lies, but of the Church, which has Power to make the Devils to speak Truth.' And to establish yet more powerfully this dangerous Doctrine, that there has been made in the said Town, and in the presence of Monsieur de Laubardemont, two Sermons in conformity to the above said Propositions. In consequence whereof, and upon such denunciations, the said Sieur de Laubardemont has again very lately, caus'd to be arrested and taken Prisoner by an Exempt of the Grand Provost, a Maid of the best Families in the City, the same having been kept two Days in the House of a Gentlemen, a Widower, then releas'd into the Hands, and under the Security of her kindred. In such sort, Sir, that the Petitioners see and know, that they strive, to establish amongst them; and in the Heart of your most Christian Kingdom, a resemblance of the Ancient Oracles against the express Prohibition of the Divine Law, and the Example of our Saviour, who has not suffer'd Devils to speak and publish things true and necessary to be believ'd, against the Authority of the Apostles, and ancient Fathers of the Church, who have always made them hold their peace, and forbid to enquire of them, or become familiar with them; And also against the Doctrine of Saint Thomas, and other Doctors and Luminaries of the Church. But besides that, the mischievous Maxims inserted in this Pamphlet, and which they wou'd now bring into credit, have been heretofore, and since the Year 1620, rejected by the advice of the most Famous and renowned Doctors of the Sorbonn, and since then condemn'd by the Decree, Censure and general Decision of the Faculty of Paris, made in the Year 1623, upon a Book publish'd concerning Three Je sons possess'd in Flanders, which contain the like Propositions with those now in question. Therefore the Petitioners induc'd by their proper interest, considering, that if they Authorise these Devils in their Answers and Oracles, the best Men, and the most virtuous and innocent, to whom consequently these Devils bear a mortal hatred, would remain expos'd to their Malice; humbly request and beseech your Majesty to interpose your Royal Authority for the putting a stop to these abuses and profanations of Exorcisms, which are daily made at Loudun, in the presence of the Holy Sacrament, wherein you will imitate the Zeal of the Emperor Charlemagne, one of your most august Predecessors, who hinder'd and did for bid the abuse which was commited in his time, by the application of some Sacraments, the usage whereof they alter'd and perverted, contrary to the design and end of their Institution. For these Reasons, Sir, may it please your Majesty, to ordain the said Faculty of Paris to examine the said Pamphlet and Censure hereto annex'd, to interpose their Decree upon the Propositions, Doctrines, and Resolutions abovemention'd, whereunto your Majesty may give them such Power as is requisite; And that it may be permitted to the said Petitioners, and those amongst them who shall be concern'd to lodge an Appeal, by Writ of Error from the Interrogatories tending to defamation, made by the said Exorcists, and from all this which ensued thereupon, and to get relief of them either in the Court of Parliament of Paris, which is the natural Judge thereof, or in such other Court as it shall please your Majesty to ordain. And your Petitioners shall continue to pray to GOD for the Prosperity, Grandure and Inlargement of your just and glorious Empire.

Sect. 49.

This Letter or Petition will not suffer the Reader to doubt of what has been related concerning the Opinions which the honest People had of the Proceedings of the Exorcists, and those of Laubardemont, who was highly provok'd by this Action, and this Resolution, as well as the other Commissaries. But because they address'd themselves to the King directly, they did not think fit to attempt any thing against those who had resolv'd it, and were contented only to make the following Order. By the KING. An EXTRACT of the Registers of the Commissioners appointed by the King, for the Judgment of the Process Criminal, made against Monsieur Urbain Grandier, and his Complices. 'WHereas it has been remonstrated by the King's Attorney General, that on Tuesday last the Eighth of this Month, the Bailiff of this Town call'd together an Assembly, compos'd for the most part of the Inhabitants professing the pretended reform'd Religion, and of Handicrafts Men, in which there was held many injurious Discourses, and tending to Sedition and popular Commotions, upon Facts falsly and calumniously averred, concerning the Exorcisms which are made publickly in this Town by the King's Authority, and other things depending on our Commission; And upon the notice which has since then been given us by him, We have heard as well the Lieutenant Criminal as the King's Advocate and Attorney of the Bailiwick of this Town, together with one General Assessors, and Sheriffs of the same, and Champion Clerk of the said Assembly; and examin'd a Memorial containing the Names of those who assisted at it, by which Act appears the Enterprize and Attempt made by the said Bailiff in the said Assembly, and the injurious Discourses which have been held there, which are disown'd by the discreetest and best qualified of the said Inhabitants, who judg'd that the Consequence thereof, might be very pernicious to the Service of the King, and to the Authority of the Court, if it were not speedily prevented. And there-upon requir'd that the said Act of the Assembly might be Cancell'd and Annull'd, and the injurious Discourses held by them may be razed and blotted out, with prohibitions, as at other times, to the said. Bailiff and all others to make the like Assembly, and in the same to propose any thing concerning the Exorcisms, and other Facts depending on our Commission; and that he was more amply inform'd of the injurious discourses tending to Sedition, held as well in the said Assembly, as elsewhere; for the information, held, made and communicated to him, Right should be done as is sitting; and having seen the said Act of the Assembly of the said 9th Day of the present Month, a List of the Names and Sirnames of some of the said Inhabitants who assisted in the said Assembly; Our Verbal Process of the Eighth and Ninth of the said Month, containing the hearing of the said Lieutenant Criminal, Advocate and Attorney of the King in the Bailiwick, and of the said Champion; The Decree of the said Ninth Day of the present Month, And all being consider'd, the said Commissaries deputed by the King, Sovereign Judges in this Cause, without having any regard to the said Act of the present Month, which we have Cancell'd and do Cancel as Null, made by attempt against the Respect and Authority given us by the King, and upon Facts calumnious and injurious, and tending to a popular Sedition, and contrary to usual Forms, by practices, and private combinations; Have order'd, and do Order, that the Minutes of the said Act shall be exhibited, and put in our Registry by Champion Clerk of the said Assembly this Day, that the same having been seen and communicated to the Kings Attorney General, We prohibit and forbid as formerly, as well the said Bailiff, General Assessors, and others, either to call together hereafter such Assemblies, or in any others, about things concerning the said Power given us by his Majesties Commission, or in any manner to meddle with the Fact hereof, upon the Penalty of 20000 Livres fine, and other greater Sum, if the Case requires it; saving to the said Inhabitants and other Persons, liberty to address themselves to us upon the complaints they would make concerning that which past at the Exorcisms, and other circumstances and dependencies of our Commission; and doing right moreover to the Conclusions of the King's Attorney, have Enacted, and do Enact, That there shall be a fuller Information made before us of the injurious and seditious Propositions which have been made, as well in the said Assembly, as elsewhere, for the said information related and communicated to the King's Attorney, to be provided such a Decree, as shall appertain thereunto. And to the end, that our persent Order may be known to every one, we command that it be signified as well to the Person of the said Bailiff, as to the General Assessors of the Town, and moreover read and publish'd by Sound of Trumpet, and fix'd to the places and Corners of the said Town, as accustom'd to be done. Given at Loudun, the--Day of August, 1634. Sign'd Nozai Clerk.'

Sect. 50.

If the Petition was an undeniable Proof of the Sentiments of the Publick, this Decree is one no less evident of the unjust and Arbitrary Power, which Laubardemont usurp'd. This little Tyrant would that they should address to him upon the Complaints they had to make against himself, and of the manner whereby abus'd the Power which he had in his Hand. He ordered that the Petitions they had drawn up to present to the King, should be suppress'd and torn in Pieces; and that there should be an Information made against the Authors of such an attempt, or rather of so lawful a Proceeding. Certainly it had been very difficult, that the Voice of a private Person, and a miserable Captive, as this Grandier was, should have been able to arrive at the Ears of the Monarch; if this of all the Inhabitants of a Town, assembled in a Body with their Officers, according to Custom, and in the prescrib'd Rules, was stifled and stopt, by artificial and violent Means.

Sect. 51.

Two Days after this Order had been publish'd and posted up, Grandier caus'd a Petition to be presented to his Judges, tending to a Second Visit; And these are some of the Reasons upon which it was grounded. 'Do not my Lords, rely upon the Visit that was pretended to have been made, you may consider the nullities by the Case which has been presented to you; But 'twas omitted that Adam the Apothecary impudently thrusting himself amongst these pretended Physicians, and Mannouri the Chirurgeon, into the Chamber where the Visit was made, he dar'd to sign the Report which was given, whereof Monsieur de Laubardemont having been advertiz'd, severely reprov'd this Man, in such manner that 'twas needful to disallow this Report; and to make another, which as 'tis said, has been done upon other like occasions.' He besought the Judges not to defer the ordering this Second Visit, which if well and duly made by Physicians of Probity and Ability, would be as a Touch-stone to discover the Truth. He remonstrated to them, That the Physicians of Villages and young Men, ought not to be call'd upon an occasion so extraordinary; That they ought not to be lodg'd in the Houses of his declar'd Enemies, nor to have daily communications with them, and with the Nuns; That the Head of Mannouri the Chirurgeon, which shook much, without doubt through some fault of the Brain, was not proper to discern the principals of the Actions in controversy, nor make a solid Judgment of them; That the surest way to penetrate into this Business, would be to do, as the Lords in Parliament setting at Thouars did, according to the Recital which Pigrai, Chirurgeon to Henry the Third, made in the Tenth Chapter of his Epitome of Physic and Chirurgery; wherein he says, that Fourteen Persons who were accus'd of Sorcery, having been condemn'd to Death by the Judges of the Places, after having been visited before them, were notwithstanding sent away absolv'd by the Parliament, upon the new Visit which was made by the Author, in the presence of two Counsellors of the

Court, appointed for that purpose, and of Three of the King's Physicians, by whom there was found neither Mark nor Appearance of those things wherewith the accused Persons had been charg'd. This Chirurgeon added, that he did not know that 'twas the capacity or fidelity of those who had given their Report; but Grandier maintain'd that he knew but two much, that 'twas the incapacity and malice of those who had visited him. This Request was not more favourably answer'd than the precedent, They have however acknowledg'd in the Extract of the Proofs which are in the Process, and c. 'That this may be said against the Instruction, That the Chirurgeon, who assisted at the Visits, was a Kinsman of the Sieur de Silly, who was said to be one of the Instruments of the Destruction of Grandier, but that he was there but as a Witness, and that they were the Six Physicians not suspected, who assisted there and gave their Report: But who will believe it?' And how can it be maintain'd, That he who manag'd the Probe, and apply'd it, was but a Witness in this Action? Can one refrain from concluding that these are the Physicians who were indeed but Witnesses? and yet Witnesses suspected, blameable and disallow'd, although by a continuation of Injustice, they have not been willing to allow of lawful causes of recusation which were alledg'd against them.

Sect. 52.

So many irregular and violent proceedings, so many denials of Justice, so many refusals to hear only the defences of the Person accus'd, to receive the Petitions and Papers which he gave, and to impart to him those which were produc'd against him; All this began to make him open his Eyes upon his approaching destruction, and to make him to understand that there was no mean between these two extreams; either that he must be punish'd as a Sorcerer and a Magician, or that a Convent of Nuns, many Monks and Ecclesiasticks, and a Number of considerable Lay-Persons should be expos'd to the Penalties which they deserv'd for the most horrid of all Calumnies, and the blackest of all Conspiracies that could be made against the Life and Honour of an innocent Person; and which Calumnies had been so visibly supported by a Bishop, and by a Commissary of the King, that they could not avoid having a part of the infamy with which the culpable were stain'd. But although he well perceiv'd that he must die an Innocent, to save a great Number of Guilty Persons, and that he had resign'd himself to the Will of GOD, he would not however abandon his own Defence; and he Wrote for this purpose the Discourse, of which mention has been many time already made; Intituled, Fins et Conclusions absolutoires, and c. Which begins in these Words: 'I beseech you in all Humility, to consider advisedly and with attention, that which the Prophet says in the Eighty Second Psalm, which contains a very Holy Admonition, and bids you execute your Offices with all Righteousness and Impartiality, considering, that being but Mortal Men you shall appear before GOD the Sovereign Judge of the World, to render him an Account of your Administration. This anointed of GOD speaks this Day to you who are sent to Judge, and says to you, GOD stands in the Congregation of the mighty, He is a Judge in the middle of Judges. How long will you have a Regard to the Appearance of the Persons of the Wicked. You are Gods Children of the most high; nevertheless you shall die like other Men, and you, who are Princes, shall fall as other Men.'

Sect. 53.

The beginning of this Discourse was grave and moving; it was presented to the Bishop, and to the other Persons of Authority, as well as to the Commissaries: The first Effect it produc'd was, that this Prelate, after having assisted at the Exorcisms, sent to Loudun a Sentence, in Form of a Decree, Dated at his House at Dissai, of the 10th of August, containing, that the Ursuline Nuns of Loudun, and the Secular Maids, were truly tormented by Devils, and possessed by Evil Spirits. This was signified to the Person accus'd, with a Copy of the Advice and Resolution of Andrew Daval, Nicholas Imbert, Anthony Martin, and James Forton, Doctors of the Sorbonn at Paris, who had deliver'd their Opinions upon the Facts which had been propos'd to them, which were absolutely feign'd and false, viz. That the Nuns had been lifted up from the Ground to the heighth of Two Foot, and that being laid all at Length, without the help either of Feet or Hands, and without bending their Bodies, they had been rais'd up. They proceeded also to his Hearing, and at length they prepar'd themselves for the Judgment of the Process. 'Father Tranquille says, That the Judges seeing themselves charg'd with an Affair, which drew upon them the Eyes of all France, and even of all Christendom, and which seem'd to be intangl'd with a Thousand Difficulties, and the Success whereof drew very great Consequences, they resolv'd all with one accord, to address themselves first to GOD, who is the Foundation of Light and Truth, and that each of them should prepare himself by Confession and the Communion often reiterated, to receive the Grace and Assistance of Heaven. They began, added he, this Action by a general Procession, to shew that they were first to excite the People to Devotion by their Examples; they continued all the Festivals and Sundays, during the Judgment of the Process, to visit also the Churches of the Town, and the Holy Sacrament exposed there, to cause a Mass of the Holy Ghost to be sung with Solemnity, with a Sermon, making publick and frequent Prayers, that it would please GOD to conduct them in their Affair, and to illuminate them with his Spirit, to render Justice to whom it belong'd, according to the Intention of his Majesty and the Duty of their Conscience.'

Sect. 54.

These Commissaries being so devoutly prepar'd, they met together the 18th of August, early in the Morning, at the Convent of the Carmelites, where they made an Order, by which, after having openly read the King's Commission, and the Papers which had been produc'd by each Side, they pronounc'd the Condemnation of Grandier in these Words; We have declar'd, and do declare, the said Urban Grandier duly attainted and convicted of the Crime of Magick, Sorcery, and the Possessions happen'd by his Act, to the Persons of some Ursuline Nuns of this Town of Loudun and other Seculars, together with other Causes and Crimes resulting thereupon. For Reparation whereof, we have condemn'd, and do condemn the said Grandier to undergo an honourable Amand, Bare-headed, a Rope about his Neck, holding in his Hand a burning Torch of Two Pounds Weight, before the principal Door of the Church of St. Peter's in the Market, and before that of St. Ursula in this said Town, and there, upon his Knees to ask Pardon of GOD, the King and the Court, and this done, to be conducted to the Publick Place of St. Crosse, and there to be ty'd to a Post upon a Wood-Pile, which shall be made in the said place for this purpose, and there his Body to be burnt alive, with the Pacts and Magical Characters remaining in the Registry, together with the Manuscript by him made against the Celibacy of Priests; and his Ashes to be cast into the Wind. We have declar'd, and do declare, All and every of his Goods to accrue and be confiscated to the King, after there has been rais'd by the sale of them 150 Livres, to be employ'd for the buying a Copper-Plate, on which shall be engrav'd the Extract of the present Sentence, and the same to be set in an eminent Place of the said Church of the Ursulines, to continue there to Perpetuity. And before the Execution of the present Sentence, we Command that the said Grandier shall be put to the Rack, ordinary and extraordinary, upon the Articles of his Complices. Pronounc'd at Loudun to the said Grandier, and drawn up the 18th of August, 1634.

Sect. 55.

Father Tranquille, and the Author of the Demonomany of Loudun, have writ concerning the Death of Grandier, abundance of false, childish and ridiculous Things They have Reproach'd him, that he had desir'd a Mitigation of his Punishment. He was much to blame, without doubt, to be mov'd with the Prospect of an infamous and cruel Death, the only Thought whereof would make one tremble with Horrour! It was, say these Writers, because be had more care of his Body than of his Soul. With like Reasons, one might easily make Criminal the most innocent Actions; but to discharge this unhappy Victim of the Hypocrisy of the Monks, Charity obligeth us to say with the Scripture, That no one hateth his own Flesh; and to believe that he had a regard for his Soul, and that he ear'd that his Constancy, his Faith and his Hope, such as they might be, should sink under the Weight of so terrible a Punishment. They have further reproach'd him, That be had not vouchsaf'd to look upon the Crucifix, nor on an Image of the Virgin; that he shook his Head when they threw Holy Water upon him; that when they offer'd it to him, be wou'd not drink, or that be drank but very little; that be invoked not the Virgin; and that be knew not the Prayer of the Guardian Angel. These are the Arguments which these Authors dar'd to alledge as demonstrative, and sufficient to prove by the Circumstances of the Death of Grandier, that he was a Magician. 'Tis true, that they add, That he neither call'd upon God the Father, nor Jesus Christ; nor that be desir'd the Assistance of any one, unless of a Huguenot Apostate and Relapse, who stood near him. This Matter has been acknowledg'd to be false by all the Spectators, who were near enough to understand what he said, and this apostatiz'd relapsed Huguenot being present and Praying alone for the suffering Person, is a Contrivance so agreeable to the Genius of Monks, that if one did not feel ones Heart fill'd with Pity, Horrour, and Indignation, one could not contain from Laughter at the Reading of it, as well as of that which they have written besides; That after his Legs had been wash'd, which had been torn by the Rack, and that they had brought him to the Fire, to recover somewhat of Spirits and Vigour, he forbore not to entertain himself with his Guards, by Discourses little serious and full of Raillery; That he did eat with an Appetite, and drink with Pleasure, Three or Four Draughts, and that be shed not any Tears whilst he suffer'd the Rack, nor after he had undergone it, nor even when they exorcis'd him with the Exorcism appointed for Magicians; and that the Exorcist said to him more than Fifty times, Præcipio, ut si sis innocens, effundas lachrymas, I command thee if thou art innocent, to shed Tears: As if Compression and Pain were not able to be natural Causes of this last Accident, supposing that it was true; and as if the Horrour and Indignation which he could not withhold himself from conceiving, were not capable to keep his Eyes dry and inflam'd; and in fine, as if nothing extraordinary could happen in a Body so horribly misus'd, and in a Mind so extreamly provok'd. But all these things were devis'd and related, on purpose to insinuate, that the Power of the Devils made him insensible of all the Cruelties which were exorcis'd upon his Person. They have further imputed to him, that he refus'd to be confess'd, by answering, That 'twas but Four Days agoe since he was confess'd, nevertheless, that he would do what they would have him: To which, Sincerity ought to have oblig'd these Writers to have added, that having not Confidence enough in Father Lactance, nor in the Capucins, he desir'd for his Confessor the Father Guardian of the Cordeliers, named Father Grillau; which was barbarously refus'd him, notwithstanding the repeated Supplications he made to obtain this last Consolation.

Sect. 56.

He demanded also in the Extremity of his Torture, of Lactance, who cry'd to him without Intermission, dicas, dicas, and who, for that Reason, was call'd by the People, Father Dicas, if he believ'd that a Man of Sincerity, ought with a good Conscience to accuse himself of a Sin which he had never committed, so much as in Thought? The Exorcist durst not go so far as to tell him that he might; whereupon the Patient conjur'd him to let him die in Peace; and this is that which they call'd Impenitence and hardness of Heart; for say they, he has confess'd greater Crimes than

Magick. But when one continues to read on, and search with Curiosity what were these Crimes greater than Magick, of which they pretend he accus'd himself of, it will be found they were Crimes of Frailty and Humane Infirmity, supposing nevertheless, that these Sins were as enormous as that of Magick; By what Consequence must it be, that he was guilty of this last, because he was of the others? In the mean time, though it pleas'd these able Casuists to make these sorts of Sins to be equal, they hindred not the Sentiments of the pretended Magician from being accounted more reasonable, and be more Universally follow'd than theirs; for see how he explains himself in his Conclusions Absolvatory, and c. upon this Subject: The Crime of Magick, is the most horrible, most abominaale, and most detestable that one can imagin, being the Crime of High Treason against God, in the highest Degree; the Fruit whereof, is Punishment without Remission.

Sect. 57.

We shall not relate here, the Testimonies that the Author of the Demonomania has drawn from the Mouth of the Devils, and which he made use of against Grandier, although they are so ridiculous and impertinent, that they would not fail to increase the Indignation of the Reader; 'tis not to be doubted, that the very Title, namely, The Testimonies of the Devil might not be taken for a Reproach, and a sufficient Confutation of all the rest which that Book contains. 'Twill then be more to the Purpose, to make a Recital of the Death of this unfortunate Man, taken from several Relations of Sincere and Unconcern'd Persons.

Sect. 58.

Friday the 18th. of August, 1634. Francis Fourneau Surgeon, was sent for by Laubardemont, and although he was ready to obey willingly and at that instant, nevertheless they hurried him from his House, and carried him as a Prisoner to the Place where Grandier was detain'd. Having been introduc'd there into the Chamber, Grandier was heard to speak to Mannouri in these Words; Cruel Hangman, art thou come to dispatch me? Thou knowest, inhumane Wretch, the Cruelty thou bast executed upon my Body; here continue, and make an end of killing me. Then one of the Exempts of the great Provost of the Hostel, whom Laubardemont caus'd to be call'd Exempt of the King's Guards, commanded Fourneau to Shave Grandier, and to take from him all the Hair upon his Head and Face and all the Parts of his Body; Fourneau going to execute this Order, one of the Judges told him, that he ought also to take off his Eye-brows and his Nails. The Patient exprest that he would obey and let him do it; but the Surgeon protested that he would not do any thing in it, whatsoever Command he might receive, and pray'd him to Pardon him, if he laid his Hands upon him. I believe, said Grandier, you are the only Person that has Pity on me; Whereupon Fourneau reply'd to him, Sir, you see not all the World. There were seen upon his Body but Two natural Spots or little Moles, the one plac'd near the Groin, and the other higher upon the Back, which the Surgeon found very sensible. When this was done, they gave him not his own Cloaths, but others very bad; afterwards, although his Sentence of Condemnation had been pronounc'd in the Convent of the Carmelites, he was conducted by the Exempt of the Grand Provost, with Two of his Guards; and by the Provost of Loudun and his Lieutenant; and by the Provost of Chinon in a close Coach to the Palace of Loudun, where many Ladies of Quality were sitting on the Judges Seats in the Chamber of Audience, Laubardemont's Lady taking the chiefest Place, although the was inferior to a Number of others who were there present; Laubardemont was in the usual Place of the Clerk, and the Clerk of the Commission was standing before him. There were Guards round the Palace, and all Avenues set by the Major Memin, who was also in the Palace standing near the King's Attorney of the Commission, and below the Ladies. When Grandier was entred into the Palace, they caus'd him to stay some time at the Bottom of the Hall, near the Chamber of Audience, and after he had been introduc'd, and that he had past the Bar, he fell upon his Knees, without putting off either his Hat or his Cap, because he had his hands bound. The Clerk having rais'd him up to make him come near to Laubardemont, he put himself again into the same posture, and the Clerk and the Exempt taking off briskly, the one his Hat, and the other his Cap, they cast them on one side of Laubardemont. Lactance and another Recollect, who had accompanied him from his Prison to the Palace, were attir'd in their Albs and

Stoles, and before they made him enter into the Chamber, they had exorcis'd the Air, the Earth and the other Elements, as also the Patient himself, to the end, that the Devil might quit his Person. Being thus upon his Knees, and his Hands joyn'd, the Clerk said to him, Turn thee, thou wretched Man, adore the Crucifix which is upon the Judges Seat, which he did with great Humility, and lifting up his Eyes towards Heaven, he continued some time in mental Prayer. When he Had put himself into his former Posture, the Clerk read to him his Sentence trembling; but he heard the reading of it with a great Constancy and a wonderful Tranquillity. Then he spake, and said, My Lords, I call to witness God the Father, the Son, and the Holy Ghost, and the Virgin Mary my only Advocate, that I have never been a Magician; that I have never committed Sacriledge; that I knew no other Magick than that of the Holy Scripture, which I have always preach'd; and that I have bad no other Belief than that of our Mother the Holy Catholick, Apostolick and Roman Church. I renounce the Devil and his Pomps; I own my Saviour, and beseech him, that the Blood of his Cross may be meritorious to me: And you, my Lords, I beseech you, mitigate the Rigour of my Punishment, and put not my Soul in despair. When these Words, accompanied with Tears, had been pronounc'd, Laubardemont caus'd the Ladies to withdraw, and all Persons who, out of Curiosity, were in the Palace, and had a very long Conversation with Grandier, speaking to him softly in his Ear, whereupon the Patient desir'd Paper; he did not cause it to be given him, but told him aloud, and in a very severe Tone, that there was no other Course to induce the Judges to remit something of the Rigour of the Sentence, but by ingeniously declaring his Complices; whereunto he answer'd, that he had no Complices, and protested his Innocence, as he had always done before. Houmain Lieutenant Criminal of Orleans, and one of the Reporters, spake to him also in private for that same end, and having receiv'd a like answer, they order'd him to be put to the Torture Ordinary and Extraordinary, which is done at Loudun, by putting the Legs of the Patient between two Planks of Wood, which they bind with Cords, between which they put Wedges, and make them enter by the Blows of a Hammer to squeeze the Legs, which are more or less, according to the Number or Bigness of the Wedges that are us'd, which sometimes go so far, that the Bones of the Legs do Crack and fall in Pieces when they are unloos'd; and that those, who have undergone this Torture, die in a little time after. They gave Grandier Two Wedges more than they usually did to the most Criminal; but they were not big enough to the liking of the Monks and Laubardemont, who threatned the Man that had the Care of the Planks and other Instruments of the Torture, to deal with him severely, if he did not bring bigger Wedges; from which he could not excuse himself, but by Swearing that he had no bigger. The Recollect and Capucins who were present to exorcize the Wedges, the Planks, and the Hammers for the Torture, fearing that the Exorcism had not effect enough, and lest the Devils should have the Power to resist the Blows of a prophane Man, such as the Hangman was, they themselves took the Hammer and tortur'd this unhappy Man; pronouncing against him terrible Imprecations. Tantæne Animis cælestibus Iræ? Can so much Gall enter the Soul of devout Persons? Yes; and with just Reason, for a Miscreant, a Sorcerer, a Magician deserves not to be spar'd, when the Glory of God is concern'd, by which one may discern the Degree of his Zeal and Fervour, by the Degree of the Transport he has against the Crime and the Criminals. The Patient Swoon'd many times during the Torture, but they recover'd him out of his Swoon by redoubled Blows; When his Legs were shattered, and that they saw the Marrow come forth, they gave over the Torture, took him out, and laid him on the Pavement. He shew'd in this Condition, an Example of Firmness and Constancy which one cannot sufficiently admire; he let not escape one Word of Repining, nor Complaint, against his Enemies; on the contrary, he utter'd, during his Torture, a proper and fervent Prayer to God; and being thus extended upon the Pavement, he pronounc'd again another, which the Lieutenant of the Provost writ down, whom Laubardemont forbid to let it be seen by any Body. This unfortunate Creature, maintain'd always in the midst of the Anguish and Blows which mangled him, that he was neither a Magician, nor Sacrilegious Person, acknowledging, that as a Man, he had abus'd the Pleasures of the Flesh, for which he was Confest, and had done Penance; but he pray'd his Judges, who urg'd him to explain himself further, that they would not oblige him to name any Body, nor to specifie the Sins, for which he believ'd he had obtain'd forgiveness by his Repentance and his Prayers; which he affirm'd to be such as a true Christian ought to make. He renounc'd again Three or Four times, the Devil and his Pomps, and protested, that he never saw Elizabeth Blanchard, but when she was confronted to him, very far from having known her, after that manner which she had declar'd. He Swoon'd once again after he had been taken from the Torture, and he came not out of that Fainting Fit, but by the help of a little Wine, which the Lieutenant of the Provost caus'd speedily to be put into his Mouth; afterwards he was carried into the Council Chamber, and put upon Straw near the Fire, where he demanded an Augustin Fryar for his Confessor, whom he saw then before his Eyes; who was also denied him, as well as Father Grillau, and he was committed, against his Will, into the hands of Father Tranquille, and Father Claude, Capucins. When they were withdrawn, they severely forbid those who Guarded him, not to let him speak with any Body, and so he was not seen during the space of almost Four Hours, but Thrice by the Clerk of the Commission, by his Confessors, and by Laubardemont, who was with him more than Two Hours, to force him to sign a Writing which he offer'd him; and which he constantly refus'd to Sign.

Sect. 59.

About Four or Five in the Evening he was taken from the Chamber by his Toturers, who carried him upon a Hand-Barrow; in going, he told the Lieutenant Criminal of Orleans, that he had said all, and that there remain'd nothing more upon his Conscience; Will you not, says this Judge to him then, that I pray to GOD for you? You will oblige me by doing it, reply'd the Patient to him, And I beseech you to do it. He carried a Torch in his Hand, which he kiss'd as he went from the Palace; he look'd upon all the People modestly, and with a settled Countenance, and desiring those whom he knew, that they would pray to G O D for him. As soon as he was come out of the Palace, they read to him his Sentence, and put him in a kind of little Chariot, to bring him before the Church of St. Peter in the Market, where Laubardemont caus'd him to come down from the Chariot, to the end, that he might put himself upon his Knees, whilst his Sentence was read to him once again; but having quite lost the use of his Legs, he fell flat to the Ground upon his Belly, where he tarried without murmuring or any Word of Displeasure, till they came to lift him up; after which, he desir'd the Assistance of the Prayers of those that were about him; Father Grillau came to him at this very time, and embrac'd him, weeping; Sir, said he to him, Remember that our Lord Jesus Christ ascended to G O D his Father, by Torments and the Cross; you are an able Man, do not ruine your self, I bring you your Mother's Blessing; She and I do pray to G O D that he would be merciful to you, and that he would receive you into his Paradice: Grandier express'd great Satisfaction at the hearing of these Words, and his Countenance seem'd very chearful; he thank'd the Cordelier with much Mildness and Serenity, and conjur'd him to be as a Son to his Mother; to pray to GOD for him, and to recommend him to the Prayers of all his Fryers, assuring him that he went with

Comfort to die Innocent, and that he hop'd that G O D would be merciful to him, and receive him into his Paradice. That edifying Conversation, was interrupted by the Blows that the Archers gave to Father Grillau, whom they thrust with violence into the Church of St. Peters by the Order of their Superiors, and Father Confessors who would not suffer the Standers by to be Witnesses of the Condition, in which the Conscience of the Patient was. He was Conducted then before the Church of the Ursulines, and from thence to the Place of St. Crosse, upon the Way from which he espied le Frene Moussaut and his Wife to whom he said, That he died their Servant, and that he pray'd them to Pardon him. When he was arriv'd, he turn'd himself towards the Fryers who accompanied him, and requested them to give him the Kiss of Peace. The Lieutenant of the Provost would ask him Pardon; You have not offended, said he, you have done but what your Office oblig'd you to do. Rene Bernier, Curate of the Town of Troismoutiers, pray'd him also to Pardon him, and ask'd him if he would not forgive all his Enemies, even all those who had depos'd against him, and if he would that he should Pray to G O D for him, and to say next Day, a Mass for his Soul? He answer'd him, He forgave all his Enemies whatsoever, even as he desir'd G O D to Pardon him; that by all means he would oblige him by praying to G O D for him, and by remembring him often at the Altar. Then the Executionor put upon him a Hoop of Iron, which was fasten'd to a Post, making him to turn his Back towards the Church of St. Crosse. The place was fill'd with People, who flock'd in Shoals from all parts to this dismal Spectacle, and came thither, not only from all the Provinces of the Kingdom, but also from foreign Countries. The place appointed for the Execution, was at last so crouded, that those who where to assist there could not put themselves in order; whatsoever endeavours the Archers us'd to make the People retire with Blows of their Halbert-staves, they could not effect it; and less yet to drive away a Flock of Pigeons, which came flying round the Pile of Wood, without being Frighted by the Halberts, with which they were commanded to strike in the Air, to drive them away, or by the noise that the Spectators made in seeing them return many times. The Friends of the Possession cried out, that it was a Troop of Devils, who came to attempt the Rescuing of the Magician, and were much troubled to abandon him. Others said, that these innocent Doves came, for want of Men, to give Testimony to the Innocence of the Sufferer. All that one can affirm here, is, that all the Facts, or at least the principal of them, are generally found in all the Relations that have been kept of them, That most of the People of Loudun (who are this Day alive) have been inform'd of it by their Parents, who had been present, and that there remain yet some living in that and Foreign Country's, particularly here in England, who can attest it, by having been Witnesses thereof.

Sect. 60.

The Fathers exorcis'd the Air and the Wood, and ask'd the Patient afterwards, if he would not confess? to whom he reply'd, That he had nothing more to say, and that he hop'd to be this Day with his G O D. The Clerk then read to him his Sentence for the Fourth time, and ask'd him if he persisted in what he had said upon the Rack? He answer'd, That be persisted therein, That he had nothing more to say, and that all that he had said was true. Whereupon one of the Monks told the Clerk, that he made him speak too much. The Lieutenant of the Provost had promis'd two things in their presence; the first, That he should have some time to speak to the People; the Second, That he should be strangled before the kindling of the Fire. But to hinder the performance of either of these Promises, these are the Courses which the Exorcists took: When they perceiv'd that he was dispos'd to speak to the People, they cast so great a quantity of Holy-Water in his Face, that he was thereby utterly confounded, and seeing that he open'd his Mouth a Second time, there was one who went to Kiss him, to stop his Words; he understood the Design, and said to him, There is a Kiss of Judas. Upon which, their Spite rose to so high a point, that they hit him many times in the Face with an Iron Crucifix, which they offer'd to him, as if they had been willing to make him Kiss it; which oblig'd him to content himself, in desiring only a Salve Regina, and one Ava Maria and c. and to commend himself to GOD, and to the Holy Virgin, pronouncing these last Words with joyn'd Hands and Eyes lifted up to Heaven. The Exorcists return'd to their Office, and ask'd him once again, if he would not confess? My Fathers (answer'd he) I have said all, I have said all; I hope in GOD, and in his Mercy.

Sect. 61.

These good Fathers, to hinder his being strangled, according to the second Promise the Lieutenant of the Provost had made him, had themselves knotted the Rope, when it had been put into the Hands of the Executioner, who providing to put Fire to the Wood-Pile; the Patient cry'd out Two or Three times, Is this what I was Promis'd? And saying these Words, he himself lifted up the Rope and fitted it. But Father Lactance took presently a Wisp of Straw, and having lighted it with a Torch, he put it to his Face, saying, Wilt thou not confess wretched Man, and renounce the Devil? 'This time, thou hast but a Moment to live. I know not the Devil, reply'd Grandier, I renounce him and all his Pomps; and I pray GOD to have Mercy on me. Then, without waiting for the Order of the Lieutenant of the Provost, this Monk taking upon him publickly the Office of the Hang-man, put Fire to the Pile, just before the Eyes of the Sufferer; who seeing that Cruelty and Unfaithfulness, cry'd out again, Ah! Where is Charity Father Lactance? this is not what was promis'd me. There is a GOD in Heaven who will Judge thee and me; I Summon thee to appear before Him, within a Month. Then addressing himself to GOD, he utter'd these Words, Deus meus, ad te Vigilo, miserere mei Deus. Then the Capucine began again, to throw all the Holy-Water in his Face which they had in their Holy Water-Pots, to prevent these last Words being heard by the People, and their being edified by them. At last, they said, aloud to the Executiner, that he should strangle him, which 'twas impossible for him to do, because the Rope was knotted; and that he was stop'd by the increasing of the Flame, into which the Sufferer fell, and was burnt alive.

Sect. 62.

Although the Commissary and the Judges of Grandier have kept secret, as much as it has been possible, all that they have done against him, and that the greatest part of their Proceedings, and the Papers, on which they have grounded his Condemnation, have been conceal'd from the Publick, whose Examination and Decision they dreaded; Nevertheless for this unhappy Priest, obtain'd of one of the Judges the Copy of the Extract of the Proofs which were in his Process. As it is the Foundation of the terrible Sentence which was given against him, and cruelly executed upon his Person, we have thought it out duty to insert it here with some Reflections, to lay open the weakness and injustice thereof. The Extract of the Proofs which are in the Process against Grandier.

Sect. 63.

As the Possession of the Ursuline Nuns is the Foundation of all the Proceeding of Monsieur de Laubardemont, and the Subject of the Process which has been made against the Parson of Loudun, it has been necessary to establish the truth by such Testimonies thereof, as could be desir'd in that Matter. Certainly the Possession is a very ruinous Foundation, and suppose that it might have been true, it does not follow yet that Grandier was the Author thereof; and though he had been the Author at first, there was no likelihood, that after he had been nam'd in the two first Possessions, to the great danger of his Honour, and his Life, he would have procur'd a Third Possession, without being mov'd thereto by any Hope of pleasure, or by any Passion of Covetousness, or of Love, Hatred, or Envy, against Persons whom he knew not, and whom he had never seen.

Sect. 64.

To that end, the Bishop of Poictiers, after having assisted at most of the Exorcisms, and sign'd the Verbal Processes which had been made, declar'd by his Sentence or Decree of the Fourteenth of the Month of August, that he judg'd the said Nuns to be possess'd, and as such, and Subjects to his Jurisdiction, he had given them Persons able to exorcise them. This Opinion has been follow'd by four Doctors of the Sorbonn, but with this difference, that the Motive of the Bishop of Poictiers, in the Judgment which he has made of the Persons possessed, has been no other than the knowledge he himself has had of all that which past; whereas the Doctors of the Sorbonn, having not been present there, were not able to decide that Question, but upon the credit of those who made them the Report, viz. That the said Nuns had been rais'd from the ground two Foot high, and that being laid at length, without the help of Feet or Hands, and without bending the Body they had been listed up. The Four Exorcists, who are Father Lactance Recollect, the Fathers Elizee and Tranquille Capucins, with a Carmelite, have also given their attestation. Father Ronceau Rector of the Jesuits, the Prior of the Jacobites of Thouars, and Revol, Doctor of the Sorbonn, have entertain'd the People in the Pulpit concerning the Truth thereof. The Physicians of Poictiers, Niort, Fontenai, Loudun, Thouars, Chinon, Mirebeau, and Fontevraut, after having observ'd the Motions and Agitations of these Maids, accounted them supernatural, and to proceed from a cause in which the subtilty of their Art has not been able to know any Thing but the effects. You have seen in this History what has been the Sincerity and Disposition of the Bishop of Poictiers, and what Exorcists and Deputies he had sent. One cannot also suffer to pass for a proof the Boldness that some Ecclesiasticks, and some Monks have had to entertain the People in the Pulpits concerning the Truth of the Possession. As for the Opinions of the Doctors of the Sorbonn, they have been given upon Facts absolutely false and suppos'd; that the Exorcists have not so much as dar'd to produce in any of their writings, nor Laubardemont to insert them in any of his Verbal Processes, as it appear'd in the Declaration of the Sentence of Death, wherein the Verbal Processes of the Vomitings and other Facts are mention'd, but there's no mention made of the Verbal Process of the Facts propos'd to the Doctors of the Sorbonn. The Testimonies of the Physicians were so exceptionable as well as their Persons, and they were drawn up in a manner so little conclusive, that 'twas impossible not to believe that the Possession was already establish'd and verified in the Minds of the Judges, before they had examin'd these kinds of Proofs. And though it be found in that Article of the Extract, and c. That there were also Physicians of Poictiers, Niort, and Fontenai, who had given their Attestation, that was in a manner different from the others, and not that they had been nam'd and appointed to this purpose; But it was because amongst the great number of People which came to see the Effects of the Possession, there were many whom the Exorcists knew themselves, either by the Relation they had with other Convents, from whom they receiv'd intelligence; they chose Physicians and other Persons distinguish'd by their Characters, to sound them, and to penerate their Opinion, and when they found them favourable to the Possession, whether by credulity, or for want of information, or by complaisance with them who supported the Party, they fail'd not to require their Attestations, and they mention'd only those of the Towns of Niort, Fontenai, and Poictiers, who gave their Opinion, though there were but some of the Physicians of those Towns, and especially of that of Poictiers, who were no ways persuaded of the Possession. But besides that, 'tis certain that there came to Loudun more than a Hundred Physicians of different Towns, adjoyning and remote, who would not give the like Attestations, though the most part were much sollicited; on the contrary, there have been some who have left Memorials against the Possession.

Sect. 65.

'So that after Testimonies so Authentick, without examining whether the Possessions of evil Spirits, are the Effects of the absolute Power of GOD alone, or whether the Magicicians, by the Covenants they made with the Devils, and by the Permission which GOD gives them, may be accounted Authors; seeing that the most knowing Persons doubt not of the First of these Things; and that the Second is not without Example. It remains to see, if by the Proofs which are in the Process, there be room to believe, that he, who has been condemn'd, was realy guilty of the Crimes, of which he has been convicted. Now these Proofs are of Two Sorts; the First, which consist in the Depositions of the Witnesses, are ordinary, and subject to the Reproaches and Exceptions of Fact and Right; the others, which are drawn from the Verbal Process of the Exorcists, and from the Visits made in Consequence thereof, upon the Person of the Accused, are extraordinary, as well as the Matter in Question, to which they are all Particular, and much more certain than the former; because of the Notoriety of the Fact, which evidenceth to us the Truth that we seek in sensible Things. As for the Proof by Witnesses, it results from Two Informations; the First is compos'd of Sixty Witnesses not sufficiently excepted against, who depos'd concerning the Adulteries, Incests, Sacriledges, and other Impieties committed by the

Person accus'd, even in the most secret Places of his Church, as in the Vestry, near the Holy Sacrament; upon all Days, at all Hours, and all Times; in a Manner, that the Church, of which he was Parson, and where, by his Example, he ought to raise in the hearts of his Parishoners a Love for Virtue, he made thereof a Place of Pleasure, and an open Baudy-House to all his Concubines. It is true, that by the Sentence of the Presidial of Poitiers, he had been remitted till new Orders should have been given upon some Matters; but besides that that Sentence was not definitive, it appear'd that he had relaps'd into a Number of the same Crimes, which render'd him yet far more culpable. Amongst the Witnesses of this Accusation, there were Five very considerable, viz. Three Women; the First whereof said, that one Day, after she had receiv'd the Communion from the Person accus'd, who earnestly look'd upon her during that Action, she was instantly seiz'd with a violent Love-Passion for him, which began with a little Shivering through all the Parts of her Body: The other said, that having been stop'd by him in the Street, he press'd her Hand, and that immediately she was seiz'd with a vehement Passion for him: The Third said, that after she had seen him at the Door of the Church of the Carmelites, where he enter'd with the Procession, she felt very great Commotions, and had such Inclinations, that she willingly desir'd to lie with him, although before that Moment, in which, they were look'd upon by him, and were seiz'd with his Love, they never had a particular Inclination for him; being otherwise very Virtuous and of a very good Reputation.' 'Tis a strange

Thing to report, and revive again the same Accusations of which Grandier had been sent away absolv'd, and the same Testimonies, which had been found insufficient by the Sentences of the Judges Ecclesiastical and Secular, and to make them one Part of the ground of a Sentence of Death. The same thing may be said, to see him boldly accus'd of relapsing into the same Crimes of Adultery, Incest, Sacriledge, and other Impieties, and the Facts alledg'd in the Depositions of these Three Women, who notwithstanding their good Reputation, and their pretended former Virtue, which then abandon'd them, might be wounded by the only Charms of Grandier's good Meen, without the Intervention of any other Enchantment, than that of Nature or rather Concupiscence: Otherwise, honest Women were much to be pitied, if Magicians could make them in Love, and inspire into them a Desire to lie with them, as often as it pleas'd those wicked Villains to look on them; or that they should touch them only with their Hand. But what Relation is there between these Accusations of Sacrileges and Incests, and the Sentence for the Death of Grandier, which was not given upon the Conviction of these Crimes? It contains not one single Word, 'tis only for the Crime of Magick, that this unhappy Man was condemn'd. Why then are all these pretended Crimes heap'd together? The greatest whereof, one has seen that he has not been guilty of; if this were not to confound the Judgment of the Reader, and to surprize him by these Appearances. Ought this to be the Design of a Judge, who Reports the Proofs upon which an accus'd Person has been condemn'd? And are they not rather the last Endeavours of a cruel, unjust, and bloodily persecuting Party.

Sect. 66.

'The Two others are an Advocate and a Mason, the first whereof depos'd that he saw the Person accus'd read the Books of Agrippa. The other being at work to repair his Study, he saw a Book upon the Table open'd at the Place of a Chapter, which treated of the Means to make Women in Love. It is true, that the first explain'd himself in some manner at the Confrontation, and said, that he believ'd that the Book of Agrippa which he had mention'd in his Deposition, on, was that, de Vanitate Scientiarum. But the Explain'd plication is very much suspected, because the Advocate vocate had withdrawn himself from Loudun, and could not undergo the Confrontation, till after he had been compell'd.' 'T would be great pity if all the Persons who have read Books of Magick, only to know them, without an Intention to make use of them, should become Magicians; 'Tis also a very forc'd Way of Arguing, to say, that the Explication of the Advocate was to be suspected, because he went aside for fear of undergoing a Confrontation. It is much more natural to conclude [as it was the Truth] that having some Remorse for having given a Testimony so little sincere, and so maliciously intangl'd, and fearing nevertheless, the Authority of Laubardemont, if he dar'd to explain himself, he fled away, and could not resolve to be of their Party; but that in the End, his Remorses, and a return of Virtue, had determin'd him to give Glory to the Truth. The Mason was a poor Rascal, who had been hir'd not to say any thing; for his Testimony signified nothing. One might add, That at making the Inventory of the Closet of Grandier, the Commissary found there no Book of Magick, and that the Devils, being interrogated upon that Point, answer'd nothing but Lies, which were verified to be such: However, these are the Five most considerable Depositions, which have caus'd a Parson to be condemn'd to be burnt; What can one think of the other Testimonies which they have not dar'd to produce?

Sect. 67.

'The Second Information, contains the Deposition of Fourteen Nuns, where of there has been Eight possessed, and Six Seculars, who have been said also to be possess'd. It would be impossible to report, in brief, that which is contain'd in all these Depositions, because there is not a Word which deserves not Consideration. 'Tis only to be observ'd, that all these Nuns, as well those that were free, as those that were molested, have had a very disorder'd Love for the Person accus'd; they have seen him in the Convent Day and Night, to Sollicite them in Matters of Love, during the space of Four Months. They have been disturb'd by a Number of Visions, of which they said they had perfect Knowledge, because the greatest Part of these Accidents happen'd to them when they were up, and at their Prayers. They said moreover, they had been struck by something which was not known by them, and which left Marks so visible upon their Bodies, that the Physicians and Surgeons have been able to see them easily, and to make the Report thereof; that all these disorders which have happen'd to them, have had their Beginning with the Apparition of one, nam'd the Prior Moussaut, who had been heretofore their Confessor; then by a Nosegay of Roses which the Mother Prioress found on the middle of the Stairs, and Three Black Thorns, which were thrust into the Hand of the said Prioress one Evening after Prayers. They said also, that the Mother Prioress imagin'd one Day, that there were Apples in her Chamber, the Kernel whereof she had a Mind to eat; whereupon, at that instant, as well as after, having smelt the Roses, and receiv'd the Three Black Thorns into her Hand, she was troubled after such a Manner, that the spoke of nothing but of Grandier, whom the declar'd to be the Object of all her Affections, and whom, as well as all the other Nuns, she has seen to approach her Bed, as she has told him, when she has been confronted to him, having maintain'd to his Face, as well as Seven or Eight others, that 'twas he himself who was often present to them. Where it must not be forgot, that all these Nuns, in making their Depositions, at the pronouncing of the Word Grandier, were seiz'd with Troubles and Convulsions, at the Confrontations where the Physicians have been present, to observe all that past which was remarkable, they were violently disturb'd, as well as all the other Seculars, who said also, they were passionately in Love with the Person accus'd.' These Nuns could no longer forbear to give this Testimony against Grandier, and the matter was come to that Point, that it was necessary, that either he must be declar'd a Magician, or that they must be declar'd guilty of the most infamous and blackest of all Cheats: So they were Witnesses in their own Cause. But these Declarations which they made, these pretended Troubles and Commotions which attended them, these Marks which they shew'd to their Physicians. Are these things so difficult to counterfeit? And is it very extraordinary and nearly approaching to an immediate Operation of the Devil, to see Women promote and defend these Extravagances and ridiculous Visions? How have they been able to know in their Convent, a Man whom they had never seen, when he was transported thither by pretended Magical Operations, and when they nam'd him for the certain Author of that Sorcery? And how should he be in Love with them, without having ever seen them? Besides, was it likely that his Magical Power had not so much Efficacy upon the Nuns, as upon the Seculars? Such were the Three Women who have depos'd as above, that they had had so great a Desire to lye with him; for if this Desire had also possess'd the Nuns, they might easily have satisfied themselves, seeing that this Lover was so often near them and in their Chambers.

Sect. 68.

'Now amongst all the Accidents wherewith these good Nuns have been afflicted, I find none more strange, than that which is befallen to the Mother Prioress, and to the

Sister Claire de Sazilli. The first, next Day after the had made her Depositions, and whilst the Sieur de Laubardemont took that of another Nun, stripp'd her self to her Shift, Bare-headed, and a Halter about her Neck, and a Wax. Candle in her Hand, and continued in that Posture the space of Two Hours, in the middle of the Court, where it rain'd very fast; and when the Parlour Door was open, she threw her self in, and fell upon her Knees before the Sieur de Laubardemont, declaring to him, that she came to make Satisfaction for the Offence she had commited, in accusing the innocent Grandier; then being retir'd, she tied the Halter to a Tree in the Garden, where she had hang'd her self, if the other Nuns had not ran to her.' That Action of the Superiour had far more Conformity to the Action of a Person constrain'd by the Resentment of her Crimes, and the Remorses of her Conscience, than to a diabolical Operation; and when the Devil had in Effect acted therein, in the Sense they would have it understood; Wherefore should he rather have spoken the Truth, when he accus'd Grandier of being a Magician, than when he confess'd that he was innocent? What way is there to know the Truth in these two Contradictory Propositions? What was the Character of Truth, which was found in one rather than in the other? All that one can reasonably inferr is this, that the Suggestion of the Devil did assuredly cause the Nun to speak, when she accus'd her Parson; and that the fear of the Judgments of G O D drew her to confess what she did against her self.

Sect. 69.

'And the Second was so tempted to lie with her great Friend, whom she declar'd to be the said Grandier, that one Day coming to receive the Holy Sacrament, she arose on a suddain and went up into her Chamber, whether having been follow'd by some of her Sisters, she was seen with a Crucifix in her Hand, wherewith she prepar'd her self to -- Modesty permits not to mention the Obscenity of this Passage.' 'Tis not to be doubted, that this infamous Action of the Sister Claire had been well concerted; and that 'twas resolv'd they should follow her, to find her in this horrible Occupation, which consider'd in it self, had nothing in it, but what might very naturally and easily be perform'd, and had no need of the Power and immediate Efforts of the Devil; so that 'twas not on that Account that it could pass for a Mark of Possession, but 'twas on that of Shame and natural Modesty, that they pretended that a Maid and a Nun could not have sufficiently lost it to arrive to such an Excess, if there had not been a Devil which had excited and transported her. This Argument is wonderfully concluding, and the Consequence thereof is very edifying; That when the Crime is so great that it passes all imaginable bounds, one must believe, that the Person, that has committed it, cannot be guilty; and that it must needs be by the Sorcery, Suggestion, or the Operation of another, that she had been induc'd to commit it; and that upon the Declaration she shall make, he ought to be burnt uppon whom she causeth the Suspicion to fall, and thereby clear her self. It must be further observ'd, that they pretended by these extraordinary Actions, on the behalf of Morality, to make amends for the deficiency of proving the Possession by supernatural Actions, which were not in the Power of Man to produce, as they had produced others.

Sect. 70.

'And to that End, It is also considerable, that Grandier had endeavour'd after the decease of the said Prior Moussaut to be Confessor of the Nuns, and that one of his most intimate Friends had a great Quarrel with the Superior about it.' All those who were not engag'd in the Cabal of the Possession have believ'd this Matter to be false; but suppose that it was true, doth it deserve to be put amongst those Reasons which have caus'd a Man to be condemn'd to be burnt?

Sect. 71.

'As for the Seculars, the Deposition of Elizabeth Blanchard follow'd, and being confirm'd by that of Susanna Hammon, is not one of the least considerable: For she depos'd to have been carnally known by the Person accus'd, who, one Day after he had lain with her, told her that if she wou'd go to the Sabat (i. e. Conventicle of the Witches) he would make her Princess of the Magicians.' Could one yet have a Regard for that extravagant and shameful Deposition of the Persons pretended to be possess'd, who were in the same

Case as the Nuns, seeing that the Justification of Grandier would also have imported their Condemnation? But this Promise, to make Blanchard Princess of Magicians, and the impudence of her Accusation, do not they make one asham'd? Surely the Devils have had very little Respect for so Powerful a Lord of the Sabat, who could make Princesses; they have never been wanting upon every Occasion, to accuse him, and to have brought him themselves to a shameful End.

Sect. 72.

'This is that which concerns the Proof by Witnesses, which consists in these Two Informations only, to which, by a single Paper, was added, the Deposition of the Sieur Barre, Curat of Chinon, who depos'd, amongst other Things, that one Day, having been sent for, to exorcize the said Nuns, and knowing that the Devil, who tormented the Mother Prioress, was call'd Astarot, he commanded him to go out; and for a Sign of his going out, to strike him, whom he said, was declar'd to be the Author of the Sorcery, who was the said Grandier, which Astarot promis'd him; and for certain, in the Time that he was to perform this Promise, Grandier absented from the Company, and having caus'd himself to be excus'd upon the Paper for pricking down the absent Canons of St. Crosse, by reason of his Sickness, That Word Sickness had been blotted out by his Hand, so that it appear'd by the Report of the said Paper; and when upon the Rack, they question'd him upon the Occasion of his Absence, he seem'd much confounded, and knew not what to answer; and many times chang'd Colour, although in all the other Proceedings he had shew'd himself very resolute.' So the Testimony of Astarot, and that of Barre, whose Way of Acting we have seen in this Affair, and who was at last condemn'd, and punish'd, as Author of the pretended Possession at Chinon, were made use of as Motives in the Condemnation of Grandier. But besides, the Animosity of this Hypocrite and his Partiality, which had been visible, ought to have hindred his being receiv'd for a Witness; wherefore, this Act was produc'd out of Season, not having been within the Time wherein the Thing should have pass'd, seeing that the Verbal Processes of that Time do not give Credit to it. That if Grandier was found to be absent at the Time observ'd by Barre, it was because he had well examin'd the Paper for pricking down the Names, to fix the Contrivance just in the Time it should have been. Is it not also an extraordinary Piece of Artifice in this Deposition, to say, that razing out of the Word Sickness, was by the Hand of Grandier? Since what time was it, that the Hand of a Man was known by a very small Razure? Grandier had no more to do, than to maintain, that 'twas done by the Hand of Barre, or Mignon, and he would have apparently affirm'd the Truth, for 'twas very unlikely that he could gain any Advantage by the striking out of the Word Sickness; it was more for his Purpose, that the Word should stand to evidence the Cause of his Absence, which could not have any other likely Pretence so probable as that. But whence did it happen, that the Devil did not strike him on the Back in Obedience to the Orders of Barre? And that the Bp. who ought not less to be obey'd, did not command him to wound this Magician in the Forehead, when he desir'd it, for this Action had been altogether convincing, and exempted from all Suspition, as may be seen in the Relation of the 23d. of June, contain'd in this History. Or how comes it, that if Barre could, by his Exorcisms, so easily drive out the Devils, he did not make use of that Power to deliver the Nuns so cruelly tormented? That if the Person accus'd has appear'd confounded at the Circumstance of the pricking down; 'tis without doubt, that hearing this Deposition, he endeavour'd to recall the Ideas of what pass'd at the Time when they mention'd to him, which was now long since, and that they qualified this Recollection, by the Name of Confusion.

Sect. 73.

As for the extraordinary Proofs, they conconsist in Two particular Points; The First is the Experiment of the Marks, which having been declar'd by Asmodee, who then possessed the Superior, together with the Places where they were, they caus'd the Person accus'd to be search'd by Eight Physicians, who have given their Report, by which they declare, that amongst all the Marks found upon his Person, those of his Shoulder and Privy Parts are suspected by them, because that a Needle having been thrust into the First, the thickness of an Inch, the Sense of Feeling there was dull, and not like to that which the accused Person shew'd to have, when they prob'd into the other Parts; and that from the one and the other there issued no Blood when the Needle was drawn out. It is true, that Asmodee declar'd, that the Person accus'd was mark'd in Five Places; but because of the Difficulty in discovering them, there were found but Two, which were suspected by the said Physicians. This is a Touch-stone to discover the Sincerity of this Body of Phsiycians and Judges who make such a Report, one of the principal Subjects of a Sentence of Condemnation to the utmost Punishment. They sound but these Two natural Spots upon Grandier's Body, the others were not seen, because, say they, of the Difficulty there was to discover them; 'tis rather, because there were none, for these so quick-sighted Eyes, which had well perceiv'd the Two First Spots, might also as readily have discover'd the Three Others. Ought one to bring such Proofs and such Conclusions amongst those which have serv'd to cause a Man to be condemn'd to the Fire? This is to pretend, that Authority ought to impose upon humane Reason. But there remains yet some Shaddow of Modesty in this Company of Physicians; they dar'd not to call these Marks, Diabolical and Supernatural, they only declare'd that they are suspicious; they durst not say that they were altogether insensible, they only reported that the Sense of Feeling there was dull; but they did not express this, which Men of Experience cannot but know, that 'tis not a Thing rare or extraordinary, that there may be some Part in the Body, where the Sense of Feeling is not so quick as in others, and especially those which are not of ordinary Conformation; such as are the Parts which are mark'd with Moles, or those which have been affected by some Distempers. Fourneau, who Shav'd the Patient on the Day of his Suffering, testified that these Moles were natural and very sensible; and if there came out no Blood, that Singularity ought to be ascrib'd to Mannouri the Surgeon, the Brother-in-law of one of the Possessed, and Nephew of Silli, who us'd a Probe round at one End, and sharp at the other, which he could not but make the Patient feel very grievously every time he pleas'd.

Sect. 74.

The Second Proof is the Scar on the Thumb of his Right Hand. For the 25th. of the Month of April, the same Asmodee having mention'd a Pact of a little Bit of Paper stain'd with some drops of Blood, be declar'd, after much Resistance, that the Blood which appear'd upon this Paper, issued from the Thumb of his Master's Right Hand; which the Sieur Laubardemont having heard, he went forthwith to the Prison with Physicians, whom after having caus'd to take Notice of a little Cut, which was found in the very Place that the Devil had declar'd, be interrogated Grandier upon the Cause of the said Hurt, who answered him, that be had not been aware of it, and had not taken Notice of it, and that it was likely to be done by flicking in some Pin, not remembring bow it should have happen'd otherwise. Nevertheless, the Physicians, after the said Visit, the 27th. of the Jane Month, made their Report, wherein they judg'd that the hurt was made by a Knife or some other sharp Instrument; and that there came out Blood, of which the Person accus'd having Notice by the reading to him the Deposition, whereas the first time he testified he had no knowledge of that Cut, he recall'd what he had exprest before, and said, that since their last Visit, he had recollected his Memory, and that he did remember that one of his Guards had given him a Knife, by which he made the said Hurt, by cutting a piece of Bread, Two Hours before the said Laubardemont enter'd the Prison; and another time he said, that the Cut was made the Day before, wherein there is a Contradiction; and besides, us'd all his Endeavours to make the said Laubardemont believe, that there came forth no Blood, because he had well taken Notice of it; and that the Report of the said Physicians was false in that Respect. After which, the 30th of the said Month, the said Sieur de Laubardemont, having again reiterated his Interrogatories upon the same Subject, he answer'd, that be believ'd that the said Cut was made the Day before the said Sieur de Laubardemont went into the Prison, and that there bad come out no Blood at it. The Declaration of a Devil, who came to bring a Pact of Paper stain'd with Blood, and the Testimony of the Physicians, who had altogether consulted in Form, to know, If a little Scar which was upon the Thumb of Grandier, was a Cut or a small Scratch; if it had been made with a Knife, Pin, or otherwise; and the Verbal Processes of Laubardemont, which thus far had any Shadow of Proof against Grandier, endeavour'd to involve him in some little Contradictions, upon a Fact which in it self was the greatest trifle in the World; all this not amounting to valuable Proofs, they relie much in this particular, upon the Astonishment of the Person accus'd, and upon the varying of his Answers. The Surprize, or rather the Reflection, which they call'd a Surprize, is upon this Occasion very natural to a Person accus'd of a Capital Crime, to whom they came upon a suddain to put Objections and Questions; he could not do less than recollect himself and reflect. The Depth of the Business was important enough, and might concern him enough to produce that Effect: But as the Circumstance, upon which they interrogated him, was in it self but a Trifle, and a little Accident which might really happen, and especially in that Condition his Mind was in at that Time, and the Wound having not drawn any Blood, as he always strongly affirm'd, 'tis no wonder that he declar'd on a suddain, that he knew not how it came; and that afterwards having recollected his Memory, he might believe he had some Representation of the Manner how the Thing happen'd; and that after he had again corrected what he had declar'd, by some more distinct Idea which was come into his Mind, seeing that such an Accident could not have made any strong Impression upon his Imagination, if he had been in a quiet Condition. On the other side, his Guards, and la Bontems his Hostess, who were continually observing him, and who had undertaken to inform them of the least Circumstances that happen'd concerning his Person, had not fail'd to acquaint Asmodee with this little Accident, which they had better perceiv'd than the Patient himself, who had his Mind fill'd with other Matters.

Sect. 75.

'This is the best Part of the Proofs, upon which there interven'd the Sentence of the 18th. of August last, in Execution whereof, the Person condemn'd, having been put to the Torture, has own'd the Book made by him against the Celibacy of Priests, out of a Design to quiet the Mind of a Maid, whom he had convers'd with for Seven Years; and of which Book, if he had not acknowledg'd it, there had been Proofs at the Trial.' That Book contain'd nothing which had Relation to Magick, it was very well written, according to the Testimony of a Physician who had seen it, and whose Opinion is set down in the French Mercury of that Time; If then that Writing had been pertinent to the Condemnation of Grandier, it ought not to have caus'd him to be sentenc'd to the Fire. His Declaration concerning that Book, which he had made an Occasion of a Marriage of Conscience between him and a Maid, has also been confirm'd by the same Physician, who said he had seen at the End of it, this Distich. If that, his Doctrine you aright conceive, Great quiet soon your Conscience will receive.

Sect. 76.

' 'Tis also very certain, whatever has been said to the contrary, that the Manner wherewith the Person accus'd receiv'd the News of his Death, is a Confirmation of his wicked Life. For in the First Place, he never took Notice of the Crucifix when it was presented to him; after the pronouncing of his Sentence, he spake of nothing but the mitigating of the Rigour of his Punishment.' Are not these Two fine Proofs of Magick?

Sect. 77.

'He refus'd the Prayers which were offer'd him.' This Matter is false, and is reported only by Authors who have writ in Favour of the Possession; whereas a great Number of Relations of very worthy Persons do mention, that he accepted of the Prayers of all those who offer'd them; as may be seen in the Account we have given of his Death.

Sect. 78.

'And he did many other Actions which testified sufficiently his Impenitence.' What were these Actions? And how could a Judge, who was not partial, bring in all those last Actions, as if they had been Proofs at his Trial? Have these subsequent Actions been Proofs to ground the foregoing Sentence upon? This is an Accumulation of all that, which for want of sufficient Proofs, they have been able to collect, to blacken and render odious the Victim which they have unjustly sacrific'd.

Sect. 79.

'All that which could be excepted against, in the Instruction of the Process, is, that the Surgeon, who assisted at the Visits, was a Kinsman of one, nam'd de Silli, who, they say, has been one of the Instruments of the Destruction of Grandier; but he was only as a Witness, and there are Eight Physicians unsuspected, who assisted there, who have given their Report.' He who manag'd the Probe was but a Witness, and those who assisted, and were presented at the Action, were Agents. So that to assist, is to be an Agent; and to act, is only to assist. By such an Inversion of Reason, one may easily burn all Mankind. It may be seen by this, of what People all that Body of Physicians was compos'd, and what Regard one ought to have for their Testimonies, as well as for the Proceedings of Laubardemont and the other Commissaries, to whom there was Complaint made of the Incapacity and Partiality of Mannouri, in demanding a new Visit; to which these Judges having not consented, they are notwithstanding forc'd to own, that there is something to be said against it.

Sect. 80.

'It may be said further, that the Apothecary, who prepar'd the Drugs to Purge and Physick the said Nuns, during the time they were sequester'd, was much suspected by Grandier, because he had had a Suit with one of his Confidents. But to that may be reply'd, that the Drugs were view'd by the Physicians who appointed them; and that the Composition was made in their presence.' Why would they acknowledge that the Apothecary was suspected without appointing another? It is because another could not be found capable of so great Wickedness. But if the Drugs had been always mingled in the Presence of the Physicians [which is not true] and that the Physicians themselves had not been suspected, they were not always present from the Moment of the Composition, to the Moment that the Drugs were administred, to know and attest that there was no change made in them.

Sect. 81.

'It may be further said, that the Sequestration of the Nuns had not been executed according to Form; because they were not all separated one from the other. But this Fault was supply'd and amended, in that they were put some of them into the House of one, who is said to be one of the best Friends of Grandier, call'd Maurat.' This is the Reasoning of a passionate and blinded Party, rather than of a dis-interested Judge. Some of the least considerable of the Persons possess'd, and who made no Figure in the Business of the Possession, are put into the House of one of Grandier's Friends, and all the Chiefest are deliver'd to his Mortal and declar'd Enemies; and the Defect of that Sequestration, in its most essential Parts, and almost in all its Parts, is said to be supply'd and repair'd, because it was a little less abusively perform'd in a small Number of the possessed; but to speak Truth, it was not done at all, since they acknowledge here, that it was intirely ill Executed in this Point, that they were not all put separately. It must then be confest, that they have been to blame for having so obstinately stopp'd their Ears, when the Person accus'd has so many times demanded a real Sequestration, and by Consequence, that he has been unjustly condemn'd.

Sect. 82.

'I forbear to speak of the Declarations made by the Devils, and which they continually repeated, viz. that Grandier was the Subject of their Mission, the Author of their Witchcrafts, and the chief Cause of all these Torments; from which these poor Maids could not be deliver'd, leaving to the Divines to know, if one may believe the Father of Lies, and if the Devils duly exorcis'd are oblig'd to speak the Truth, and if the Conditions requisite to make a perfect Exorcism, are as possible, as necessary. As concerning the Host, whereon they say, there were some drops of Blood; besides, That this Miracle doth in no wise serve for the Conviction of Grandier, and that it happen'd after his Death; having not been an Eye-witness thereof, I refer the curious to the Information which the Lieutenant Criminal of Orleans has made thereof.'

Sect. 83.

To overthrow all at once the Testimonies of the Devils and Persons possess'd, we shall relate here an Act of the Sorbonne, more Authoris'd and more decisive, than all the Arguments we can use. 'We, subscribed Doctors of the Faculty of Paris, concerning a certain Question which has been propos'd to us, are of Opinion, that one ought never to allow the Devil to accuse others, and less also to make use of the Exorcisms to discover the Faults of any one, and to know if he be a Magician and when the said Exorcisms shall be made in the presence of the Holy Sacrament, with an Oath drawn from the Devil, by making him Swear, which is a Ceremony we do not approve of, however, one ought not for that to believe him, being always a Liar, and the Father of Lies; the Exorcisms also being not in all Kinds infallible, to produce such Effect as is pretended, and so it is held by most of the Doctors. Considering also, that the Devil is greatly delighted in Calumny and Imposture, and is the Sworn Enemy of Mankind, so that notwithstanding the terrible Torments which he endures by the Exorcisms, being adjur'd by the Name of God in the Presence of the most Holy Sacrament, he had rather suffer all that Evil in lying impudently, provided he may discharge and execute his Rage upon him, against whom he has a Design: Whereunto may be added, that if this Door be once open, the honestest Persons would not be in safety, considering that 'tis at those that the Devil chiefly aims; for this Reason St. Thomas, Book 22. Quest. 9. Articul. 2. maintains with the Authority of St. Chrysostom, that Dæmoni etiam ver a dicenti, non est credendum, the Devil must not be believ'd, tho' he speak the Truth. And in Effect, our Saviour, in St. Mark, Ch. I. and St. Luke, Chap. the 4th. suffers not the Devils to speak, but enjoyns them Silence, although though they speak the

Truth in calling him the Son of GOD. Whereby 'tis manifest, that one ought in no wise to proceed against those that the Devil shall accuse, when there are no other Proofs. And also we see this well observ'd in France, where the Judges do not take Cognizance of such Depositions. And on the other side, all the Discourse held by the Devil, so as it had been related to us, is particularly suspected, for being too long, of one Tenour, and without Intermission. Made at Paris the 16th of February, 1620. Signed Andrew du Val. P. Gamaches, and N. Imbert.'

Sect. 84.

'The reading of this Act, all the Decisions whereof so well agree with the Business of Grandier, do clearly shew the Injustice of the Sentence given against him.'

THE HISTORY OF THE Devils of Loudun:

Or, an Account of the
Possession of the Ursuline Nuns.
AND THE
Condemnation and Punishment of
URBAN GRANDIER,
a Parson of the same Town.

THE THIRD BOOK.

Sect. I.

IT was with much astonishment and displeasure, that the Monks beheld the courage and resolution that Grandier shew'd, even to the last breath of his Life. They did not believe that a Man who had liv'd in ease and pleasure, was capable of so much constancy. They did hope that he would have been shaken by the prospect of the Torments which were provided for him, and by the promise they would have made him for the mitigation of them; Or that at least the Torments themselves would have forc'd from him the Confession of a Crime, whereof they would have made him guilty, and were perswaded that if they could not bring him even to charge those whom they had design'd to make his Complices, they should not fail to draw Consequences very dangerous for them by that Confession, which being ready drawn in such terms as they thought fit, should be presented to him to sign; whereby it might be concluded, that if he did own no more, it was to spare them, and not to expose them to the rigour of the Punishments to which he was condemn'd. 'Twas upon this consideration that Laubardemont spake to him very low, and discours'd him a very long time in the Chamber of Audience, when he denied him the Paper which he ask'd for, wherein doubtless he intended to write quite other things than the Confession they exacted of him, which was once again tender'd to him in vain by the same Laubardemont, all written and ready to sign, after he had undergone the Torture, and that he was in the Council Chamber upon the Straw near the fire. This Obstacle, which they did not expect, or which at least they did assuredly think to surmount, had so highly rais'd the Spirits of the good Fathers, that they proceeded to execute upon his Person the Excesses which have been mention'd: But it serv'd to secure the Bailiffe, the Lieutenant Civil, Magdalane de Brou, who was Grandier's most intimate Friend, and many other Officers and good Catholicks, as well as most of the Protestants, upon whom they pretended to make dangerous attempts in consequence of the Declarations which they endeavour'd to extort from the Sufferer in his Torments.

Sect. 2.

Things being in this Condition, and the Exorcists not being yet satisfied, because they had not hitherto found out ways to establish their Inquisition, by causing to be drawn before the Tribunal of the Judges, all those against whom they had a Mind to act in pursuance of Grandier's attestation; they were constrain'd to have recourse to other means, and to endeavour to do by the testimony and power of the Devils, what so many diabolical Actions had not been able to effect.

Sect. 3.

Altho' the number of the Persons possess'd were very great, it was seen nevertheless that there were but a very few that were become famous in these Exorcisms and proper to perform the postures, and to fall into Convulsions. As the Superior excell'd amongst the Nuns, Elizabeth Blanchard carried the Prize amongst the Seculars. She had the confidence to maintain to Grandier's Face, that he had carnal commerce with her. And that he had promis'd to make her Princess of Magicians, if she would follow him to the Sabat, although he had protested that he never saw her before the day she was confronted to him. She said she was possess'd by fix Devils, by Astarot and the Coal of Impurity, who were of the Order of Angels, by Belzebuh, and the Lion of Hell, of the Order of Archangels, and by Perou and Marou of the Order of Cherubins. Astarot had promis'd to raise her up six foot from the Gound when he went out, and the Lion of Hell to pierce her Foot, the others boasted of nothing: These Miracles promis'd by the two Devils were expected with impatience, when there was another substituted in their place.

Sect. 4.

The third day after the death of Grandier in the Evening, the Father Peter Thomas de St. Charles, a Carmelite, Exorcist of Elizabeth Blanchard, having given her the Communion, she was much agitated by one of her Devils, who would not tell his Name. During this Struggle the consecrated Wafer was held by one of its edges and raised its whole length upon the lower lip of the Person possess'd, and was seen by all the Assistants to be red and mark'd with Blood in many places, particularly on the most elevated part. The Exorcist interrogated the Devil in Latin, and commanded him to tell him what the Prodigy meant? The Possess'd answered in French, That it was the Blood of Jesus Christ, thus shed upon the Consecrated Wafer, to convince the wicked and incredulous, who said it was but Bread; which was confirm'd by great Oaths, and a new Miracle, which the Devil did in this manner. Two Recollects who stood far enough from the Possess'd, agreed together, whispering upon a Motion that she should perform, in an act of Adoration which should be commanded her, to know thereby if she were really possess'd, and if the Devils knew what past in secret. She fail'd not to perform that Motion in saying, I adore the precious Blood of Jesus Christ there present, or at least the two Recollects protested that she had done it; so there is no room to doubt it, and it ought to be believ'd, notwithstanding the suspicions there were that she had been advertis'd before by these two fellow Friars of Father Lactance, and notwithstanding the complaints that were made, that this sign had been declar'd to no Body but to these two Monks. It happen'd further to the first of these Prodigies, that there were a great many Persons in the Assembly who would search that Maids Mouth, and who consider'd her Tongue, her Lips, and all their Parts, without finding either Wound or Scratch, or Fistula, or any appearance that there had issued out thence Blood that day. In fine, the Exorcist took the Bloody Host, and being devoutly follow'd by all those People who were perswaded and believ'd, he carried it in Procession to the Convent of the Carmelites.

Sect. 5.

The next day in the Morning, August 22th. Elizabeth Blanchard was Exorciz'd again in the Church of the Carmelites. The Exorcist demanded of the Devil, Of what Church doest thou believe the Authority? Who answer'd nothing to that Question: But the Maid said by her own Motion, I have enough to do to speak of that Blood. Of what Blood, said the Carmelite to her? 'Tis not they Blood, reply'd she, 'tis the Blood of a Master who is Almighty. Whereupon the Exorcist having commanded her by the Virtue of that Blood, to tell him, Who was that great and Almighty Master? She utter'd an Oath so horrible, that instead of daring to write it here, it makes one tremble to think of it only; and afterwards she answer'd, If I bad it thou shouldst never have it. The Exorcist proceeded. Q. I command thee by the Virtue of that Blood, to tell me who is that Almighty Master? A. I will not answer thee concerning that Blood. Q. Whose is that Blood? A. I am inrag'd, thou know'st it well; keep it safe that it be not spill'd, thou shalt answer for it, God must be serv'd; She pronoun ed these Words swearing again horribly by the Holy Name of God. Q. For what is this Blood? A. God has made this to the end that more Reverence may be given to the Holy Sacrament: I am obliged to say it by the Almighty Power of God. Q. Whose is that Blood which torments thee? Say, if thou obey'st not-- A. Thou know'st it, I told it yesterday, I cannot tell it without suffering pain. She utter'd not these words before she had gnash'd her Teeth, turn'd her Eyes, and seemed to suffer some convulsions. Q. Tell it, to the end that the Assist mts may now bear it. A. We cannot think of God but it increaseth our Torments, I am inrag'd. She renounc'd God in concluding that last answer. Q. Whose is that Blood? A. 'Tis the Blood--There she stopt short, and fell into another Convulsion. Q. Whose is that Blood which was shed yesterday? A. 'Tis the Blood of the Son of Man. Q. And who is the Son of Man? answer. A. 'Tis the Blood of the Son of the Virgin, I am inrag'd, I will not tell it, this makes me mad. Upon which she made frightful Grimaces with her Teeth, and dreadful cries. Q. Who is the Son of the Virgin? A. 'Tis a little Baby. Q. Who is that? A. 'Tis the little Jesus; After she had said that she had many convulsions. Q. Whose Blood is that which was shed yesterday? A. 'Tis the Blood of Jesus Christ: She stopt short again, and the Exorcist having commanded her to adore it, as a sign that she had spoke the truth, she rais'd her self up, and went to put her self on her Knees upon the lowest Steps of the Altar, where she stretched out her Arms in the form of a Cross, the palms of her Hands turn'd outwards, her head bow'd downwards, and her face towards the ground, the Exorcist commanded her to adore with words plainly pronounc'd. I adore, said she, the Blood of Jesus Christ which was shed yesterday for the incredulous. Proceed, said the Exorcist. That word imprudently let fall, was taken hold of by one of the Standers by, who said that that signified that she had not recited all that was contain'd in her Part; but he who had been so rash for making that remark, was very fortunate that he could slip amongst the croud, and so get away. The Possessed in the mean time proceeded thus, He shed his Blood yesterday for the Incredulous, to the end they might believe it was not an Imposture; God at the end of Judgment will condemn them, and then his Anger shall appear, and they shall be more damned than the Devils. This strange Dialogue being ended, two Carmelites went to find Lauberdemont, and they related to him the great Miracle that was done the day before, and what happen'd again at the last Exorcism, as if he had known nothing of it. Whereupon Lauberdemont and the Procurator General Deniau went to the Convent of the Carmelites, with the Clerk of the Commission. When they were near the great Altar of the Church, the Host was presented to them; they found it mark'd with Blood in several places, being a little more full of Spots on one side of the edge than elsewhere, the Marks being more red, and bigger, and all the Blood of a Vermilion colour, although it was quite dry. Laubardemont himself would draw up an Act, but 'twas now past noon, and each of the Spectators, for whatsoever reason it was, exprest so great a desire to be gone, that at the request of the King's Procurator, the Commissary caus'd an Act, which had been already drawn up by a Carmelite, to be read immediately, and he oblig'd all the Standers by, of whom some would have been willing to be further off, to swear upon the Holy Gospels, and to attest that that Act contain'd the Truth, afterwards it having been sign'd by the Order of the same Commissary, by all those who could write, and in Particular by the Priests, and Friars, who had assisted the precedent Evening at the Exorcism at St. Peter du Martrai, it was sent to the Registry, and the Host was carried in a little Tabernacle, near the great Altar, on the Gospel-side, whereof Laubardemont took the Key. The Relation of that Miracle was no sooner printed, but 'twas contradicted by the Incredulous, who maintain'd, that the Exorcist might easily put an Host stain'd with Blood upon Blanchard's Mouth; That the Devil himself was honest enough not to speak of Blood going out of the Host, but of Blood shed: That the Carmelite in imitation of him had sufficiently discover'd, that that Part had been devis'd and suggested, when he said to the Person pretended to be possessed, Proceed, as 'twas well observ'd by him, who was fain to go out of the Church; And that thence it followed, that the Blood of Jesus Christ had been twice shed, the first time upon the Cross for the expiation of the Sins of Men; and the second upon the Host for the Conviction of the Incredulous, who look'd upon the Possession at Loudun as a gross and ill contriv'd Imposture, and which was supported but by the violence of Authority; the Doctrine whereof contain'd so many absurdities and blasphemies, that one cannot too much wonder that there had been Christians in the World who durst introduce and support it.

Sect. 5.

That double Miracle was too famous not to deserve to entertain the Reflections of devout Souls for a long time, and 'twas to give them leisure to feed their Holy Avidity, that the Persons possessed stopt, and offer'd them nothing extraordinary. But the Devils, who are active, could not so continue in Idleness. Here follows what they did, as it is contain'd in a Book printed at Poitiers by Authority by Anthony Meusnier, in the Year 1635. intituled, A Relation of what pass'd in the Exorcisms at Loudun, in the presence of Monsieur the King's Brother, Pag. 22, and 25. wherein the Author having maintain'd, That the Exorcists do almost all, more or less, partake of the Effects of the Devils, by the Inconveniencies and Disturbances they receive, and that few Persons have attempted to expel them, but they have been exercis'd by them. "He adds for a Witness, the late Father Lactance Gabriel of happy Memory; who whilst he was in that Employment, wherein he gloriously died, after he had expell'd three Devils out of the Mother Prioress, felt great Molestations by those Evil Spirits, loosing sometimes his Sight, sometimes his Memory, and now and then his Understanding, suffering Pains at his Heart, Infestations in Spirit, and divers other Molestations." That is, to speak plainly, and without any disguise, that Father Lactance died the 18th of September, just a Month after the Death of Grandier, and that he was almost continually mad, and inrag'd during his disease. If he had some interval during his Frenzy he employed it in Uttering merry Jests, such as when he said to his Physician, That he pray'd him to prepare in his presence the Medicines he had order'd him, because that all that came from Adam, savour'd of Original Sin, quibbling so upon the Name of Adam his Apothecary. You are very happy, said he, another time to the Wife of du Fresne Moussaut, who tended him, and at whose House he lodg'd; You are very happy for this, that the Providence of God has made me thus fall into your Hands, and you have obtain'd an opportunity to render me the good services which you do: And looking with contempt upon the young Monks who were put about to watch with him, Is it not a lamentable thing, cry'd he, That a Man of Weight, Desert, and Importance, as I am, should be serv'd and assisted by such Monkeys and little Hobgoblins? Certainly if one will not believe with the most Catholick Author of the Relation abovemention'd, that he has been possess'd by real Devils, at least one must agree, that his Conscience did serve him instead of an Executioner and a Devil, since it is certain that he died in such a fit of Madness and Despair as are not to be express'd. It must not be omitted here, that a few days after the death of Grandier, that good Father beginning to find himself seiz'd with the Distemper whereof he died, what, ever it was, he purpos'd to make a Journey to our Lady of Ardilliers at Saumur, he had a place in the Coach of the Sieur de Canaye, who went to divert himself at his Estate of Grandfons, with a company of Persons who were not greatly scrupulous, as he himself was not. They knew already that 'twas nois'd about, that the Father was really possess'd, and they flirted out against him some jesting passages upon that Subject, when all upon a sudden going on gently in an even way, the Coach overturn'd, the top of it falling undermost without any Body's being hurt, or receiving any inconvenience. Whatsoever courage the Company had, they were surpriz'd at that Accident; and when they were come to Grandfons, being at the Table, they discours'd very seriously concerning the Devils of Loudun, and the death of Grandier, with Father Lactance. He seem'd sad and disorder'd, and spake little in that Conversation; he only acknowledg'd that he repented of his advising that they should deny Father Grillau to be Confessor to Grandier, who had desir'd it with so much earnestness. The next day they proceeded on their Journey for Saumur, where the Coach was again over-turn'd after the same manner, in the middle of the great Street of the Suburb of Fenet, which leads to the Chapel of Ardilliers, and which is also very plain and even, which gave a great Reputation to the Noise that was spread abroad of the

Possession of Father Lactance by evil Spirits, and that rumor yet made a far greater Impression upon the People, when they had seen that Father die mad and in despair. But that which did fully confirm that Belief, was the applause which the Monks gave it; for it concern'd them so exceedingly to make the Possession find Credit, that to remove all doubts, and to have an essential Proof, they would readily agree that Father Lactance did die possess'd, saving that they might the better turn that Possession to the Glory of the Church, and of the late Matyr, and to the advantage of the other Exorcists, even as it appear'd in the Relation printed at Poitiers above cited.

Sect. 6.

The Lieutenant Civil of Loudun, Lewis Chauvet had testified by his Proceedings and oppositions to the Procedures of the first Exorcists, that he gave no credit to those Devils, and did not fear them. However he could not overcome the fear which seiz'd him, and so far possess'd him, that it never forsook him during the remainder of his Life. That Magistrate had Wit, Politeness and Honesty: But as he had not been willing to applaud the Possession, the Cabal, to cause him to be suspected, had had recourse to the ordinary and general means, which was to accuse him of Magick by one of the Possess'd. At first he laugh'd at the Accusation, and accounted it as ridiculous, as indeed it was. But when he had seen the tragical End of Grandier, his courage was shaken, and he began to be afraid. In that disposition he took a Journey to Poitiers, where the Assizes were held; he met with a Man there of consideration and quality, by whom he was particularly known; he had a long conference with him upon the Subject of the Possession at Loudun, and of the condemnation of Grandier: Whereupon that Friend assur'd him, that after he had well consider'd all the circumstances of that Affair, it was his persuasion, that all those who had been accus'd of that Magick, and should be for the future, would be in great danger to lose both their Honours and Life; And that if he saw himself accus'd of that Crime, as Grandier had been, he should think himself lost without hope, whatsoever Credit, Friends, or good Reputation he had. This Declaration surprized the Lieutenant Civil, he was confounded and the Agitations of the fright seiz'd so violently upon his Spirit, that they overturn'd it, and reduc'd him to such a condition, that since he was never restor'd to his right Understanding.

Sect. 7.

The Carmelites of Loudun heretofore had been possess'd of the Power of working Miracles; they had an Image of our Lady, call'd our Lady of Recovery, who fail'd not any one of those in what they requir'd of her devoutly, and in the requisite form. But since that Image of Ardilliers came to be set up at Saumur, in the Neighbourhood of the former, as if she had been her Rival, she usurp'd all her Power and Credit; and 'tis no great wonder; for doubtless there's no body in the World, who does not agree, that the Priests of the

Oratory are more able and cunning People than the Carmelites. At that time all one Quarter and a Suburb of Loudun, which was fill'd with Inns for Pilgrims, remain'd unpeopled and desolate, and the Carmelites without Presents, Votaries, and Gospelmoney. What was there to be done in such a Desertion? They employ'd Humane Means to reestablish the Work, which the Image had not been able to support, and which she had suffer'd to decay: They pierc'd the Wall of the Altar upon which she was plac'd; they drew a Branch of a Vine, which was planted behind it, and brought it through this Wall just to her Eyes; and at the time when the Vine us'd to weep, the Image in the presence of a number of People assembled to hear Mass and the Sermon, wept at several times for their want of Devotion, and for the Contempt they made of her Altar and her Power. But that Contrivance having not succeeded happily, because of the great multitude of Protestants which were then at Loudun, who had maliciously examin'd the Miracle, and discover'd the Artifice, those good Fathers were very glad to find in the Possession, and in the Authority of its Confederates, a way open to save their Credit, in spite of the piercing and malicious Eyes, and indiscreet Tongues of Hereticks, who were constrain'd to keep silent, by the Terror of Loubardemont, which, to use the Scripture Language, was fallen upon them, and gave them deadly Alarms. These Fathers knew readily to lay hold of the opportunity in the Exorcism of Elizabeth Blanchard on the 21st of June, wherein was produc'd the Host stain'd with Blood; and believing that after that Proof, there were no more Miracles which they were not able to perform, they attempted to cause a Devil, or a Magician, to bring a Copy of the Instrument in Writing, which Grandier had given to the Devil, when they made their Agreement. To attempt and to succeed was the same thing for these good Fathers, who pretended to be invested with the Authority of the Church. Having got that Copy, they caus'd it to be Printed, and fix'd in several places, to the end that if there were yet any Incredulous Person in the World, he should be fully convinc'd of the Possession by a Proof so solid and so evident: Whereof these were the Contents; My Lord and Master, Lucifer, I acknowledge you for my God, and I promise to serve you as long as I shall live; I renounce any other God, and Jesus Christ, and other Saints, and the Apostolical and Roman Church, and all the Sacraments of the same, and all the Prayers and Orisons which may be made for me; and I promise you to do all the Mischief I shall be able, and to entice as many Persons, as I can, to do hurt: And I renounce the Chrysom and Baptism, and all the Merits of Jesus Christ and his Saints: And in case I fail to serve, adore, and do homage to you thrice a day, I give you my Life, as belonging to you. The Original is in Hell, in a Corner of that Country, in the Cabinet of Lucifer. Sign'd with the Blood of the Magician. 'Tis not to be doubted but that this is the Stile of the Court of Hell; for either the Devils themselves drew up this Act, or else it must be forged in the Convent of the Carmelites; and if so, one may be bold to say, that there are Monks, who are skilful enough to imitate the Stile of Devils, and are so learn'd in their Languages and Customs, that one may easily take the Acts which they make in the obscure Retreat of their Cloisters, to have been fram'd in the very Darkness of Hell. It is a Truth whereof one may be entirely convinc'd by the inspection of this, that it cannot be denied but that Diabolical Spirits were the Authors of it.

Sect. 8.

The Place of the Reverend Father Lactance having continued void by his Death, 'twas very fit that they should cast their Eyes upon a Jesuite to supply it. For why should not that Order, so famous, so pious, and so proper to make every thing succeed that they undertake, have been call'd in to combat against the Devils? Seeing that every one of them who enters therein, is born, as they themselves boast, with a Helmet on his Head, and arm'd with all sorts of offensive and defensive Weapons? 'Tis true, that Father Joseph would not suffer it, whilst he thought himself able to perform the Office of Exorcist, and he caus'd almost all that Mission to fall into the Hands of the Friars of St. Francis; but after that he was disgusted, and that he had refus'd to be concern'd himself in that Business, the way remain'd open to the Jesuits, who enter'd it with Joy. It was not less worthily supplied by Father Surin, of whom they made choice amongst themselves for that purpose, than it had been by his Predecessor. That Father came to Loudun the 25th of December; and to be well inform'd with what he did there, it may be learnt from his own

Writings, wherein he says, 'That he endeavour'd to discover with Evidence, the Possession of the Devil in the Mother Prioress; That this was the first Obligation, he believ'd, was incumbent upon him in the first entrance upon his Office; That he had found unquestionable Proofs, and could swear before God and his Church, That more than two hundred times the Devils had discover'd to him things very secret, concealed in his Thought or his Person.' One must believe this Testimony of a Jesuit in favour of the Devil, and to the prejudice of God, who thereby is found to have no longer, and to the exclusion of all others, the sole Power of Searching the Hearts, the Reins and the Thoughts. How important and terrible soever this Opinion might be, it is hereby become probable, or rather Father Surin deserves well to be believ'd on his Word. But if one were yet too obstinate and incredulous not to be perswaded of the Truth of the Possession, upon the Faith of such a Voucher, one need but consider, without Prepossession, the new and unquestionable Proofs which hereafter follow.

Sect. 9.

The Relation of what past in the Exorcisms at Loudun, in the presence of Monsieur, printed at Poitiers, which has been already quoted, relates, 'That the Devils threatned at first the Father Jesuit, by the Mouth of the Mother Prioress, who had been given him in charge, to use him very ill, and to be fully reveng'd of him; and as he pursued daily his Design, they attempted, being sollicited, as they said, by some Magicians, to disturb him extraordinarily, to cause him to quit his Employment: So that he began, since the 19th of January, 1635, to be sensible of divers Signs of the Presence and malicious Operations of Devils; and that it was observ'd at that time, that performing his Exorcism, he lost his Speech upon a sudden; so that they were oblig'd to call in some other Exorcists, who applying the Holy Sacrament to his Mouth, freed him entirely; That that accident continu'd a long time, and even in the presence of the Bishop of Nimes; who, whilst the Devil nam'd Isaacarum took possession of the Countenance of the Mother Superior, and spake by her Mouth, he saw how the Devil audaciously threatning the Father to impose Silence upon him, disappear'd on a sudden from the Countenance of the possess'd, and at the same time attack'd the Father; that he made him change Colour, that he squeez'd his Breast, and stopp'd his Speech; and that quickly after, obeying that command which was given to quit him, he return'd to the Body of the. Prioress, spake by her Mouth, and shew'd himself extreamly hideous and horrible upon her Countenance; That the Father renewing the Combat, continued his Function with the same Liberty, as if he had not felt any Assault of the Devil; and so one Afternoon he was assaulted and acquitted seven or eight times one after another. That these Assaults have been follow'd by others much stronger, which began before the Passion Week, when the Devil said often to the Exorcist by the Mouth of the Possess'd, I will make thee suffer the Passion this Passion Weeek, my Friends are taking pains about it, intending to speak of some Magicians. And that really on good Friday about the Evening, the Father being in his Chamber, in the company of eight or ten Persons, he felt great pains at his Heart, and certain impetuosities which mov'd him inwardly, and constrain'd him to twist himself, as it happens in the extremities of the Cholick, That these Assaults which began at home, continued afterwards in publick, according to the Threats which the Devil often made to the Father; protesting that he would make him quit his Trade, and compel him to return from whence he came. That 'twas seen during the Exorcisms, that the Devil exorciz'd by the Father, leaving the Prioress, struck the Exorcist inwardly, as with a Dart, and threw him on the Ground, so that he cried and was shaken by his Adversary and Atagonist; That after he had continued in that condition about half an hour, or an hour, by the Succours of other Exorcists, and the application of the Holy Sacrament to the Places where he was sensible of the presence of the Devil, one while in the Breast, and another while in the Head, which he shew'd with his Hand, (as being always himself, and in liberty of Spirit,) and the rest of his Body, he was deliver'd, and that that Devil went to appear in the Countenance of the Prioress; where the Father being relieved, with a holy Vengeance he went to pursue him, as if nothing had happen'd, and forc'd him to adore the Holy Sacrament in the manner that is practised in those Exorcisms.'

Sect. 10.

But possibly one may believe a Letter which the Father Surin himself writ to Father D'atichi, who was then at Rennes; 'tis of the 3d. of May. 1635. and has been Printed under this Title.

A LETTER Of the Reverend Father Surin Jesuit Exorcist of the Ursulin Nuns of Loudun, to one of his Friends, a Jesuit. PAX CHRISTI To my Reverend Father. 'THere has been scarcely any Body, to whom I take the Pleasure to relate my Adventures but to your Reverence, who hears them willingly, and forms thereupon thoughts which happen not so easily to others, who know me not as you do. Since the last Letter which I writ you, I am fallen into a condition very remote from my foresight, but very conformable to the Providence of God in relation to my Soul; I am no more at Marennes but at Loudun, where I have receiv'd yours lately. I am in a prepetual conversation with the Devils, where I have had the Adventures which would be too long to mention to you, and which have given me a greater cause than ever I had to acknowledge and admire the Goodness of God. I will tell you something, and I would tell you further, if you were more secret; I am combating with four Devils, the most powerful and malicious of Hell, I my self, say, whose infirmities you know. God has permited that the Combat has been so rude, and the Approaches so frequent, that the smallest Field of Battle was the Exorcism; for the Enemies declare themselves in secret by Night and by Day, and in a thousand different ways. You may conceive what pleasure it is to find ones self at the Mercy of God alone. I will tell you no more, it sufficeth me that knowing my condition, you will take an occasion to pray for me: So it is, that for three Months and a half, I never am without a Devil exercising of me. Things are come to that pass, that God has permitted, I think for my Sins, what one could never be able to have seen in the Church, but in the exercise of my Ministry, the Devil passes from the Body of a Person possessed, and coming into mine, assaults me, overthrows me, tosses me, and visibly troubles me, by possessing me many hours as a Demoniac. I cannot explain to you what passes in me during that time, and how that Spirit was united with mine, without depriving me either of the knowledge or liberty of my Soul, making himself nevertheless as another my self, and as if I had two Souls, one of which was dispossest of its Body and the use of its Organs, and keeps it self apart, beholding the other act, who has introduced himself there. These two Spirits combat together in the same Field which is the Body, and the Soul is as it were divided; according to one part of its self, it is the Subject of diabolical Impressions, and according to the other, of the Motions which are proper to it, or what God gives it. At the same time I feel great quiet under the good pleasure of God, and without knowing how there come an extream rage and aversion to him, which produceth as it were some impetuosities to be seperated from him, which astonisheth those who see them, and at the same time a great joy and delight, and on the other part a Sadness which shews it self by lamentations and howlings, like to those of Devils. I feel the State of Damnation, and apprehend it, I feel my self as pierced with the points of Despair in the stranger Soul, which seems to me to be mine; and the other Soul which is in full confidence mocks at those Sentiments, and curseth with all freedom him who caus'd them; truly I find that the same cries, which go out of my Mouth, come equally from these two Souls, and I can hardly distinguish, whether it is pleasure that produceth them, or the extream madness that filled me. The tremblings which seize me, when the Holy Sacrament is apply'd to me, come equally, as it seems to me, from the horrour of its presence, which is supportable, and from a Cordial and pleasing Reverence, without being able to attribute them to the one rather than to the other, and that tis not in my power to retain them. When I would, by the motion of one of these two Souls, make the sign of the Cross on my Mouth, the other turns away my Hand with great quickness, and seizeth my Fingers with his Teeth, for to bite them with fury. I scarcely ever find Prayer more easie, and quiet, than in these agitations, whilst the Body rolls through the Place, and the Ministers of the Church speak to me as to a Devil, and load me with Curses; I cannot tell you the Joy that I am sensible of, being become a Devil, not by rebellion to God, but by the calamity which gives me a lively Representation of the estate wherein Sin has reduc'd me, and how appropriating to me all the curses which are given me, my Soul has cause to sink it self into its nothingness. When the other Possessed behold me in that condition, 'tis a Pleasure to see how they triumph, and as Devils mock me, saying, Physician heal thy self, be gone, get thee up into the Pulpit, 'twill be a pretty sight to see him preach, after he shall have roll'd through the place; Tentaverunt, subsannaverunt me subsannatitione frenderunt super me dentibus suis. What a cause of Blessing is this, to see ones self made the Mock-game of Devils? And that the Justice of God calls me to an account in this World for my Sins. But what favours! to experience from what an estate Jesus Christ has delivered me, and to feel how great that Redemption is, not by hearsay, but by the impression of the same estate, and how good it is to have at the same time the ability to understand perfectly this calamity, and to give thanks to the divine Goodness who has deliver'd us with so great trouble and pains! This is the condition I am in at this time, almost every day. This gives occasion to great disputes, and factus sum magna quæstio, whether it be a possession or no, whether it be possible for the Ministers of the Gospel to fall into so great inconveniences? Some say, that 'tis a chastisement of God on me for the punishment of some Illusions; others say, some other thing; and for my part I would not change my Condition with another, having a firm perswasion that there is nothing better than to be reduc'd to great extremities. That wherein I am is such, that I have few operations free. When I would speak they stop my Mouth; At the Mass I am hindred from going any further; At Confession I forget my Sins all at once, and I feel the Devil go and come in me as into his House; When I awake he is there at my Prayer; He bereaves me of my thought when he pleaseth; when my

Heart begins to dilate it self towards God, he fills it with rage; He casts me into a Sleep when I would wake; And publickly by the Mouth of the possess'd, he boasts that he is my Master; against which I have nothing to say, having the reproach of my Conscience, and upon my Head the Sentence pronounc'd against Sinners; I ought to submit to it, and to reverence the order of the Divine Providence, to which every Creature must be subject. 'Tis not one Devil that torments me, there are usually two; The one is Leviathan oppos'd to the Holy Ghost, for as much as they say that in Hell there is a Trinity. That the Magicians worship Lucifer, Belzebub and Leviathan, who is the third Person of Hell; And some Authors have observ'd and writ of it heretofore. Now the Operations of this false Paraclete are all contrary to the true one, and imprint a desolation, which one cannot well represent. He is the chief of all the Band of our Devils, and he has the Government of all that Affair, which is one of the strangest that possibly was ever seen. We see in this very place Paradice and Hell; I mean the Nuns who are as so many Ursula's, taken in one Sense, and in the other, worse than the most Profligate in all sorts of Disorders, Beastlyness, Blasphemies and Madness. I do not desire that your Reverence would make my Letter publick, if it please you. You are the only Person, to whom except my Confessor and my Superiors, I have been willing to say so much. It is but to entertain some Communications, which may assist us to glorifie God; In which I am your most humble Servant, John Joseph Surin.' And by a Postscript. 'I pray you to procure for me Prayers, having need of them. I am for whole Weeks so stupid towards Divine Things, that I should be glad that some body would make me pray to God like a Child, and would expound to me the Pater Noster. The Devil said to me, I will deprive thee of all, and thou will have need that thy faith continue, I will make thee become stupid; he has made a Pact with a Witch to hinder me to speak of God, and to have power to restrain my Spirit, which he performs very faithfully as he promis'd, and I am constrain'd to have some Understanding, to hold often the Holy Sacrament upon my Head, using the Key of David to unlock my Memory.'

Sect. II.

But in a Manuscript Copy, which some have in keeping, there is a second Postcript, which has not been Printed, and 'tis this. 'I am content to die, seeing our Lord has done me the favour to have withdrawn three consecrated Wafers, which three Witches had put into the Hands of the Devil, who brought me them publickly from Paris, where they were under the Mat of a Bed, and left the Church in Possession of that Glory, and to have in some measure render'd to her Redeemer, what she had receiv'd of him, having redeem'd it out of the Hands of the Devil. I know not whether our Lord will soon take away my Life, for when I was in pain about that affair, I gave it him freely, and promise to quit it for the Price of these three Waters. It seems that the Devil by these bodily evils that he caus'd me, would make use of his right, and consume me by little and little.'

Sect. 12.

They who publish'd the Letter, have questionless judg'd it fit to suppress that last Postscript; and they had done well also to suppress the whole Letter, and the horrible Things it contains, which will not fail to induce the Reader to think seriously of the condition wherein the Exorcist has been, as well as his Predecessor the Father Lactance. In effect, if it be true, that that there are Sorcerers, Magicians and Persons possess'd, or that there may be, as none can doubt, is there not evidence enough, that God for the just Punishment of these Wicked Persons, who upon this occasion so impudently mock his divine Majesty, has permitted, that their abominable and diabolical dissimulation, should become a truth, and that they should be really possess'd by the Devils, whom they would counterfeit, testifying by so many horrid Actions, that they believ'd not their Existence, nor that of God himself; seeing that if they had believ'd it, they would have trembled, and never dare to attempt to make it their Pastime in so wicked and insolent a manner, Certainly if they have not been actually possessed, and by real and bodily Possession which is pretended here, it is however certain that the Devil had fill'd their Heart, that he presides over their abominable Acts, that he was the Author, and that one may say in that sense with much justice and reason, that they were absolutely possess'd. But to omit nothing of what concerns the Truth of the Facts, leaving otherwise to the Reader the liberty to judge according to his Sentiments, one cannot refrain from declaring here that all the Relations do mention that the Fathers Lactance, Tranquille and Surin, after the death of Grandier, were troubled by Devils, and that all the Protestants or Papists who have been discourst with upon that Subject, who had assisted at the Exorcisms, and had knowledge of the death of the Recollect and that of the Capucin, have agreed of all the Facts, which are related here concerning their condition, as of the greatest part of the other Acts which are contain'd in the Relation of what past in the Exorcisms at Loudun in the presence of Monsieur, the Duke of Orleans, and in the Letter of Father Surin, and they have all protested that they did not believe that all the abominable things which they had seen and heard, could have been produced by the only power of Nature, nor only by the perversity thereof, but that it must needs be that Devils intermeddle, and that they had really possess'd those pretended Exorcists. Whereupon 'tis to be found in the Relations that were then writ, that they reproach'd the Jesuit that he resembled not the Apostles, nor the Exorcists of the Primitive Church, which fail'd not to expel readily the Devils in the Name, and by the Authority of Jesus Christ, without being either abus'd, or insulted, or much less possess'd, but that his Exorcisms were like those of the Jews, of whom it is said in the Acts of the Apostles, who attempted to invoke the Name of the Lord Jesus over those who had evil Spirits, saying, We adjure you by Jesus Christ, whom Paul preach'd, to whom the evil Spirit answer'd, Jesus I know, and Paul I know, but who are ye? and the Man in whom the evil Spirit was, leaping upon them, and mastering them, us'd violence against them; So that they fled away naked and wounded out of the House.

Sect. 13.

Much after this manner was the Condition of Father Surin; for besides his Sufferings either real or feigned, he perform'd more than a Year the Function of Exorcist, without expelling any Devil: In the mean time some days after that he writ the terrible Letter, the Copy whereof you have read, Monsieur the King's Brother came to Loudun, to see the Wonders of that famous, Possession, which made so great a noise both within the Kingdom and without. The Author of the Relation printed at Poitiers, reports that Monsieur arriv'd at Loudun the 9th of May. 1635. 'That his Highness went presently to the Convent of the Ursulines, where being at the Grate, and being informed by them of their condition, Sister Agnes seem'd a little troubled, and made some tremblings, which shew'd the presence of the first of the four Devils which possess'd her, nam'd Asmodee when 'twas resolv'd to exorcise her presently, and that Asmodee delay'd not long to discover his greatest rage, shaking divers times the Maid backward and forward, and making her batter as an Hammer with so great great quickness, that her Teeth crash'd, and her Throat made a forc'd noise; That during these Agitations, her countenance became so altogether chang'd as not to be known, her looks furious, her Tongue prodigiously great, long, and hanging down out of her Mouth, livid and dry to that degree, that the want of Moisture caus'd it to seem all rough and shaggy, without being in the mean time any ways press'd with her Teeth, and her breathing being always equal; That Beherit, who is also another Devil, made appear a second Countenance smiling and agreeable, which was again diversly chang'd by two other Devils, Achas and Achaos, who shew'd themseves one after the other; That Asmodee being commanded to continue still, and the others to retire, her first countenance return'd; That the Devil being adjur'd to adore the Sacrament, said presently, That he would himself be ador'd, but at last he obey'd, prostrating his Body on the Ground; That after divers other Countenances the Sister Agnes brought one of her Feet by the hinder part of her Head, even to her Forehead, in such a manner that her great Toe almost touched her Nose; That the Exorcist having commanded him to kiss the Pix, and to tell who it was that he had ador'd, the Devil, after he had made many difficulties, obey'd the former of these commands, but that he refus'd to obey the second; That laying his Hand on the Pix, he swore, By the God who is there, I will not tell; That as the Father insisted, commanding him absolutely to tell it, the Devil reply'd as it were mocking him, perceiv'st thou not that I have just now nam'd him. That then he withdrew, and the Maid came to her self, and said to Monsieur, that she remembred some of the things that were done, but not all, and that she heard the Answers that came from her Mouth, as if another had spake them; That her arm having been felt by a Physician and a Surgeon of Monsieur, her Pulse was found to be equal after so many shakings and violent agitations.'

Sect. 14.

'The day following Monsieur went to St. Cross, whither they brought Elizabeth Blanchard, to make her take the Communion in his presence: The Relation of that day mentions, That one of the six Devils which possess'd her, nam'd Astarot, appear'd presently and troubled her; That her Exorcist having commanded this Devil to approach the Maid, she fell into a general Convulsion of all her Body; That her Face chang'd both the form and colour, appearing livid, and much swollen, and her Tongue going all out of her Mouth, very much charged, and of a length, thickness, and bigness altogether extraordinary; That in this Condition the came rolling and wriggling even to the Feet of the Priest, who laid the Holy Sacrament upon her Lips, commanding the Devil to hinder that the Elements should not be moistn'd in any manner, and forbidding him to commit or suffer that any of his Companions practise any Irreverence against that adorable Mystery; That the Maid was immediately thrown upon the Floor, where the Devil exercis'd great violences upon her Body, and gave horrid marks of his rage; That he turned her thrice backwards in the form of a Bow, in such a manner that she touch'd not the Pavement but with the tip of her Toes, and the end of her Nose, and that she seem'd as if she would have made the Holy Host to touch the Ground, bringing it near almost as within the thickness of a leaf of Paper; but the Exorcist reiterating his former prohibitions always hinder'd it; That the Devil raising himself up, blew against the Holy Host, which was seen upon the Lips of the Possess'd, shaken like a leaf of a Tree, when a violent Wind strikes upon it, and passing it divers times from one Lip to the other; That Beelzebub having been commanded to come up to her Face, there was to be seen a beating of her Throat, which swell'd it exceedingly, and made it hard as a piece of Wood; That Monsieur having desir'd to see all the Devils appear which possess'd that Maid, the Exorcist made them come into her Countenance one after another, rendering it very hideous, but every one making a different Deformity; That when Astarot had been commanded to appear, there was observ'd under the left Arm-pit a great Tumour, with a quick beating which was admir'd by all the Assistants, and even by his Highnesses Physician; That the Devil being retir'd from that place by the command of the Exorcist, he went to seize her Visage, and let the Host fall upon the Paten, wherein it was seen to be very dry, without leaving any mark whereby it had stuck to her Lips, which the Devil had so dried, that the Skin appear'd white and standing up; That the Exorcist touch'd with his Fingers all the edges of the Wafer without sticking to it, to shew that it had not been retain'd upon her Lips by any moisture; That that same Exorcist wip'd the Teeth of the Maid with his Surplice, and laid the Holy Host on one of the Fore-teeth of the upper-row, and that it hung in that manner a long time, laid cross the edge of the tooth, and not holding there but by a bare touch of the point of its circumference, notwithstanding the violent agitations of all the Body, the strange contorsions of the Mouth, and a very vehement blast which Astarot made to throw it out; That after all the Species were swallow'd down by the command of the Exorcist, who pray'd Monsieur's Physician to search the Mouth of the Maid, to see if the Wafer were there; which he did, putting his Fingers within the Gums, and thrusting them to her Throat, and found that there was nothing; that after that they made the Maid to drink a draught of Water, and caus'd her Mouth to be search'd once again; that at last the Exorcist having order'd Astarot to bring back the Water, it was seen presently after upon the tip of the Tongue, and that this Experiment was try'd two other times again. So this Wafer serv'd for a Pastime to the Devils: Thus was it exposed to their blasts and violences, to be seen, and not to be seen, to be swallow'd and to be cast up again; to be held on one Lip, then repell'd upon the other, and in the end to suffer all the Indignities that could be pretended to be necessary to serve for Proofs of the Possession, and to confirm it, for want of miraculous Effects, which they might have produc'd, if it had been real and true, as to raise the Bodies of the possessed many foot high from the Ground, and to hold them so sometime hanging in the Air, and many others, whereof there has been already spoken, and of which we shall speak hereafter, which is the reason that we pass them by at this present in silence.'

Sect. 15.

After that the Author of the Relation has thus mentioned the Feats of Activity of the Devils of Elizabeth Blanchard, he also speaks of those of the Sister Claire de Sazilli, and says. 'That Monsieur being come to the Ursulines in the afternoon of that very day, that Nun was exorcis'd in his Presence; That the Devil, the Enemy of the Virgin, appear'd according to the command which the Father Elizee Capucin, her usual Exorcist, had given him; That he made her supple and pliant as a Plate of Lead; That the Exorcist afterwards bow'd her Body in several fashions, backward and forward, and on each side, so that the almost touch'd the Ground with her Head, the Devil keeping her in the Posture wherein she had been put, till 'twas altered by them, having not during that time, which was very long, any breathing through her Mouth, but only a little blowing through her Nose; that she was almost insensible, seeing that the Father took the Skin of her Arm and pierc'd it through with a Pin, without any Blood coming thence, or that the Maid seem'd to have any sense of it; That Sabulon appear'd after, who roll'd her along the Chappel, and caus'd her to make several contorsions and tremblings; That five or fix times he brought her left Foot over her Shoulder to the Cheek, embracing in the mean while her Leg on the same side; that during all these Agitations, her Countenance was very deform'd and ghastly, her Tongue thick, livid and hanging down even to her Chin, and no ways press'd by her Teeth; That her breathing was equal, her Eyes fixed, and always open without winking; That there happened to her after that an extension of her Legs so wide, that she touch'd the Ground with her Perinæum; That whilst she was in that Posture, the Exorcist made her hold her Body upright, and to joyn her Hands together; That Sabulon being conjur'd to adore the Holy Sacrament, made some resistance, but that being press'd to it, he dragg'd the Body quite bowed, the Hands a little distant one from the other without joyning, her Face half turn'd, and painted like a representation of Hell, and went to kiss the Foot of the Holy Pix which the Exorcist held in his Hand, testifying by his Gestures, Tremblings, Crys, and Tears; both Horrour, Reverence, and Despair; That the Exorcist having ask'd him, What be had ador'd? he said, after some denial, 'Tis he who was put upon the Cross; That Monsieur having seen and admir'd all these things, agreed secretly with Father Tranquille upon a thing which he desir'd that the Devil would find out; That the Exorcist conjur'd him to obey, saying, Obedias ad mentem Principis, and that the Devil having cast a frightful look upon Monsieur, he fell upon his Knees, his Hands being joyn'd towards the Father Elizee, and kiss'd his Right-Hand. Whereupon Monsieur exprest himself to be mightily satisfied, saying aloud, There is no more to be said. I desir'd that be would kiss his Right-Hand, be has exactly obey'd; That the Mother Prioress being come into the Lifts, the Devil Balaam appear'd at first, but that quickly after he gave place to Isaacarum by the order of Father Surin her Exorcist; That this last ador'd the Sacrament as the others, by giving marks of a horrible despair. The rage, said he, which I have for having lost it, takes from me the liberty of adoring it; But that the Father repeating the command he had given him, he put the Body of the Prioress into a frightful Convulsion, and drawing out a Tongue horribly deform'd, blackish, and grain'd like Spanish Leather, without being press'd by the Teeth, and so dry, as if it had never had any Moisture, and being not out of breath; That there was observ'd in other Postures such an extension of her Legs, that there were seven Foot distance from one Foot to the other, the Maid being but four foot high; That after that the Devil threw her with her Belly on the Ground at the Feet of the Father, who held the Sacrament in his Hand, and that having her Body and Arms in the form of the Cross, he turn'd first the Palms of her Hands upwards, he brought them afterwards quite round, so that the Palm of each Hand touch'd the Pavement, and that he brought the Hands so turn'd, by joyning them at the end of her Back-bone, and that presently after he brought the two Feet so joyned, so that the two Palms of her Hands touch'd the two out-sides of the Soles of her Feet; That the continued in that posture a great while with strange Tremblings, not touching the Ground but with her Belly; That being rais'd up, the Devil was once again commanded to come near to the Holy Sacrament, and to shew by his Countenance the opposition there is between Jesus Christ and him; That thereupon, he shew'd such a rage which cannot be conceiv'd, if one had not seen it: Ah! said he, crying out, It is impossible to shew it, there is too great a distance from the one to the other; That being ask'd what was that distance? It is, said he, an Epitome of all Goodness, and I of all Calamity: That having utter'd these Words, he became again more furious, and discovered a great rage for what he had said, biting his Arms, and horribly distorting his Limbs round. That the agitation ceas'd a little after, and that the Maid came perfectly to her self, having her Pulse no more mov'd, than if nothing extraordinary had past; But that almost at the same time that Father Surin spake to Monsieur, and that he went to finish the Exorcism, he felt the Assaults of Isaacarum, who threw him down twice, and shook his Arms and Legs with quakings and tremblings; That the Devil; constrain'd to retire by the Holy Sacrament which was apply'd to him, enter'd again upon a sudden into the Body of the Prioress, who was two paces from him, speaking to one of Monsieur's People; and in a moment he made her Visage horrible and furious, and that at the same time the Exorcist being again rais'd up, he went to combat with Isaacarum, of whom Father Tranquille demanded, whence he had the boldness to torment the Father? He answer'd in a rage, addressing himself to Father Surin, It is to revenge me of thee. That then having receiv'd a command to retire, and to leave the Prioress free, he obey'd, and that so there was an end put to the Exorcism. The same Relation imports further, that Monsieur having seen what past at the Exorcisms on Wednesday in the Evening, and all Thursday, his Highness, to demonstrate the satisfaction which he had receiv'd, gave the next day the following Attestation.' We, Gaston, Son of France, Duke of Orleans, do certifie, that during two days having assisted at the Exorcisms which were made in the Churches of the Ursulines and St. Cross in the Town of Loudun, upon the Persons of the Sisters Jane des Agnes, Ann de St. Agnes, Claire de Sazilli, Ursuline Nuns, and of Elizabeth Blanchard a secular Maid. We have seen and observ'd many Actions and strange Motions, surpassing the natural Powers, namely at the Communion of the said Elizabeth Blanchard, have seen the Holy Host abiding upon her Lips altogether dry, notwithstanding a vehement blast from her Mouth, which Host having been swallowed down by the said Blanchard, at the command of the Father Exorcist, the said Host has been brought up out of the bottom of her Stomach, and laid upon the Tongue of the said Blanchard, after she was made to drink Water, and searched if any thing were in her Mouth, which was done three several times, by command given to the Devil nam'd Astarot. All which we have judg'd to be super-natural; And having moreover desir'd to have an exact sign of the real Possession of those Maids, we did agree secretly, and in a low voice with the Father Tranquille Capucin, to command the Devil Sabulon, who actually possess'd the said Sister Claire, that he should go and kiss the Right-hand of Father Elizee her Exorcist; the said Devil as punctually obey'd according to our desire, which has made us assuredly believe, that what the Fryers performing in the Exorcisms of the said Maids, have told us of the Possession, is true, there being no appearance that such Motions and Knowledge of Secret Things, could be ascribed to human Powers. Whereof being willing to give a Testimony to the Publick, We have granted this present Attestation, which we have sign'd with our Hand, and caus'd to be subsign'd by the Secretary of our Commands, House, and Finances of France, the 11th day of May 1635. Sign'd Gaston, and lower Goulas. 'Monsieur, says also the Author of the Relation, having given this Attestation, and left to the Ursulines illustrious Marks of his Liberality, as well as of the Judgment he made of them, wherein he was imitated by the chief of his Court, went to hear Mass in the Church of the Fathers Carmelites, and having been told that for seven or eight Months there was kept an Host, upon which there was seen Blood, when Elizabeth Blanchard had it upon her Lips, he desir'd to see it and adore it; For that purpose Father Peter Thomas Carmelite took it in his Hand, and a little while after commanded one of the Devils of Elizabeth, who was there present to tell whose was that Blood with which the Host seem'd stain'd, to whom the Devil, after several difficulties, contorsions, and agitations, answer'd in these Terms; I adore a Man full of Charity, who is not contented to shed his Blood once for the Redemption of Sinners, but a second time has caus'd it miraculously to appear here for his Glory, and for the confusion of the Incredulous, and confirmation of Believers. Upon which the Exorcist, seeing Monsieur very attentive to what pass'd, ask'd his Highness, if he would be pleas'd that some secret Sign should be prescrib'd to the Devil, for a proof of the Truth of what he had said, touching the miraculous Blood shed upon the Host; With which his Highness testifying that he should be well satisfied, he said to him in a low voice and in his Ear, that he would command the Devil to kiss his Cross, and his Stole on the right side, which the Father did, not saying any thing to the Devil, but that he was to obey the intention of the Prince; and quickly after the Devil obey'd, discovering that he suffer'd great violence by that action, as by all others, whereby he is oblig'd to bow under the Authority of the Church. This [adds our Author] with what we have said before, made Monsieur say, that one must be a Fool not to believe the Possession of these Maids. But least one should wonder that the Devil heard a word which has been said in a low voice and in the Ear, he said, that the Devils which possess'd these Maids, answer'd often the Questions which were put to them by the Exorcists, without having exprest them otherwise than by the inward direction of their thought, of which he alledg'd some Examples; and because that is hard to believe, as being directly contrary to the Text of the Holy Scripture, he maintains, That one ought not to wonder, since the Devils and Angels speak only by the means of the inward Acts, which they form in themselves. At last, having related, many other things upon this Subject, he says, That the very day of the arrival of Monsieur, a Huguenot Apothecary of Loudun named James Boisse, took upon him to speak to his Highness's Apothecary, and to pray him to come and lodge at his House, whither having conducted him, he entertain'd him with a discourse of the Ursulines, and assur'd him, that all which pass'd was but feign'd and an Imposture; that they had no other design, but that of putting Grandier to death, as they had done, and that there was in that Town a Protestant Maid, who, by the flexibleness of her Body, made contorsions and motions, as much if not more strange than those which were seen amongst the Ursulines. Where upon Monsieur's Apothecary, who had seen the same Evening the prodigious Agitations and Postures of Sister Agnes, told him, that he could hardly believe it, and that he would advise him not to hold such discourse; for should Monsieur know that he spoke at this rate, it would be sufficient to ruin him, as a Calumniator; To whom Boisse reply'd, that he was ready to maintain in his Highness's presence what he had said, and that he desir'd no better; which Monsieur's Apothecary having made known the next day to his Highness, Boisse was presently sent for, and confirm'd before his Highness what he had said the Evening before; but being urg'd to name and shew the Maid, whereof he spake, he said, in Truth, he had not seen her, but that he had, what she had said, from a Chirurgeon nam'd Fourneau, professing also the Protestant Religion. Fourneau being call'd, and ask'd whether he had seen the Maid, he said no; Boisse reply'd to him, that he had then known of her, what he had heard him say; Fourneau denied that again, and protested he knew nothing of it, that he had never spoken of it, and that it was a thing devised by him Whereupon, they who were present, cry'd out against Boisse, that he deserv'd to be whipt for having had the boldness to advance so notorious a falshood in Monsieur's presence; Who, to shew that he desir'd to partake as well of the Title of Just, as he was a-kin by Blood to him who acquir'd it so lawfully, instead of causing him to be punish'd presently, would observe the forms of Justice, and straightway aster that Action, being gone to hear Mass in the Church of St. Cross, his Highness told the King's Advocate of Loudun, who was there present, that he would have this audacious Fellow chastis'd, sending also the next day for the Lieutenant Criminal and the King's Attorney, to tell them the same thing; whereof Boisse having had notice, he thought it the best course for him to run away.'

Sect. 16.

When that Writing was publish'd, the Incredulous fail'd not to make their Reflections upon what it contain'd, as they had already done upon the others which preceded it. They maintain'd that Monsieur had been prepossess'd, and that his Devotion had been impos'd upon; That they had put upon him such Feats of Activity and Leggerdemain, as Juglers and Tumblers usually do upon the Stage or Rope, for such true Marks of Possession, as those are which are set down in the Ritual. That to blow and play with the Host upon the Lips, as Elizabeth Blanchard had done, which Action seem'd most astonishing to his Highness, was the most easie of all the other Illusions; and that upon the whole Matter it expos'd the Christian Religion to the Derision of Jews and Mahometans; That it his Highness had told his Secrets to any others than those Monks and Exorcists, or rather if he had kept them himself conceal'd in a Paper without imparting them to any Body, the Devils had not guessed them, but that there was such a Juggling amongst the Exorcists, that it cannot be doubted but they had agreed upon certain Signs to speak by, and to understand one another; That this Invention was not extraordinary, seeing that the very Children perform the like in their Pastimes, and know very well to speak, and to entertain themselves that way; But that this Highness having thought fit to rely upon the Honesty of the Fathers, he could not fail to be cheated by Masters so experienc'd, who had taken care to instruct and fashion such apt Scholars, for a long time together.

Sect. 17.

The truth of the Matter, which concern'd Boisse the Apothecary, was, that a Maid bred up a Protestant, who out of Levity had embrac'd the Roman Religion, and had thrown her self into the Convent of the Ursulines, was there found fit to perform the part of a Person possess'd: And in effect she profited well by the care that was taken to instruct and prepare her: But just at the time of being produc'd in publick, she got away out of the Convent; and whether it were by a sincere return, or by a continuation of her Whimsies, she return'd to the Communion of the Protestant Church. As the managing of the Possessed was a continual matter of Entertainment and Conversation for People of all sorts and conditions, that Maid who was the friend of Fourneau's Wife, perform'd often in her presence, and of divers other Women, what postures, grimaces, and contorsions she had learnt, which were not at all inferior to those of the Nuns. Fourneau having been made acquainted with it by his Wife, had in confidence told it to Boisse, who made that ill use of it as has been related, and exposed himself to a danger, in which he was abandon'd by Fourneau, because the consequence of his imprudence did not seem to be so dangerous for him, as it would have been for that Maid, by the Spite and Resentment which all the Cabal of the Monks, and Confederates of the Possession, would have had against her, if it had been discover'd, and publish'd what she had done, and what she was able to do.

Sect. 18.

But as those Actions and Motions, which were shew'd in the presence of the Duke of Orleans, were not ordinary, and might deceive the Eyes of some of those who have little experience, or knowledge of what pass'd in the World; it will not perhaps be unserviceable to make here a small Abridgment of what was then printed upon that Subject. The unfortunate Grandier had already said in his Case, That the Art of Man could do things more approaching to supernatural, than all that which had been seen done by the Nuns; He cited for a Witness Philip Camerarius in his Historical Meditations, Chap. 75. and another Historian, who relates many surprizing things which a Polander did at the time of the Circumcision of the Son of Amurath. How many Rope-Dancers, added he, and other such like People, Men and Women, do perform things extraordinary? Which however are done by Art, and are far worthier of admiration, than any of those that have been perform'd by those Maids. Duncan expresseth himself in his Book in these Words; 'What has there been supernatural in all this? There needs no more than the Testimony of St. Augustine to condemn rash Judgments, and those who are so bold as to set bounds to the power of Nature; possibly it will have more Efficacy upon the Exorcist and other Friars, than if it had been taken out of the Writings of Aristotle, Hyppocrates and Galen. That Father in the 24th Chap. of the 14th Book of the City of God, declares, that he knew People, who made their Bodies to perform things, which other Men would hardly believe. That there were some who mov'd their Ears, and others who made their Hair to fall down upon their Fore-head, and rais'd them up again without moving their Heads; Others who so exactly imitated the Voices of living Creatures, that one could not have been able to know the Deceit, without having seen them: Others who made a strange noise so long a time as they pleas'd, and seem'd to sing from behind them: Others who shed Tears in an extraordinary abundance. That there was a Man who could sweat whensoever he would; That a pretended Prophet, nam'd Restitutus, fell into an Extasy as often as he pleas'd, and that he remain'd without breathing like a dead Person, in such manner that he was prick'd and pinch'd, and sometimes had Fire apply'd to divers parts of his Body, without any signs that he was sensible of it. That Author adds, That no Body would have admir'd the motions of the Nuns, if they had been done by Jugglers and Tumblers upon the Stage; and that these Nuns had been instructed and practis'd to do them a far longer time, than most of these People employ'd to learn what they present to the Eyes of the Publick; But that however these Motions were not common to all these Maids; each of them perform'd only some particular ones, viz. those for which she was found most apt, whether it were by the Conformation and natural Disposition of her Body, or by Exercise and Custom; That if the Exorcist had commanded the Superior to do what Elizabeth Blanchard and the Sister Agnes usually did, he had not been obey'd; That not any of these Maids had rais'd herself up into the Air, the height of two or three Pikes, and had not remain'd suspended there some notable while; That none of them had flown or vaulted into the Air, or climb'd an upright Wall without a Ladder, or such other help, or walk'd upon the Water without sinking; In which cases there would have been something more than humane; But that a Man must have a Mind wonderfully prepossess'd to believe, that to roll, vault, or crawl on the Ground is a thing supernatural; That they had not done any thing more surprizing, than it was to see a Man walking upon his Hands holding his Feet on high, which is however very common, and us'd for a Pastime by Children; That 'twas a thing strange enough to see that the Devils so obedient to the Exorcists when they commanded them to make contorsions, were not more readily driven out and expell'd by that wonderful Power which the Church had to make them obey, and that 'twas not made use of but to make a show to the People, to amuse them with trifles, to command one Devil to appear, and to make him retire having plaid his Part; and to call another, and cause him to do the same thing, instead of using that Power to drive away the Infernal Troop, and speedily to deliver the Nuns, whom they pretended to be tormented with so much violence.'

Sect. 19.

Duncan adds many other Reflections, drawn from the Conformation of a humane Body, and from the disposition of the Members, by which he makes it clearly appear, that the pretended Possess'd did not any supernatural Motions, as it would have been to shut the Hand outwards, so as one closeth it inward; To bend the Thighs backward, in such a manner that the Hamstrings might touch the Shoulders, and 'c. That all their Motions were only ordinary in themselves and owing either to the faculty of Nimbleness and Swiftness, or extraordinary Extensions, such as a long Exercise, or a Disease, or violent Remedies might cause, whereof he cited some Examples, too long to be here related. It is more proper to mention some Questions which were then propos'd to the University of Montpellier by Santerre Priest, and Promoter of the Bishoprick and Diocess of Nimes, who had recourse to that Remedy, when he saw that the contagious Air of Loudun began to spread it self to Languedoc.

Sect. 20.

The design of the Cabal of Monks, and some over-zealous Catholicks, being to authorize, as much as it was possible, the Propositions whereof there has been mention made before, tending to establish a kind of Inquisition upon the Testimony of Devils, they thought to find a good Advancement in it, by the Success of the Possession at Loudun, and judg'd it fit to make possessed Persons appear in a great many places of the Realm at a time, and to cause them to speak the same Language. Jane de Ruede of the Village of Blast near Tournon, gave out that she was possess'd by four Devils, Beelzebub, Barrabas, Guilmon, and Carmin, which were sent to her by a Wizzard and a Witch of the same Country: She was brought to be exorcis'd in the Chappel of our Lady of Roquefort, famous for the Miracles which were wrought there: But Mazarin, then Vice-legat of the Pope in Avignon, whereon the Chappel depended, not being of the same Opinion, as the greatest part of the Ecclesiasticks of France, he enjoin'd Silence to the Exorcists and Person possess'd; and the Devils obey'd far better the Orders of that sort, which were given with the Threats of the Civil Power, than those which had been made them by the Authority of the Church. Santerre being not of humour to be engaged in the Diabolical Commerce of the Possession, which they would have establish'd in the Diocess of Nimes, he examin'd the Possess'd, their Postures and Contorsions, which were the same that were made at Loudun, as one may infer by the reading of the Questions following: And he consulted afterwards the University with intent to support and authorize his Sentiment, to evidence to the Publick what they ought to think of the Possessions that were in vogue, and to repel the Complaints and

Reproaches which he must have undergone from the Monks and Bigots, whom he went directly to encounter, by opposing their Intrigues in his Diocess, to nip the Bud of that infernal Seed, before it had time to sprout and spread deep Roots.

QUESTIONS
Propos'd to the University of Montpelier.

QUESTION I.

Sect. 21.

'WHether the bending, bowing, and removing of the Body, the Head touching sometimes the Soles of the Feet, with other Contorsions, and strange Postures, are a good Sign of Possession?'

ANSWER I.

'Vaulters and Tumblers make such strange Motions, and bend and bow themselves in so many Fashions, that one may believe that there is no kind of Posture, of which Men and Women may not render themselves capable by diligent Study and long Practice, being even able to make extraordinary Extensions, and spreading out of the Legs, Thighs, and other parts of the Body, because of the Extension of Nerves, Muscles, and Tendons, by long Custom; therefore such Operations may be done by the Power of Nature.'

QUESTION II.

Sect. 22.

'Whether the quickness of the Motion of the Head forward and backward, bringing it to the Back and Breast, be an infallible Mark of Possession?'

ANSWER II.

'That Motion is so natural, that one needs not add Reasons to those which have been said upon the Motions of the Parts of the Body.'

QUESTION III.

Sect. 23.

'Whether a sudden swelling of the Tongue, the Throat, and the Face, and the sudden alteration of the Colour, are certain Marks of Possession?'

ANSWER III.

'The lifting up, and agitation of the Breast by Fits and Starts, are the effects of drawing and holding the Breath, being ordinary Actions of breathing, from which one cannot infer any Possession. The swelling of the Throat may proceed from holding of the Breath, and that of other Parts from Melancholy Vapours, which are often seen to wander through all the parts of the Body:

Whence it follows, that this Sign of Possession is not to be allow'd.'

QUESTION IV.

Sect. 24.

'Whether Dulness and Senselessness, or the privation of Sense, even to be pinch'd and prick'd, without complaining, without stirring, and even without changing Colour, are certain Marks of Possession?'

ANSWER IV.

'The young Lacedemonian who suffer'd his Liver to be knaw'd by a Fox which he had stoll'n, without making any shew os feeling him, and those who suffer'd themselves to be scourg'd before the Altar of Diana, even to Death, without knitting their Brows, shew that Resolution may well enable one to endure the Pricks of a Pin without crying out: Besides, it is certain, that in a Humane Body there is in some Persons certain little parts of Flesh, which are without feeling, although the other parts which are about them are sensible, which most commonly happens by some precedent Disease. Therefore such an Effect is equivocal to prove a Possession.'

QUESTION V.

Sect. 25.

'Whether the Immobility of all the Body, which happens to the pretended Possessed by the command of their Exorcists, during and in the middle of the strongest Agitations, is a certain Sign of a truly Diabolical Possession?'

ANSWER V.

'The Motion of the Parts of the Body being voluntary, it is natural to Persons well dispos'd to move themselves, or not to move themselves, according to their Will. Therefore such an Effect, or Suspension of Motion, is not considerable to infer a Diabolical Possession, if in the Immobility there has not been an entire privation of Sense.'

QUESTION VI.

Sect. 26.

'Whether the Yelping or Barking like that of a Dog, in the Breast, rather than in the Throat, is a Mark of Possession?'

ANSWER VI.

'Humane Industry is so pliant to counterfeit all kinds of Actions, that there are daily seen Persons expert in expressing exactly the Actions, the Cry, and the Voice of all sorts of Animals, and in imitating them without moving their Lips but unperceivably: There are found also very many who form Words and Voices in the Stomach, which seem rather to come from elsewhere, than from the Person who forms them after that manner; and they call those People Eugastrimuthi, or Engastrologi; i. e. those that speak in their Bellies. Therefore such an Effect is natural, as Pasquier observes in the 38th Chapter of his Inquiries, by the Example of a Buffoon nam'd Constantine.'

QUESTION

Sect. 27.

'Whether a fix'd steady Look upon some Object, without moving the Eye on either side, be a good Mark of Possession?'

ANSWER VII.

'The Motion of the Eye is voluntary, as that of other parts of the Body; and 'tis natural to move it, or to keep it fix'd: Therefore there is nothing considerable in this.'

QUESTION VIII.

Sect. 28.

'Whether the Answers that the pretended Possessed make in French, to some Questions that are put to them in Latin, are a good Mark of Possession?'

ANSWER VIII.

'We affirm, that to understand and speak the Languages, which one has never learn'd, are things Supernatural, and which might make one believe that they are done by the Ministry of the Devil, or of some other Superiour Cause: But to answer to some Questions only, that is altogether Suspicious; a long Exercise, or a private Intelligence between Persons, being able to contribute to such Answers; it seeming to be a Dotage to say, that the Devils understand Questions which are put to them in Latin, and that they always answer in French, and in the natural Language of that Person whom they would make pass for Possessed. Whence it follows, that from such an Effect the Residence of a Devil cannot be inferred, most especially if the Questions do not contain many Words and many Discourses.'

QUESTION IX.

Sect. 22.

'Whether to vomit such things as People have swallow'd, be a Sign of Possession?'

ANSWER IX.

'Delrio, Bodin, and other Authors say, that by Witchcraft Wizards do sometimes cause Nails, Pins, and other strange things to be vomited by the Work of the Devil: So that in the really possessed the Devil can do the same thing. But to vomit the things as they have swallow'd, that is natural, there being found Persons who have a weak Stomach, and who keep for many Hours what they have swallow'd, and then cast them up again as they took them; and the Disease call'd the Lienteria rendring the Aliments through the Fundament, as they had been taken by the Mouth, without any alteration, is a fuller Proof of it.'

QUESTION X.

Sect. 30.

'Whether the Prickings of a Launcet upon divers parts of the Body, without Blood issuing thence, are a certain Mark of Possession?' ANSWER X. 'That ought to be attributed to the Disposition of a melancholick Temper, the Blood whereof is so thick, that it cannot issue out through so little Wounds; and 'tis for that Reason that many being prick'd even in the Veins and natural Vessels, by the Launcet of a Chyrurgeon, bleed not one drop, as 'tis seen by Experience: Therefore there is nothing extraordinary in it.'

Sect. 31.

That Question made it appear, that there happen'd things as surprizing in the Possessions of other Countries as in that of Loudun, where this last Effect has not been observ'd, and to which it can have no relation, seeing that there is nothing alike, either in the printed Books, or Manuscripts of that time. Nevertheless the Possession in the Diocess of Nimes, where that pretended Miracle was done, has not been truer, nor judg'd such, because the Promoter of that Diocess had more Modesty and Honesty than many other Ecclesiasticks of his time.

Sect. 32.

These are the Decisions of the University of Montpellier, which have been here related to shew of what Nature those Miracles were which past in the presence of the Duke of Orleans. To which may be added further, to omit nothing which may not be alogether clear, and that the quiet and repos'd condition of the Possess'd at the end of their Agitations, where they seem'd to have suffer'd nothing, and where their Countenance recover'd in an instant its natural Form, is so far from being a good Proof of a true Possession, that 'tis an evident Mark of the contrary, seeing that 'tis not the Custom of Devils to be contented to do feats of Activity, by the Bodies which they possess, and to leave them afterwards sound, well dispos'd, and free from Pains. The Gospel teacheth, that these terrible Guests made some of the Possess'd deaf and dumb; that they caus'd others to fall into the Fire and the Water; that they made others to foam at the Mouth, or made them wither'd and consumptive, or tormented them as if they would break or tear them in pieces, and after the Agitations and Torments they left them feeble and tir'd, and sometimes half dead. So that there has been reason to conclude that the Motions which begin and end at the Will of an Exorcist, jubentis aut prohibentis, commanding or forbidding, as the Book of Demonomany mentions, are Motions studied, concerted, and done out of a Design, and that they who do them, being far from the being possess'd by Devils, they possess themselves so well that they stop and return to their natural State as soon as they please. Duncan assures that the same thing happen'd in his Presence, and that in publick, upon the Stage, where a young Maid turn'd about for half an hour with so wonderful a swiftness, that the Sight was troubled to follow it; then she stopt all on a suddain, and made her Courtesie with so good a Grace, and so clam an Air, as if she had continued always still.

Sect. 33.

It were but to tire the Reader, to make all the Reflections that offer themselves upon the behaviour of the pretended Possess'd, and to relate all the examples of the Jugling Tricks, and other Actions counterfeit or natural, far more wonderful than those of the pretended Devils, which are contain'd in the Books of the Fathers of the Church, and in those of a great number of Authors ancient and modern. 'Tis therefore much better to resume the Order of things which past in that accursed and abominable Intrigue at Loudun.

Sect. 34.

The Expectations of a great Repute had doubtless flatter'd the Nuns, but they were not less touch'd with the hope of Plenty and Wealth, of which they were destitute. Their Expectation was not deceived; Their Reputation had flown into all Quarters, although it was not in a manner so advantagious as they were persuaded; And they were from that time freed of their Indigence by the officious care of the Exorcists, and by their sollicitations to Persons pious, credulous and charitable. The Author of the Demonomany saith, 'That Alms were sent them from all Parts, and that if they had not receiv'd a sufficient Charity, they would make a Gathering for them in the Towns.' The Generosity of the Nobility of the first Rank, and above all that of the Duke of Orleans, and all his Court, as we have seen before, put them altogether into a wealthy Condition.

But that was not yet enough; all this was done but by the way of Persuasion, or by the Motions of Compassion and Charity, which were only commendable, and which did not suit with the Character of the Commissary, nor with that of the Authors of the Contrivance, nor with that of the Exorcists who directed it. To fill up these Characters, and to bring by little and little the Work towards the principal End which was propos'd, they began to declare War against the Protestants, and to invest themselves with their Spoils. The Protestants enjoy'd one part of the Church-yard of Loudun, which after many contestations had been left them by Rochefort, and since confirm'd by Mangot and Douville, all three Commissaries of the King in that behalf, successively and at divers times, But Laubardemont by Virtue of a Commission obtain'd upon false Informations, took from them that Possession, and depriv'd them of their Right, by a Sentence which he gave the 23d. of January 1634. permitting them by a particular favour, to buy with their own Money some Gardens for their Burying-place. He order'd also the Protestant Inhabitants, who had Houses in those Streets thro' which the Procession was to pass, upon the Festival call'd Corpus Christi day, to hang and adorn the Front of their Houses, and also commanded them and the Consistory to take care of the Execution of the said Order against each of them in particular, who were not obedient, upon the Penalty of 500 Livres Fine, and suspension of their Offices, if they had any, and the interdiction of the Exercise of their Religion within the Town and Suburbs: Which Order the Protestants vigorously oppos'd in consequence of the secret Articles of the Edict of Nants, and they could not be induc'd to obey it, neither by the Intrigues which were imploy'd for that purpose, nor by the Threats which they made use of to terrifie them. They were again sent for another time by the same Commissary, who order'd them to assist at the Exorcisms, which they refus'd to do, as well because of the Places where they exorcis'd, as the Ceremonies which they us'd during the Exorcisms, and of the use which they made there of the Sacrament; which oblig'd the Assistants to pay those Respects, to which their Conscience could not submit. Laubardemont told them that they were afraid to be convinc'd by the Evidence of Truth to give Glory to God, and to acknowledge the Possession; To which they reply'd, that supposing that the Possession was true, it would no ways prejudice them, nor their Religion, and that so the fear to be oblig'd to own it, would not give them so much trouble as he imagin'd. But however, said the Commissary to them, if the Possession were acknowledg'd, one might infer thence divers Conclusions in favour of the Roman Religion, and against the Doctrine of Protestants. If it were permitted us to write, answer'd James de Brissac Sieur Desloges, one of the Ministers, there is nothing in the World more easie, than to prove that the Possession does not establish at all the Roman Religion, nor that it destroys that of the Reformed. Why do not you write then? reply'd Laubardemont, Who is it that binders you? The Threats that were made to Mr. Duncan, answer'd the Minister, and the Displeasure which we are told that

Court and your Lordship have shewed against him; But if you please to grant us liberty under your Hand, you shall quickly have the satisfaction to judge of our Reasons, and the Publick may judge of them likewise. But, said he, your design would be possibly to oppose the Possession, and 'tis that which cannot be tolerated, after that the Question has been judg'd in a legal Manner. We will suppose the Possession, reply'd the Minister, and the intent of the Writing will be only, that the Roman Catholicks cannot draw thence any advantage against the Protestants. Most of the Roman Catholicks there present, amongst whom was the Marquiss de la Rochepozai, would have been glad that the permission which the Minister desir'd might be allow'd him, but Laubardemont, who perceiv'd well the consequences, and who would not expose the Propositions of the Exorcist to the Confutation of the Ministers, sent them away without allowing them that liberty.

Sect. 35.

The Protestants who [by Virtue of the Edict of Nants] had a Right to keep little Schools for the instruction of Youth, and the Right whereof had been confirm'd by the Commissaries of the King, and by the Decree of the Parliament of the 30th of August. 1613. had in their Possession a pretty large House, wherein they caused the Greek and Latin Tongue to be taught. That House seem'd convenient to lodge the Nuns of St. Ursula, who yet liv'd in an hir'd House: And 'twas believ'd that 'twould not be difficult to take it from its Owners, and to put it into the Hands of the Nuns. For that purpose James Denieau the King's Attorney in the Commission which concern'd the Affair of the Possession at Loudun, remonstrated to Laubardemont the 18th of January 1634, that the Lodging of Ursulines was inconvenient, because of the smalness of its Extent; That they could not perform there the Exorcisms but with much difficulty, and that there was not in the Town a sufficient number of Churches to Exorcise conveniently, by Reason of the great concourse of People, who came in Crouds from all Parts to assist thereat. But that the Reformed, to whom it was not permitted to keep Schools, had a Colledge, which was a large House, and was very fit for the Reception of these Nuns; That he requested that it would please Laubardemont to go thither and visit it; and then order what he should think good. The Commissary agreed to go thither, which he did the very same day, with Denieau. He found in the Colledge but two Regents, who told them that the Sieurs Desloges Minister, and Martin Counsellor of the Bailiwick, were the Directors of it: He order'd that these Directors should be appointed to appear before him, that the matter might be determin'd according to the Conclusions of the King's Attorney. They appear'd but would not acknowledge Laubardemont for a competent Judge, as not having any Commission for that purpose; however he omitted not to make some Procedures, and to give some Orders, notwithstanding the refusal made by them. Whereupon the Protestants signified that they appeal'd from his Orders, as being an incompetent

Judge, and that they took upon them the Defence in their own Private Names: And to prevent all other Proceedings which he might make thereafter, they sent Deputies to Paris to complain to the King, and to maintain their Right. In prejudice thereof Laubardemont gave the 29th of January a Sentence, importing, That whereas the Protestants have establish'd a Colledge without the King's Permission, and to the Prejudice of his Edicts, he commands them to clear the House of the said Colledge of the Bodies and Goods, and to put the Keys into the Hands of the King's Attorney, three days after the intimation of the present Order; and that the said time being past, they shall be compell'd thereto whatsoever opposition or Appeals notwithstanding. That Order was signified the day following, and they caus'd all the Ecclesiasticks, and Religious Orders of the Town to prepare to make a solemn, Procession, and to conduct the Ursulines with pomp, and, as it were, in triumph into the House of the Protestants, where in case they refus'd to let them in, they purpos'd to break the Doors open. The Protestants went to Laubardemont and remonstrated, That as soon as they should have understood by their Deputies the King's pleasure, they would wholly submit to it, and that they besought him to grant them so much time. Upon the refusal which he made, they signified to him their new Protestations, Appeals, and c. and afterwards went to the ordinary Officers of Loudun, before whom they made a long Verbal Process, containing all their Reasons and their Offers to obey the Will of the King, when it should be made known to them. Upon this the

Catholick Officers fearing that the Populace would raise some tumult prejudicial to their Interests and to the Town in general, they sent to desire of the Commissary a Delay for eight days, but he granted them but four, which he after revok'd the same day, and the 4th of February the Provost of Thouars came to Loudun with all his Company of Guards; which having caus'd much uneasiness to the more moderate Inhabitants of both Religions, and to all those who desir'd to live in Peace, the Lieutenant Civil and the Judge of the Provostship made many Proposals to each Party, to oblige the Protestants to sell their House, and the Nuns to buy it: But that was not the design of those Ladies, nor what was promis'd them. So the Magistrates having not succeeded in that Negotiation, they saw all the Town in trouble and tumult; for as they knew the imperious and violent Humour of Laubardemont, they judg'd that he would not easily relinquish his design. In effect the Provost of Thouars made himself ready to go with his Guards into that House, but they met in the Streets the Protestant Women of all Qualities and Ages, with their Aprons full of Sand and Ashes, which they pretended to cast into the Eyes, to blind, as much as it should be possible for them, all those that should attempt to go and force the Colledge; Whilst their Husbands, who had understood that there were come from Poitiers 800 Men, besides all the Marshalseas of the neigbouring Towns, were in an extream Consternation, being uncertain of the Issue that an Affair of that Consequence might have. But Laubardemont seeing that it took such a Course, and finding in the Protestants more Obstinacy than Menuau the King's Advocate, and the rest of his Adherents had made him believe, he probably fear'd that that Attempt which be had made without any Order of the Court, should be disavow'd; and so durst not proceed to Extremities. However it was, he sent away the Provost of Thouars, and caus'd not the others to come, according to the Threats he had made. In the mean while he drew up a bloody Verbal Process against the Protestants, and caus'd Informations to be made full of Calumnies and odious Imputations. The Lieutenant Criminal made also one on his part, upon the Demand of the King's Attorney; and 'twas hop'd by one or other of these Informations, wherein the Protestants were strangely aspers'd and blacken'd, they would reduce them to ask for Favour, and to offer gladly what they had denied with so much resistance and resolution. They did not fail on their part to take care of themselves, by presenting their Petition to the Chamber of the Edict, where they obtain'd a Decree the 8th of February, which imports, That the Court receiv'd their Appeal from the Procedure made by Laubardemont, who was forbid to proceed further in the execution of his Order, till they had taken Cognizance of that Matter, upon the Penalty of Nullity of the Proceedings, and of all the Costs, Damages, and Interests. This Decree having been signified to the Commissary Denieau, the Lieutenant Civil, and the Judge of the Provostship, with a Summons to appear at the Court, Lauberdemont departed the 15th of February, to go to Paris, and carried the Informations of the Lieutenant Criminal, and the Verbal Processes which he himself had made; wherein he charg'd the Protestants with having caus'd a Sedition and popular Commotion. He fail'd not to be favourably receiv'd and heard by Cardinal de Richelieu, and by the King's Council; where all he had done was approv'd of, and confirm'd by a Decree, with Prohibitions to the Parliament to take Cognizance of that Affair, and with a command to the Protestants to obey the Orders and Edicts of Laubardemont, of the 29th of January, and the 3d of February, and all that should be ordain'd by him, touching the Business of the Colledge. There was also a Commission dispatched to d'Etampes, Master of the Requests, to proceed to a new Information; and he had a Warrant of Imprisonment granted against fix of the principal Protestants, which cast them all into great trouble; whereunto the return of their Deputies from Paris did not put a stop; for they understood that the Court was prepossess'd against them to such a degree, that they would not consent to grant any Audience to those who demanded it on their behalf; and that they had condemn'd them without hearing. Upon this they sent again new Deputies, some whereof having rid Post, confirm'd what the former related, and said, that they were advised to consent to a voluntary Sale of the House in Question. But they resolved rather to suffer it to be taken by Force, than to receive the Price which had been offer'd for it; which was so low, that the Offer might rather pass for an Insult on the part of their Enemies, than for a serious Proposal of Persons, who, in good earnest, sought for an Accommodation. In the mean while the Deputies who had remain'd at Paris, writ that the Marquiss du Rivau had in his Hand a Letter of Privy-Seal, by which he was commanded to disarm the Protestants of the Town of Loudun; That he was to depart from Paris for that purpose, and that Laubardemont would come back with him; which he did not however so suddenly; and during that time, Regnier, and Dumoutier Bourneuf, who were of the number of the Six, against whom he had caused a Warrant to be decreed to seize their Persons, surrendred themselves in the Prison of Fort l'Eveque, where they were heard and interrogated, whether there had not been a popular Commotion at Loudun; and if it had not been resolv'd before to make it, in an Assembly held by the Protestants, where the Ministers had assisted? Whereunto having answer'd very pertinently, they were at first set at liberty under Bail; and some days after their Sureties were discharg'd, and they dismist.

Sect. 36.

At length, the 5th day of December, Laubardemont being return'd to Loudun, signified the Decree of the Council of State abovementioned, dated the 23d of May; to which the Protestants by a Verbal Process having offer'd to obey, with a Protestation to address themselves by their most humble Remonstrance to his Majesty, against that Decree which had been granted without their being heard or call'd, they deliver'd the Keys of the House, and the Nuns were put into possession of it, and made very quickly after other Purchases of some neighbouring Houses, and the nearest

Gardens: And since that time they have added such considerable Room, rais'd so many Buildings in their Convent, and bought so many Tythes, Rents, and other Lands and Demains in the Country, that one may be assur'd, that not only their pretended Diabolical Possession has put them out of the State of Indigence, wherein they were, but that their House may at this Day pass for one of the richest Communities of their Order.

Sect. 37.

The noise which that Affair made, had drawn all the Attention of the People; and the Devils, who seem'd to have no other end than to divert and please them, seeing them thereby drawn off from the Contemplation of the Miracles of the Possession, continued quiet, and took that time to recover their past Labour, and to prepare themselves for new Endeavours at the return of Laubardemont, their famous Protector, who caus'd them to understand, that he would shortly return to favour and shelter them with his Authority. Father Surin, whose Direction had not yet produc'd any thing extraordinary, except in his own Person, found it convenient, while they expected the Commissary, to raise by some Miracle the Reputation of the Exorcisms, which began to diminish. There remain'd in the Body of the Superior, four Devils, Leviathan, Behemot, Balaam, and Isaacarum, after the Expulsion of the three others, Asmodee, Aman, and Gresil, which had been effected by Virtue of the Exorcisms of Father Lactance. The Jesuit attempted not to drive them out all at once, for it was of too great importance to cause always the best Actresses to appear upon the Stage; and he accounted it much better to use moderately the Authority of the Church, in not delivering altogether that poor possess'd Person according to the Power which he had, and according to which Charity seem'd to require it, than to suffer the most famous of the Possess'd to retire, who could best of all impose upon the Eyes of the Publick. 'Twas therefore resolv'd to expel only Leviathan at that time, who was an eloquent Devil, and who sometimes made long discourses, as it appeard in a Book intituled, The Glory of St. Joseph, and c. printed at Saumur by Lewis Mace, second Edition; In which this Devil is made to say, 'That his principal business was to hinder the Love of God to his Creatures, and that of the Creatures to God; That in that employment he suffered a new Hell, because he could not prevent, but that some would advance towards God; That he was very unfortunate in being come to Loudun to act the Nun; That they made him fast in spite of his Teeth, and wear Sackcloth, and that this was worse to him yet than a Hell; That he would long since have quitted the Body of the Superior, if God had not constrain'd him to continue there; That he had made it all along his Business to possess Bodies, but that he never was so much molested in any other as in that: To which the Author of the Book adds, That he was to be pursued with great Application of Spirit, through all the Faculties and Operations of the Soul, where he had insinuated and intrench'd himself, fortifiying himself in the natural Inclinations, and the Roots of Imperfection, in which he maintains himself as in his own Territories; That when he had lost one Intrenchment, he entred into another; That 'twas necessary to seek him every where, and to root him out by little and little; That he made then great complaints and cry'd out, Thou takest from me my Nest, where shall I be now? Meaning by that Nest, not great Failures, but petty Faults, which others would call Virtues; That this Devil resisted the designs of the Exorcists, one while by violence, exercising cruelties, which God permitted him for her greater Merit, and another while by Craft, making use of his rights of Temptation and Possession; That they had experimented against him the Assistance of the Holy Guardian Angels, and that of Providence, and that with incredible Labour they were assisted by Grace against Nature supported by Satan; That this Conflict had continued several Months, and that they had seen with admiration the things which pass'd in the Secret of Hearts, to become sensible and visible; That at last the Devil had yielded, choosing rather to be dismist, than kept in possession, seeing that his House was chang'd into a Prison. That Book imports further, That the Possession of Loudun was one of the strangest and delicatest that had ever been seen; That 'twas founded upon the Operation of Magick, and upon the Wicked usage of the Liberty of Men, to which God condescended very much, respecting the Free-will of his Creatures; That the Principal design of the Magicians was to conceal the residence of Devils in those Bodies, and that for these reasons the exterior effects which were seen in other Possessions, and were supported by the

Power of Satan alone, were neither so numerous, nor so great.'

Sect. 38.

That Devil having been expell'd, they gave notice of it to the Bishop of Poitiers by a Letter, to which they added the Extract of the Verbal Process of the Exorcisms; whereof this is the Copy. 'Monday the 5th of November 1635. after the Devil nam'd Isaacarum, one of the four possessing the Mother Prioress, had made this Adoration to the Holy Sacrament in the Church of the Ursulines, where the Reverend Father Surin of the Society of Jesus exorcis'd him, the Body of the Possess'd has been suddenly rais'd upon her Feet, and Leviathan, chief of all the Troop of the Possession, appear'd on a sudden in the Place of the said Isaacarum, manifesting himself by disdainful frowning and proud Gate as of a Queen, with a very fair and shining Countenance: Whereupon the Exorcist speaking Latin, according to his custom, said, Here's a Devil who makes himself a Beau, but for the Glory of God and the Edification of Souls, I intend presently to make him shew his ugliness and deformities: And the Hymn Gloria and c. having been sung to that end, the Body of the said Prioress was cast to the Ground, shewing a very hideous and frightful Visage, with strange contorsions in all her Members, turning her Face towards the Earth, that it might not be seen, and then lifting up her self with a very majestick Countenance, went and set her self proudly in a Chair, nodding her Head with Gravity, and seeming to desire to say something; But the Exorcist having constrain'd her by a speedy command to humble her self and to cast her self on the Ground, asking the Devil if it were not true that Jesus Christ had vanquish'd him in that Maid, and by her answer'd with Blasphemy in a doleful tone, and a dejected look, It is but too true for me. Moreover being urg'd again to finish his Adoration, he cast himself at the Feet of the Father, rolling himself along with frightful Agitations, embracing them divers times, and whilst the Magnificat, and c. was sung, she extended her Arms and Hands, making them become streight and stiff, and her Head lean'd on the Foot of the said Exorcist, upon the middle of the step of the Altar, she did turn it side-ways towards some of the Spectators, on the side of the Window, and shew'd a wound in form of a Cross; Blood dropping from it of a fresh and Vermillion Colour; the first and second Skin which they call the Dermis and Epidermis were scratch'd and a little open'd, and that Cross was near of the same length that appears in this Figure.

Sect. 39.

'At the same time the Father, who knew the Sign by the last going out of the chief Devil, promis'd and sign'd by the said Leviathan since the 17th. of May in the presence of the Lord Bishop of Poitiers, cry'd aloud, Behold, Sirs, God be thanked, the sign of the Ejection, Leviathan is gone out, and then the said Prioress appear'd on a sudden with a Countenance so modest and serene, and a Spirit so quiet and settled, that the Spectators well perceiv'd, notwithstanding the Blood which was upon her Fore-head, that indeed the Finger of God and the Ray of his Mercy was there, which oblig'd them to sing presently, with Tears of Joy, the Hymn Te Deum, and Thereupon the Exorcist being resolv'd to make Isaacarum appear again, and make him give an account of that Wound, and having sung to that end Memento salutis Author, and c. the said Isaacarum shew'd himself upon her Visage with a frightful aspect, then with an insolent Joy he cry'd aloud thrice, I am now Master my self, I am now Master. Being ask'd how? He answer'd, That the chief is gone away. Being urg'd whether he spake true, being so great a Liar? He reply'd, Tis as true as that the Flesh of God is in that Tabernacle there. Being ask'd where is Leviathan at present? He answer'd, What do I know? In Hell, I think; Being demanded from whence came that sudden Departure, he said, renouncing God as 'twas usual with him, That he knew nothing, adding, Joseph came, who has driven him away, intimating to him on the behalf of God, that there was now no longer time to resist the Ministers of the

Church, and that he bad triumph'd enough. Finally, being urg'd to tell whether the Bloody Cross which was on her Forehead, was a wound by a Mans Hand? he said, No, and swore. Upon which the Father Exorcist declar'd succinctly three things to the Assistants, That the Prioress, by the advice which had been given her since the time he had begun to Exorcise her, had put her self under the special Protection of that Holy Patriarch; That for these two Months past, she had very much increas'd her devotion towards him; and that in fine two Days ago she had made a Vow to say the little Office of the Saint every day for the space of a Year. This Act is sign'd by the Register of the Commission, by Laubardemont, and by eight Exorcists, Jesuits, and Capucins, some Priests, Curates and Nuns, and some Officers as well of the Bailiwick, as of the Province of the general Assessors, and Office of Salt at Loudun.'

Sect. 40.

After such a Verbal Process so authentickly attested and sign'd, can one doubt the truth of the Miracle? And was it not imprudence in the Incredulous to say, that the Nun might have made that Wound whilst she roll'd her self, and that she might have had an Iron Cross hid in her Clothes, or in her Hands, which were at liberty, and have made a slight Wound, having not judg'd it fit to make a deeper? 'Tis true, that to support that Suspicion and their Prejudices, they alledg'd, that the Wounds made by the three former Devils, who were already gone out of the same possessed Person, having been suspected, as it was clearly manifested, and even by a Writing, those Devils, who seem'd to be so well dispos'd, and to have a mind to confound the Incredulity of Gainsayers, ought to use more Precaution, and not to forget any Circumstance which might have satisfied the Publick, and convinc'd them wholly of the truth of that Action. But would it have been reasonable to give one self so much trouble to satisfie the Whimsies of the Publick? What needed there more? One Devil had promis'd in the presence of the Bishop of Poitiers, a good while ago, he had now perform'd his promise: Another Devil serv'd for a Witness, the had made his Deposition, and confirm'd it by a solemn Oath in proper Terms, without any Equivocation, As true, as that the Flesh of God was in the Tabernacle. And all these things were well attested by a number of Friars, and other Persons of Quality, all good Friends of these Devils, who frequented them often, had Commerce with them, and had known their Sincerity. What could then have been said against it? And what ground of Unbelief must not one have had to resist so many Proofs?

Sect. 41.

This last Miracle was followed quickly by a new one, done upon the same Person, by the Expulsion of the Devil Balaam. This is the Verbal Process that was then publish'd. 'Thursday the 29th of November 1635. We, James Denieau, Counsellor of the King at the Presidial Court of la Fleche, and his Attorney in the Commission given by him for the Fact of Exorcisms to Monsieur de

Laubardemont, Counsellor of his Majesty in his Council of State and Privy-Council, being at the said Loudun in the Church of the Ursulines, with James Nozai, Register in the said Commission. The Reverend Father Surin of the Society of Jesus, having receiv'd a Letter from the Lord Archbishop of Tours, by which he recommended to him to cause that Mr. Montague, a Noble Englishman, might receive Edification by the fight of what pass'd at the Exorcisms; The said Father Surin should diligently apply himself to exorcise the Mother Prioress of the said Nuns, in the presence of the said Mr. Montague, Mr. Killegrew and Mr. Scandret, English Gentlemen, and of many other Persons of Quality: In performing of which Exorcism, the Devil Balaam appear'd counterfeiting the Postures and Motions, which Isaacarum and Behemot have been accustom'd to do: Whereupon the Father supposing that it was Isaacarum, he commanded him to give the reason of an Accident that happen'd eight days since to the said Mother Prioress, which was an extraordinary wandring of her Spirit, with a perpetual Inclination to eat and sleep, whereby she felt an extream pain, as of things unusual and very violent. To whom the said Devil answer'd, That 'twas an Enterprize; and as the Father pursu'd him to know that Enterprize, the Devil retir'd: Then the Hymn Magnificat, and c. being sung, he appear'd again in the very shape of Isaacarum; and the Father forbearing to continue his Demand, enjoyn'd him to prostrate himself as he us'd to do, and to adore the Holy Sacrament; to which having been obedient, as he was in the middle of the Action, he stopt on a sudden, and the form of Balaam appear'd in her Visage sad and hideous, making however some shew of Laughter, which caus'd him to be known. Then the Father told the Spectators, that it was Balaam, which the Devil own'd; and as it was observ'd, that the Face became wan, and like one dead, the said Father Surin said to him, Thou look'st pale, as one guilty; what hast thou done? He answer'd, 'Tis true, 'tis I who have done the Evil whereof thou complainest. The Father urging him to tell plainly what it was, after some little delaying, he said, 'Tis my self, who these days past have caus'd to the Diseas'd that extraordinary Hunger and troublesome Sleep, and who have kept her from all the Exercises of Prayer and Piety, which she had been accustom'd to do. Whereupon the Visage continuing to appear still more pale, and tending to an Extremity, the said Father perceived that the Devil could hold out no longer, and conjecturing that he was ready to go out of the Body, he commanded him with great Fervour to do it. Then the Body of the said Maid, being upon her Knees, would be bow'd backwards upon her Heels, and stretching out her Left-Arm in the Air to the fight of all, We saw, with many others of the Assistants, viz. the Sieur Demorans, the Vicegerent of the Bishop of Poitiers, the Father Anginot and Bacheterie Jesuits, Exorcists, Father Luke Capucin, Exorcist, the said English Gentlemen, the said Nozai Register, the Sieur de Fresne Burgess of Loudun, and especially the said Father Surin Exorcising bloody Characters, forming themselves upon the Back of her Hand, which compos'd the Name of Joseph; this being perceiv'd by the said Father, he said, that 'twas the sign of the going out of Balaam: The said Name is written in Roman Letters, and in the form and bigness almost as this is, J O S E P H; which Sign the said Father had extorted from the Devil the 1st of the Month of October last, which happen'd in this manner. The said Father Surin having taken notice that the Mother Prioress receiv'd the special Favours of God, by the Intercessron of St. Joseph; and that the Devil Balaam had own'd that the said Saint was his particular Enemy in Heaven, he purpos'd to compel him, for a sign of his final departure, to write the Name of Joseph on the back of the Left-Hand of the possessed Maid, instead of that of Balaam, which two Years before he had promis'd to write; the Father thinking it more decent that a Religious Person, should have upon her Hand the Name of a Saint, than that of a Devil. Having therefore several times commanded that Devil to promise this Sign, without being able to engage him to consent to it, he resolv'd to perswade the Maid to perform some Devotion for that End; which was, to receive the Sacrament nine days together, and to do some Austerities every day to the Honour of St. Joseph; that being done, the ninth day at the Exorcisms, without the Fathers seeming to enquire into that Affair, the Devil Balaam appear'd in a terrible Form, contrary to his ordinary Practice; and biting with rage the back of her Left-hand, confest that he was compell'd by the Guardian Angel of the Maid, on the behalf of St. Joseph, to make the Sign commanded at the very time of his last going out; after which he promis'd him, and swore upon the Holy Sacrament, not without regret, saying, That be intended, being not able to go to Heaven in Person, that at least his Name should go thither, being ingrav'd upon the Hand of that Maid: In conformity to his Promise, that being come to pass which has been represented above: And the said Name being mark'd in such a manner, that the first and second Skin, and the Flesh, seem'd pierc'd; after which, the Maid being come to her self, they sung Te Deum Laudamus, and c. Then 'twas advis'd to make some of the Devils to appear, to know how the matter had passed. Upon that the Father, having the Holy Sacrament in his Hand, commanded that Devil who should be in the Body, to appear and answer to what he should be interrogated; and presently Behemot appear'd with his frightful Countenance, who being commanded to tell who had writ that Name upon her Hand, answer'd, That 'twas Balaam, who had appear'd alone, counterfeiting the others.. Being ask'd if he were truly gone out, he answer'd, Yes, by the Flesh and Blood of God which is there, making a Sign towards the Sacrament. Being ask'd, who compell'd him to go out? Stretching out his Hand, he said, Tis his Enemy, He whose Name is written there, who is come, and hath commanded him to leave his Dissimulation, and to appear in his own Countenance, and to declare that he was the Author of the Disorder that happen'd eight days since to the Prioress, and for the punishment of that disorder, to go out presently. Being ask'd more expresly of the Cause of his going out, he said, That be was driven out, because be bad hindred the Works of God. Being ask'd, what Works? he answer'd, Prayer,

Abstinence, Penance, and all other Recollections of Spirit, by the irregularity of the abovesaid natural Actions. Being urg'd to tell plainly, what Irregularity? and in what? he reply'd, That it was, as he had said, by making her eat continually, by sleeping, doing idle Tricks, and hindring the other Nuns in their Devotions and Offices. Whereupon the Father having said to him, Thou wilt play the same Pranks one of these days; and for a Punishment thou shalt be constrain'd to go out, as well as he, he answer'd, swearing, I would it were in my Power to obey, I would go hence without being entreated; for I am too much tormented. And as he looked steadfastly on the Pix, the Father having said to him, What do you look on so much? he answer'd, I look upon him who is not to be seen by bodily Eyes; and upon that he withdrew. Upon which, We, the said Attorney of the King, have made and drawn up our Verbal Process, and caus'd it to be sign'd by the Persons present, for a Testimony of the Truth which it contains; after which the same was read aloud by the Register. Thus Sign'd: Denieau. John Joseph Surin of the Society of Jesus. Montague, as having seen the Letters of the Name of Joseph mark'd upon her Hand. Thomas Killigrew. And below the said Subscription there is written in English, which has been translated into French, by Mr. Montague, I saw her Hand white as my Hand, and in an instant change Colour all along the Vein, and become red, and all on a sudden a Word distinctly appear'd, and the Word was JOSEPH.'

Sect. 42.

Thus these wretched Possessed continued molested and tormented by the Devils, without their Exorcists giving themselves the trouble to deliver them, but when they were concern'd to edifie some great Persons of Quality, and to satisfie the Prelates, whose Recommendation these Honourable Persons brought. Some Chyrurgeons being sent to view the Impression of that Name, they perceiv'd an Inflammation, which made them suspect that it had been done, not by the Operation of a Spirit, but by Humane Art; knowing, that in other matters 'twas very easie to make a like Impression with Aqua fortis, or some other Compositions. But Denieau kept the Verbal Processes, and suppress'd them, and caus'd other Chyrurgeons to be sought for, who should speak a little more favourably, but who however durst not, or could not, so well disguise the matter, but that the Exorcists were oblig'd to own in their Books, 'That there happen'd a thing very remarkable to that Name of Joseph writ by Balaam; which was, that after its having been for fifteen days very well mark'd upon the Hand of the Superior without any Inflammation or Suppuration happening there, the Devil Isaacarum, had in his Rage bit it in such a manner, that it became a great Sore on her Hand in the place of that Writing; That after a Swelling and Inflammation there grew a Scab, which had entirely taken off, and erac'd the Name of Joseph, which was seen no more, and continued ten or twelve days without appearing; after which, the Scab, being dried and fallen off, the same Characters that were first form'd, by little and little return'd, contrary to all appearance, shewing themselves as fair as ever; which could not happen naturally, according to the Report of the Chyrurgeons, whereof a Certificate was made.' To which they added, That Behemot being thereupon interrogated about that matter, said, That in truth naturally these Characters could not return; but that God had constrained Isaacarum, who by his biting had defac'd that Name, to restore it to its former condition. 'Moreover, they say further, they plainly perceiv'd therein the Providence of God, as well to favour the Piety of a poor afflicted Maid, as to support the Proofs which have been given of her Deliverance; and that there is a great appearance that these Names and those which were written afterwards, would continue imprinted all the time of that Maid's Life.' But the Incredulous were of an Opinion very contrary to the Testimony of Behemot; for they believ'd that the Inflammation had been caus'd by the anguish of the Wound which had been made by writing the Name Joseph; and that the Characters which were defac'd by time, and which they said to be from time to time renew'd by the Guardian Angel of the Superior, were also refresh'd, not by the Operation of that Angel, but by the use of Aqua fortis: And in effect those Characters did wholly disappear towards the end of her Life, when the leanness of her Hand had made it uncapable of receiving that Impression, as shall be told hereafter.

Sect. 43.

During this time the Possession at Chinon went on, although it made little Noise, the Court being not so favourable to it, as to that of Loudun, because of a report which was made to the King by the Cardinal of Lions, and the Bishops of Nimes, Chartres, and Angers, or rather because that the Cardinal de Richelieu was not concern'd for it, and that there was no Body at Chinon who had been render'd odious to him, as Grandier had. The punishment that that unhappy Priest had undergone would not permit those four Prelates, who met together at Bourguil in the Month of November, in the Year 1634. to concern themselves with the matter of the Possession at Loudun, which had been declar'd real by the Sentence of the Bishop of Poitiers, and afterwards by a Decree of the Commissaries of the Court; But also reflecting upon the Scandal which these Possessions had caus'd to some good Catholicks, and upon the Scoffs that the Hereticks had taken occasion to make upon the unworthy manner in which they made use of the Authority of the Church, and wherewith they profan'd the Sacrament, they resolv'd to examine that of Chinon, in favour whereof no Court either Ecclesiastical or Civil had yet given their Opinion. For that purpose they sent for Barre, and order'd him to bring the Maids, which he usually exorcis'd, to Bourguil. The Order of the Prelates was executed, but the pretended Possess'd were so confounded and dazled by their presence, that they durst not open their Mouths to speak one single Word. The Cardinal of Lions put to them several

Questions in vain, they continued always Silent. They ask'd Barre, why they did not answer? It must needs be, said he, that there has been a Compact of Silence agreed on between the Devils who possess'd them and the Magicians; They told him, that he ought to break that Pact, in the Quality of Exorcist, who labour'd in the Name and in the Authority of the Church; but he refus'd to do it; and Prelates so discerning as these, fail'd not to see whence the cause of his refusal proceeded: The suspicions which they seem'd to conceive against him, made him uneasie, he fear'd the consequences thereof, and to prevent them, he took the Sacrament in his Hand, and protested in the presence of all the Company, that he believ'd the Devils possess'd the Maids whom he exorcis'd, after the same fashion, and with as much certainty as he believ'd that the Body of Christ was contain'd under the Accidents of Bread and Wine. Whereupon these Prelates told him, that he was very insolent, to advance such a Proposition; That he had not a sufficient Authority to decide so important a Question; That although these Maids were not effectually possess'd, they might believe they were so upon his word, as well because of their Melancholy, as because of the good Opinion which the possess'd had of him. There was one of the Prelates that told him, that if he was under his Jurisdiction, he would assuredly cause him to be chastis'd. Some time after, the Cardinal of Lions being at the Court, made a Report to the King of the things which pass'd at Bourgueuil in his presence, and so well perswaded his Majesty, that those Maids were not possess'd, that the King sent a Letter of Privy-

Seal to the Archbishop of Tours, which was afterwards printed, and whereof this is the Copy. My Lord Archbishop of Tours.

Sect. 44.

'Having been inform'd that one named Barre, Curate of St. James of Chinon, contrary to all sorts of Advice and reasonable Counsel, which have been given him, exorcis'd a number of Maids and Women of Chinon, who are not possess'd, as it has been related to me by several Prelates fully inform'd of that Affair; especially by my Cousin the Cardinal of Lions, in whose presence they have been exorcis'd by the said Barre; wherefore it being necessary to take care of this matter, and to prevent the evil Consequences which may happen; I have been willing to write this Letter by the Bishop of Nimes, whom I have sent express to you, to the intent he might confer with you upon the Subject of that Irregularity, and to exhort you to interpose your Authority for the stopping of these Proceedings, according as he shall acquaint you with my Intention, wherein you may give him entire Credit. Wherefore referring my self to him, I will no further express my self, and pray God, my Lord Archbishop, to have you in his holy Protection. Written at St. Germains in Laie the 19th of December 1634.'

Sect. 45.

The Archbishop of Tours having receiv'd that Letter, gave notice to the Court, that there would be need of a very considerable Sum of Money to proceed to the Instruction of such a Process; for which, seeing that he was not provided, and besides having no ill will neither for the Devils nor for the Exorcists, he caus'd not any Proceedings to be made against Barre, who continued exorcising, and added to the Exorcisms frequent Sermons against the Corruption of Manners, aggravating with so apparent a Zeal the Faults of the Age, that the common People took him for a Saint, and that there were even Persons of Merit and Quality, who were seduc'd by his extraordinary Hypocrisie. There was of this Party one Duclos a Physician, who maintain'd the truth of the Possession at Chinon, being engag'd to it by the Judgment which he had already given in favour of that at Loudun; but he had for an Antagonist, another Physician, named Quillet, who publish'd in the Year 1635. an excellent Latin Poem dedicated to the Clergy of France, which was then assembled at Paris; therein he ridicul'd all the Contrivances of the Exorcists, and shew'd that Melancholly, or rather the Frenzy of Barre and the Maids whom he exorcis'd, were the only Devils that possess'd them: And infine, after having prov'd, by very solid Reasons, the Falshood of such Possessions, he solicited the Clergy to employ their Authority to suppress the Audaciousness of those who use such scandulous Practices, by inflicting on them severe Chastisements. The Clergy was not at all mov'd by the reading of that Poem; and the Language of the Gods seem'd not to touch the Ears of the Ecclesiasticks, who were assembled for other Affairs more important for their Interest, than that of the Possessions of Chinon and Loudun.

Sect. 46.

In the mean time Father Surin, continuing his Exorcisms with success at Loudun, apply'd himself at the beginning of the Year 1636. to the Expulsion of Isaacarum out of the Body of the Superior. But as this Devil seem'd very obstinate, and that he would not obey nor go out by the commands which had been given in the name of Jesus, the Exorcist happily bethought himself of invoking the names of Mary and Joseph. This is what we learn in the little Book which has been publish'd under this Title; The Glory of St. Joseph, victorious over the Principal Devils of the Possession at Loudun, wherein is particularly to be seen what happened on Twelfth day in this Year 1636. in the going out of Isaacarum from the Body of the Mother Prioress, dedicated to Monsieur the Duke of Orleans, the King's only Brother. That Book imports, 'That the Father Jesuit having known the Condition of the Mother Prioress, and consider'd that she, as well as he, had need of the assistance of Heaven, and the experiments heretofore made upon several occasions, having inform'd him of the benefits which the Souls receiv'd in this World by the aid of St. Joseph, he purpos'd to take that great Saint, next the Holy Virgin, for a special Protector in in all that Affair.' 'Twas said that this Saint had been chosen for the Conformity of his Name with that of the famous Father Joseph Capucin, who had been the Protector of the Exorcists, next to Cardinal de Richelieu, because that Cardinal seem'd no more to be so much concern'd for the Possession, after Grandier had been executed, and that 'twas with difficulty he caus'd the Pensions to be paid, which had been granted to the Exorcists. It is further mention'd in that Book, 'That Isaacarum is one of the Devils who has given most disturbances to the Mother Prioress, and who had caus'd her greatest vexations; That he had declar'd, that he would go out at Saumur at the Feet of the Holy Virgin, in the Chappel of Ardilliers, as Behemot had already promis'd to go out at the Tomb of the late Bishop of Geneva, Francis de Sales; for although this Saint had not yet been canoniz'd, they had invok'd him since the beginning of the Inchantment, and he had assisted to expell the former Devils. It was in acknowledgment of that favour, that the Community made a Vow to sing to his Honour, every day till Easter, the Psalm Laudate Deum Omnes, and c. and that new Devotion was countenanc'd by the favour that God did to the Superior in advertising her by a Revelation which she had, being awake, that Behemot should go out at the Tomb of that Prelate.'

Sect. 47.

But Laubardemont, who return'd then, as it has been already said, and brought a new Commission for the Exorcisms, thought it not convenient, that she should take a Journey to Geneva, which was long and troublesome, the Season it self being incommodious;

'Twas therefore advis'd, that 'twould be better to publish Declarations at the Exorcisms, whereby it might be concluded, that the Orders of Heaven for the going out of those Guests were chang'd, and that so they were not oblig'd to keep their promise. In the mean while his Affairs calling him into Guienne, he departed and went thither. A little while after the Superior related to her Exorcists a Dream which she had had twice, and as it was found very considerable, and had relation to the Orders which Laubardemont had left, they oblig'd her to put it in Writing, which she did in these Terms. 'The first day of the Year 1636. about two Hours after Midnight, being gone to Bed after our Prayers, where having recommended my self to the Glorious St. Joseph, and having pray'd him to take me into his particular Protection the whole course of that Year, and to obtain of our Lord for me, that he would do me the favour to take from me all the inward Impediments which hinder me from the Union of his Love and Service; after I had fall'n asleep I seem'd to feel a particular Emotion accompanied with an exceedingly sweet smelling Odour, and quite different from that of Perfumes of the World; and I heard at the same time a Voice, which said to me, Behold him to whom thou hast recommended thy self. Immediately the thought of that Holy Patriarch return'd into my Mind, and my Heart was full of a great respect and love towards him, and to my thinking I saw a clear Light much more bright and resplendent than that of the Sun, and within that Light I saw a Face full of Majesty, accompanied with so perfect a Beauty, that I have not Words to express it, nor can I find any

Comparisons which can come near it. From this Visage proceeded a Sweetness and Modesty very admirable, which spake to me, as I thought, in these Words.' Have constancy and patience under the Impediments which you feel, support them with resignation, and forget your self, God will do you good. Tell your Father Exorcist, that if Men do not, in a little time, take pains for your Recovery, God will provide for it by some other way, and that your Exorcist continue with patience to exorcize you, whereby he will much content our Lord by labouring in his work, and that he shall drive out by his Ministry, if there be no order taken, the Devil, who does most retard your Recovery. 'After which the whole disappear'd, but the Odour continued yet for some time after, and being awake, methought that all my Bed was perfum'd. The thought of that Dream all the day long in my privacy gave me great Sentiments of Confidence in our Lord, and a particular assurance of the Assistance of St. Joseph in my necessities, however I neglected to speak of it, not regarding the whole but as a Dream. The night following the same thing, with all the circumstances as above related, happen'd to befal me again in my Sleep, but the beautiful Visage seem'd to me a litle more stern; It ask'd me what was the reason that I had not told my Exorcist what happen'd to me, and that I should not fail to tell him, which I did the next day. Sign'd by Sister Jane des Agnes, Ursuline Nun.'

Sect. 48.

The Favourers of the Possession put this Dream in the Rank of those which God promis'd to his Children by the Prophet Joel; They compar'd it to those of the two Josephs mention'd in the Scripture, and all the proof that they brought for that purpose, besides the Account of the good Nun, was drawn from the Authority of the Devils, for they write, 'That when the Prioress related that Dream to her Exorcist, One of the Devils stopt her Speech and seiz'd upon her Spirit, testifying a great fury, and that the Exorcist having demanded of him what he thought of that Dream, he answer'd, I know not what to say, I was not in her Body that night, nor the precedent, my Companion and I were at the Witches Subat; I can only say, that when we return'd into her Body, we were sensible that there was a marvellous sweetness, and an extraordinary quiet in her Soul.'

Sect. 49.

The Incredulous, whose Sentiments were more ready to agree with the testimonies of Devils, than those of the pious Exorcists, were not however satisfied of the truth nor sincerity of that Dream, they believ'd that those words, Tell your Exorcist, that if Men take not pains for your Recovery, God will do it some other way, ought to be thus explain'd; Say, that if they will not conduct you to Saumur into the Chappel of Ardilliers, to the Feet of the Image of the Virgin, the place from whence Isaacarum was to make his going out, that Devil shall in fine be expell'd at Loudun, by the Ministry of the Exorcists, and by that means one shall save them, and also you, not only the trouble, Costs and Fatigue of a Journey to Geneva, but also the trouble of that to Saumur. In effect, Father Surin having heard the relation of that Dream, said to the Superior, That we must wait in humility for what God will do; and that if it please him, he can easily change things by the effects of his Providence, as he had already done, and that the events would justifie the whole.

Sect. 50.

The Exorcist often interrogated this Devil; he commanded him to tell him, by what Artifices he debauch'd Men from the service of God? Isaacarum was not then pleased to answer that Question, he chose rather to amplifie the reasons for which he was fill'd with rage against God and Men. These Reasons were, That God had not equally treated Men and Angels after their fall; That he shew'd favours to Men, which the most part abus'd, and that he deny'd them to Devils, who would not have abus'd the same, and that nevertheless he oblig'd them to adore the humane Nature in his Son. The Father ask'd him afterwards, what was the best way by which the Creature, which was gone astray from God, might return to him, and which he would make use of, if it were in his power? 'Tis the Love of God, reply'd Isaacarum, and if I had the liberty as Man has, I would employ all my power by the Virtue of that Love, to produce Works to satisfie him. That

Doctrine of a Devil, who Authoriz'd the Freedom of the Will, and humane Satisfactions, began that day to be suspected by very good Catholicks, because of the Channel through which it pass'd.

Sect. 51.

The Exorcist continued to demand of the Devil, If since his fall he had ever tasted of the Sweetness of divine Love? No, said he, and I am glad of it, presupposing that I ought to loose it, because it would be a very great Misery to me to call to mind so great a good. Thou bast however receiv'd Charity and Grace reply'd the Exorcist; 'Tis true, answer'd the Devil, but I have never produc'd an act by which it has been able to continue in me an impression of that sweetness of Love. The Exorcist proceeded afterward to another Question, viz. What is the strongest of all the bands which may keep a Man ty'd to the Creature? Where-unto he answer'd, after some resistance, That 'tis the Pleasure of the Senses, preceded by the forgetting of God, and that the cares of Life, the fears, and the troubles, which one has to enslave himself, are the means which the Devils make use of to produce this Oblivion in the Mind of Men.

Sect. 52.

The Devil continuing to discover the infernal Artifices, and to furnish Men with Reasons how to avoid them, which was properly to divide his Kingdom, and to put it into a Condition to subsist no longer, as the Gospel speaks, said, That he destroy'd very many Persons by Incontinence; That he had acquir'd very much Credit with Lucifer by the fall of Macaire the younger, by visiting him in his Desart, and intrapping him by the means of a Woman's Shoe, and a perfum'd Handkerchief, which he put in his way; That for three days he made the relish of Sin to increase by that perfum'd Handkerchief, which he saw and smelt often; But that he recover'd his former State, and for Penance made a Pit, wherein he buried himself up to the Neck, leaving no more than his Head out to look up to Heaven. The Devil added, That Alumette, another Devil, by whom Elizabeth de la Croix was possess'd, intrapp'd Martinien after the same manner by a Courtesan, which he had sent to him. He was also interrogated, If there were Persons in Hell, who had very much tasted of the divine Love upon Earth? He answer'd, That there were some who had tasted of that Love in perfection, but there were very few; That those kind of People could not be surpriz'd, and fell not but by a secret Vanity, and that their torments proceeded from calling to remmembrance the favours of God. These Questions were not much more extended, and at the end Isaacarum seem'd inraged, making frightful howlings, and endeavouring to strike the Exorcist, Because, said he, that he constrain'd him to speak to the Advantage of Men, whereas he desir'd but to destroy the Works of God, and to annihilate himself, repenting that ever he became into a Body, wherein he serv'd the Counsel of God against his Will; That 'twas a long time that he toyl'd in the World, altho' Behemot had labour'd much longer, and that he had been employed from the beginning against Job, whom he had not only tormented in his Body, but that he had also besieg'd his Soul, and that 'tis thence that those Words proceeded, which seem to approach to Despair, and which have given so much trouble to Interpreters; and 'twas also for that reason that he sinned not in all that he said. This Discourse was mightily applauded by all the Exorcists that were present, although to convince him of a Lie that made it, there needs but to relate the very Words of Job, who said, I am terrified for having spoke thus, and I repented my self in Sackcloth and Ashes, which shew'd his Sin and the Sentiments that he had of what God himself had reprov'd.

Sect. 53.

But behold another discovery which Isaacarum made (for he always lov'd to make long Harangues) he said, That before the Incarnation, the Devils did not possess Men, as they have done since; That indeed they had not, during the Life of Jesus Christ, understood the manner of the Union of the Word to Man to conform themselves to it; That they knew not even the Divinity of the Son, nor how the Motherhood of Mary could he join'd with her Virginity; That when Lucifer tempted Jesus Christ in the Wilderness, his design was to penetrate into that Secret; but these Words, Thou shalt not tempt the Lord thy God, left him in blindness as to that Mystery; That since the Death of Jesus Christ, the Devils have endeavour'd to imitate him, and to be incarnate in some sort, possessing be perceiv'd; and that the Magicians serve them most in the Design. All these things having been utter'd by the Mouth of the Superior, Father Surin, after the Devil was retir'd, ask'd her, if she remembred well that she had said for two Hours? To whom she answer'd, That she did not; so that some of the Exorcists doubted whether that was Isaacarum that had spoke by her Mouth. She then entreated the Father to give her leave to perform nine days Devotion to the Honour of St. Joseph, to obtain that her Prayers might not be so often troubled and interrupted; which was readily agreed to by the Exorcist, who doubted not of good Success by that extraordinary Devotion, and who promis'd on his part to say Masses for the same purpose; for which the Devils were inrag'd; and to be reveng'd, on Twelfth-day, which was the third of that nine Days Devotion, when the Possessed would have sung the Office of that Day, they disturb'd her, made her Face blewish, and caus'd her to fix her Eye steddily on the Image of the Virgin, Twas already late; but Father Surin resolv'd to exorcise her powerfully, and to cause the Devil with fear to worship him, before whom the Wise-Men prostrated themselves. For that purpose he made the Possessed go from the Convent into the Chappel, where she spake many Blasphemies, endeavouring to strike the Assistants, and striving to abuse the Father himself, who brought her however quietly to the Altar, where he caus'd her to be bound on a Bench; and after some Prayers, he order'd Isaacarum, who appear'd instead of Behemot, and who was taken for him, to prostrate himself on the Ground, with a sign of Reverence and Subjection, to Honour the Child Jesus Christ, ador'd heretofore by the Wise-Men, which the Devil refus'd to do, blaspheming horribly. Then the Exorcist sung the Magnificat, and c. and when he came to these last Words, Gloria Patri, and Filio, and Spiritui Sancto, the wicked Nun, whose Heart was really fill'd with the Devil, cry'd out, Cursed be the F--- Cursed be the S--- Cursed be the H---G. and cursed be Mary, and all the Heavenly Court. The pretended Devil redoubled yet his Maledictions against Mary, upon the occasion of the Ave Maria stella, and c. which was also sung; and said, That be fear'd neither God nor Mary, and that be defied them to drive him out of the Body which be possessed. He was ask'd, why he defied a God that was Almighty? I do it for madness, reply'd he, and henceforward neither I, nor my Companions, will do any thing else: The more we go on, the more we conceive a Hatred against God; because we see that he is well serv'd, and that thereby Men are fortified against us. Then he began his Maledictions again, and cursed at the same time the nine Days Devotion of the Superior. Whereupon Father Surin advertis'd the People to observe the spite of this Devil, because that good Nun had begun a nine Days Devotion in Honour of St. Joseph: And he again commanded Isaacarum to adore the Child Jesus Christ, and to make Satisfaction as well to the Divine Infant, as to the Holy Virgin, for so many Blasphemies which he had vomited against them. Isaacarum was not tractable; he refus'd to obey, saying, That he should be better pleas'd to swallow the Exorcist himself; and the Gloriosa, and c. which had been sung at that time, serv'd but to make him utter new Blasphemies against the Virgin. Fresh instances were made to oblige Behemot to beg Pardon of Jesus Christ, and Isaacarum of his Holy Mother; during which, the Superior having had great Convulsions, she was unty'd, because they imagin'd the Devil would obey: But Isaacarum suffering himself to fall to the Ground, cry'd out, Cursed be Mary, and cursed be--- whom she has born; the Exorcist commanded him at that instant to make Satisfaction to the Virgin for these horrible Words, by winding himself on the Ground like a Serpent, whose Head she has crush'd, and licking the Pavement of the Chappel in three places, and to ask pardon in express Terms before the Image that was in that place; but he again refus'd to obey for that time, until they came to continue the singing of some Hymns. Then the Devil began to twist himself, and by winding and rolling himself, he brought his Body to the end of the Chappel, where he thrust out a great Tongue, very black, and lick'd the Pavement, with Tremblings, and Howlings, and Contorsions very horrible. He did the same thing also again near the Altar: After which he rais'd himself up from the Ground, and continued upon his Knees, with a Countenance full of fierceness, making a shew of his unwillingness to proceed any further. But the Exorcist, with the Sacrament in his Hand, having commanded him to give satisfaction for the Words, his Visage chang'd and became hideous; and the Head turning backward, he was heard to pronounce with a strong and quick Voice, which came from the bottom of the Breast; Queen of Heaven and Earth, I ask pardon of your

Majesty for the Blasphemies which I have utter'd against your Name: Which the Father having heard, he cry'd out with a loud Voice, He is going out. And altho' Isaacarum had never promis'd to change the Sign of his going out, however the Exorcist vehemently commanded him in Latin to write the Name of Mary. Then lifting up the Left-Arm, and shewing the Hand all uncover'd, with Cries and redoubled Howlings, he quitted the Body, leaving upon the Hand, in the sight of Persons who were nearest, the Holy Name MARIA, writ in the Flesh in very fair Characters, and so perfectly, that 'twas not in the Art of Man to imitate them, in such a manner, that that Event was miraculous, and a certain Proof of the going out of the Devil. But to confirm it yet, the Sieur de St. Marte, and a Gentlewoman whom he accompanied, testified that they had seen a kind of Vapour go out with impetuosity, at the place where the Name was writ, which was seen and kiss'd by the Spectators, some whereof shed Tears; and the Mother Prioress immediately came to her self, and was full of Joy. They sung Te Deum, and c. and the Exorcist having commanded Behemet, who continued alone, to appear, and to give an Account of what had happened; that Devil declar'd, That Isaacarum was gone out by the Virgin's command; who, during the Vespers, had order'd him at his going out, to write the Name of Mary near that of Joseph, and him, Behemot, to write that of Jesus, upon the Right-Hand, when he went out; That that command was brought to Isaacarum by the Guardian Angel of the Nim; and that when be began to ask pardon of Mary, she had made him feel her Power, and commanded him from Heaven to go out; That he did not go out at the Chappel of Saumur, because Men had not endeavour'd to perform what God had ordain'd, and to make that use of it to which it was destined; That Joseph had requested Mary, and that Mary had consented that that Miracle should be done at Loudun, and not at Saumur, because it had been so delay'd; That as for him, he knew not whether he should go out at the Tomb of the Bishop of Geneva, or elsewhere; That he had not learnt any thing of late concerning it; That he would do harm enough before that should come to pass; That God might hasten his time, but let him do it is be would; as for me, said he, with Eyes full of Tears, I care not, I am mad to be here; in the mean while I will do the worst I can against God. Upon which Father Surin curs'd him, and commanded him to worship with trembling the Divine Majesty in the Sacrament: Which Order he having obey'd with great Convulsions; he lay upon the Ground, and winding his Arms twice, he joyn'd his Feet and Hands together backward; after that he retir'd, leaving the Prioress the use of her Understanding, and full of Joy, for having her late Dream so quickly and so happily accomplish'd.

Sect. 54.

The Author, whence this Relation has been extracted, says further; 'That Behemot had promis'd to raise up the Mother Prioress, and to hold her suspended in the Air, as long as one could be in singing the Psalm Miserere, and c. But that the Superior having earnestly desir'd to bear on her Hands the Name of Jesus, with that of Mary and Joseph, with intent to have before her Eyes, whilst she liv'd, the principal Objects of her Devotion, she had entreated that Favour of our Lord, by the Intercession of St. Joseph: So that upon the simple Wish of that good Maid, and without any command of the Church, 'twas enjoyn'd that Devil to add this second Sign to the former already promis'd, in conformity to that pious Desire.'

Sect. 55.

The Night which follow'd Twelfth-day, in which that famous Miracle happen'd to be wrought, the Superior had a Vision, which she her self writ down in these Words, 'I find in my self a great consolation of Spirit, and a lively imagination of the great St. Joseph, and at the same time I have smelt a very sweet Odour, and seen a very clear Light, out of which proceeded a Voice exceedingly agreeable and courteous, which said to me these Words.' Tell your Father Exorcist, that the Holy Mother of God desires that be go to Saumur with another Father, to celebrate in her Chappel some Masses, as an Action of Thanksgiving, for that she had permitted that the Devil Isaacarum should go out; and say also to him, that be use all the diligence he can, to prepare what is necessary for the rest of your Cure. And as for you, do you learn to confide in God; complain not of the great hindrances which he will suffer to befal you by the Devil who remains in you, he will relieve you by the help of your Exorcist. After which all disappear'd. Sign'd by Sister Jane des Agnes, Ursuline Nun.

Sect. 56.

When the precedent Relation was publish'd, the Author well imagin'd that 'twould be rejected by the Incredulous, and that so many Visions and Dreams would effectually be consider'd as meer Dreams. Wherefore he exprest himself in this manner, ' 'Tis very credible that this Relation which we have made will be diversly consider'd by Men who shall read it; Worldly Persons will say, that these are Fables which are mingled with Devotion, and that the Imagination has a great Share in these Matters, and they will think that their Judgment is founded upon the Strength of their Wit. They who distrust the whole, will suppose, that one cannot see clearly into these Affairs, wherein the Devil intermeddles, and that 'tis difficult to lay any solid Foundation upon the things related.' That Author was not deceiv'd in his Conjecture; for some maintain'd, That the Decrees of God are unchangeable; that the Negligence of Men, or any other Reason or Accident, could not be Cause sufficient to change them; That the Divine Power should at least have as well inspir'd Men with the Design of bringing the Superior to Ardilliers at Saumur: They pretended that she had made known, by her Dreams and Visions, that the Orders of his Providence were chang'd, because Men had broke his former Measures; That 'twas certain and notorious, that Isaacarum had promis'd at other times, for a sign of his going out, to split the Thumb of the Left-Hand of the Superior, so that it should divide the Nail on both sides; and that this Sign had not been chang'd, but because the other which had been put in its place was more easie, less painful, and less dangerous; That there was no appearance that God out of Complaisance to the Desires of the Superior, had been willing to contradict himself, seeing he had already said in the Scriptures, You shall not make any Cuttings in your Flesh for the Dead; You shall not stamp any Marks upon you, I am the Lord. Because that if it was not permitted to make those kinds of Characters on ones self, it was far less lawful to desire to do it by the Ministry of the Devil, whether in respect of Joseph or of Mary, or of any other deceased Person: And, in fine, the uttering of so many Curses, Blasphemies, and Impieties, was accounted abominable, seeing the Exorcists had not, since the beginning, any ways prohibited the Devils from speaking them any more, nor interpos'd the Authority of the Church for that purpose.

Sect. 57.

These Reflections disturb'd a little the Exorcists upon the going out of Behemot, who was appointed to go out at the Tomb of Francis de Sales, Bishop of Geneva; and they were hard put to it to invent plausible Reasons to authorize the change of the Declaration which had been made. The Book intituled, The Glory of St. Joseph, and c. imports further, 'That they desir'd that Men should favour the Design of God, to the Glory of that Prelate, and to the Confusion of Hereticks; and that they would not restrain Providence, which changeth its Effects according to the necessity of those whom it loves, to provide by any other way the relief of that afflicted Num.' But whilst all the Cabal employed themselves to make the Expulsion of this last Devil successful, whether by the Course already observ'd, or by some other which might authorize the Reasons of a Change, and give them a resemblance of Truth, see what happen'd again at Chinon.

Sect. 58.

Santerre Curate of St. Louaud, and Canon of St. Memes, having been accus'd of Magick by the pretended Devils which Barré exorciz'd, he briskly prosecuted that Exorcist, and the possessed Maid, whose Confessor Barré was, before the Parliament of Paris; the Matter was referr'd to the Officiality of the same City of Paris, where a Decree was made against Barré, and the pretended posses'd. But Santerre being return'd to Chinon to put that Decree in execution, he acquainted the Lieutenant General of that Town with it, and shew'd him his Papers. He had receiv'd many Civilities and Offers of Service before his departure for Paris, and he seem'd at that very time fully perswaded that all that Affair was but an Imposture contriv'd by Barré. But this Magistrate, who had been one of the Judges of Grandier, and to whom Barré had been very much recommended by the Marquiss du Rivau, who otherwise was a Person of Honour, had his Head fill'd with the

Hypocrsie of that Exorcist, and look'd upon it as a real Sanctity; this Magistrate, I say, who all his Life time had not been over scrupulous, fail'd not to discover the secret of Santerre to Barré, who secur'd the possess'd in the Castle of Chinon, and address'd himself to Laubardemont, who had then been made Intendant for the King in the Provinces of Touraine, Anjou and Maine. This Intendant made an Order the 15th of March, whereby he forbid Santerre to apply himself elsewhere than to him for the Fact of the Possession. Nevertheless Paul Bonneau Sieur Desgenetes Counsellor at Chinon, did not scruple to go, accompanied by the Register, and three of the Guards, to the House of Jane le Tailleux and others Possess'd, and summon'd the Kindred of these Maids to produce them immediately, in default whereof he would carry them away the next day. Hereupon Barré put up his Petition to Laubardemont, and remonstrated, that these Maids, vexed and tormented by Devils, had need to go to places of Devotion, and to pray to God, that they might receive some spiritual Consolation, and especially at that time, which was that of Easter; That in the mean time, they durst not go from the Castle of Chinon, for fear that Bonneau and his Guards should attempt something against them, and should do some injury to their Kindred, under the pretence of Justice; That he intreated him that he would be pleased to reiterate the prohibitions which he had already made for Santerre to address himself to any but to him, to make void and annual all the Judgments and Decrees given by other Judges, and forbid Bonneau and other Officers from executing the said Judgments and Orders. It was order'd by the Intendant, upon the hearing of the King's Attorney in that Commission, That the Judgment given the 15th of the Month should be executed according to its form and tenour, and prohibitions made to Bonneau and all others to oppose it, upon the Penalty of 1000 Livres. In effect none durst gainsay that Order, because of the Authority wherewith Laubardemont was invested in Quality of Intendant of the Province, and the matter continued in that condition.

Sect. 59.

Since the Expulsion of Isaacarum, there was no Wonder done at Londun, till the beginning of the Year ensuing; but in the mean while there happen'd some things from time to time which very much vexed the Exorcists, amongst which was the Dissimulation of the Count du Lude. He came to Loudun out of Curiosity, and having seen the Contorsions and Convulsions of the Possess'd, he seem'd very well satisfied, and told the Exorcists that he doubted no more of the truth of the Possession, than that of the Gospel, wherewith the Fathers were very well contented, and they thought him fully persuaded. He told them after that, that he had brought a Box of Reliques, which had been left him by his Ancestors; That he really believ'd that there were some true Reliques worthy of Mens Veneration, but that there were some also that were false, and that he would fully know of what Order his were, and whether they deserv'd his esteem or contempt; That he had hopes to know the

Truth infallibly at Loudun, because if the Reliques were true, the Devils would be sensible of the Virtue and Efficacy, and seem disturb'd when the Application should be made. The Exorcists assur'd the Count that he could not put his Reliques to a better Trial; wherefore they took them from his Hand, and apply'd them to the Prioress, after having made a sign hat she understood very well; but whereof the Count; who observ'd them, had also taken notice. She made at the same time hideous Cries, and frightful Contorsions; One would have said that she was consum'd by an invisible Fire, so extraordinary were her Torments, and her Agitations violent: In the height of that fit of Rage, the Box of Reliques was taken off her, and in an instant she seem'd as cool and calm, as she was before. The Exorcist then turn'd himself to the Count, and said to him, I don't believe, Sir, that you question now the truth of your Reliques; I doubt no more of it, reply'd the Count, than of the Truth of the Possession. The Father express'd, that he desir'd to see those precious Reliques, and the Spectators signified that they had the same desire. The Count permitted it, the Box was open'd, and the Exorcist confounded and non-plust, who found therein nothing but Feathers and Hair, instead of the Reliques he sought for. Ah! Sir, said he, why have you mock'd us? But, Father, reply'd the Count, why do you mock God and Men?

Sect. 60.

Madam de Combalet, otherwise call'd the Dutchess d' Aiguillon, being at Richelieu, would also go to Loudun to see the Miracles which were done there; She was accompanied by Mademoiselle de Rambouillet, the Marquiss de Breze, the Marquiss de Faure, an Abbot, an Almoner, Cerizantes Governour of the Marquiss de Faure, and Son of Duncan Physician of Saumur, and many other Persons. The Abbot and the Almoner disputed continually upon the Subject of the Possession; the Almoner believ'd it real, and the Abbot derided it as an Imposture ill contriv'd. The principal Persuasion of the Almoner proceeded from this, that the Possess'd reproached Persons unknown, who came a great way off, with Sins which they had actually committed, and whereof they were convinc'd by the testimony of their own Conscience. The Abbot maintain'd, that not using it so indifferently towards all Strangers, but only in regard of some, one must necessarily conclude, according to what he had heard, that these Travellers who were the most curious and most simple, or the most bigotted, address'd themselves to the Exorcists, and told them, That being come from far to be Witnesses of the effects of the Possession, they earnestly desir'd to see some extraordinary Sign before their Return; That the Exorcists advis'd them first to patience, and told them; That one ought not desire, nor curiously seek after Signs; That when the Curious grew weary of attending and made fresh importunities they were told at last, that 'twas expedient that they should pray to God, to the end that he would grant them the favour that they desir'd, and that the best way to obtain it, was to prepare themselves by Prayer, Confession, and the Communion; That these Persons fail'd not to confess themselves either to the Exorcists or to other Confessors, who were all of Intelligence with them. That in the Confession 'twas commanded them to prostrate themselves before a certain Image, to repeat the Prayer of the Guardian Angel, or to make some other Devotion of that Nature, whilst others were busie about the Exorcisms; That when the Prioress, or some other Person possess'd, whom they exorcis'd saw the Penitent kneel before the Image, she said boldly, that Man repeats the Prayer of the Guardian Angel, which he must needs grant to be true. Upon which the Possess'd upbraided him with all the Sius which he had pour'd into the Breast of his Confessor, of whom this Penitent having too good an Opinion, and not daring so much as to think of having been betray'd, he continued persuaded and convinc'd, that 'twas the Devil who had revealed his Secrets. Madam de Combalet, who was often as President in that Dispute, acknowledg'd that all the Abbot said seem'd not impossible, but she objected to him two things, which held her Mind in suspence, and which hinder'd her from determining against the Possession; and that was, the Marks that were seen upon the Hand of the Superior, and the Trouble that one had to lift up the Possess'd, when they were stretch'd upon the Pavement, for they became so stiff towards the Ground, that when one took them by the middle of the Body to lift them up, they were found to be as heavy, as if they had been lead. But Cerizantes promis'd to shew that the first of these might be done by Art; And for the second he said, that the difficulty that there was to lift up those Bodies, when they were so laid, proceeded doubtless from their situation, rather than from any supernatural Virtue which ty'd them to the Ground, which he hop'd to prove upon occasion. In effect, the next day he shew'd his Arm before all the Company who were in the Castle of Richelien, and they saw a Name as well mark'd and as red, as those which were writ upon the Hand of the Superior; And since that time in the year 1652. the Queen's Maids who went to Loudun, having been brought to the Grate of the Ursulines to see those wonderful Impressions, they derided them openly both at the Court and in the Citizens Houses where they lodg'd, because they said that their Gallants without any other Magick then that of Love, bore their Mistresses names upon their Arms. Cerizantes having so well succeeded in that first Experiment, he caus'd at the same time a Carpet to be spread on the Pavement and he lay down upon it in the same posture that the Possessed of Loudun plac'd themselves; He was found as heavy as they, and they had not less trouble to lift him, when they took him by the middle of the Body, but when he told them that they ought to put their Hands under his Head, there was not any who could not raise him easily. Mademoiselle de Rambouillet desir'd passionately to make the same Trial upon the Possess'd, and it was partly to satisfie her, that all the Company of Richelien resorted to Loudun. When the Superior and the other Possess'd saw the Persons of Quality, they came forward commonly and call'd them by their Names with intent to persuade'em that that knowledge of their Names proceeded from the Devils. Cerisantes who was well instructed in all that pass'd, said to Madam de Combalet, That there were at Loudun Confederates in the Possession, who took care to give notice to the the Exorcists and the Possess'd of all the Strangers that arriv'd there, were they but any ways considerable, and that they made a description of them, or told them some other circumstances, by which they might distinguish them; That 'twas probable that on the present occasion they would content themselves in saying to these good Maids, that the Marquiss de Brezé; took place of the Marquiss de Faure, without troubling themselves to describe them more particularly, being both almost of the same Age. That 'twould be very proper to begin that way to discover what one should think of that great Affair, the conduct whereof was imputed to so many People, and that for that purpose the Marquiss de Faure should go in before the Marquiss de Brezé. That proposal having been perform'd, the Devil fail'd not to take the one for the other; however, the possess'd took courage, and made their usual Contorsions, amongst which the Situation of their Bodies, whereof I have already spoken, was not forgot. The Exorcist perceiving that Mademoiselle de Rambouillet seem'd more curious than others, he entreated her to satisfie her Curiosity, and to endeavour to lift up from the Ground the Nun whom he exorciz'd. The Lady, at first seem'd in no wise to doubt of the Possession, but at last seeing her self urg'd by the Exorcist, who would confirm her in the belief, she gave her Gloves to her Woman, and taking hold of the Nun, who seem'd to be as heavy as lead, not by the place where they us'd to take her, and which the Exorcist directed her to, but by that which Cerizantes had shew'd her, she lifted her up without trouble, to the great amazement of the Standers by, and to the great Mortification of the Exorcists.

Sect. 61.

There were yet other means, whereof these Fathers, and the Favourers of the Possession, were accustom'd to make use of to know the humour, quality, and adventures, of those who came to behold these Wonders. The Persons who gave themselves the trouble to come so far, were not usually of the meanest sort of People; they scarce left the places of their Abode, but the Convents of the Capucins, Carmelites, Recollects, or Jesuits, who were settled there, had some knowledge thereof, and they gave notice of it to the Exorcists of their Order, with whom they entertain'd a correspondence, and to whom they sent Accounts of what concern'd the Travellers: Besides that there were a hundred several Accidents which happen'd there, that the Devils knew well to make advantage of, and from whence they took occasion to shew that they could discover things very secret. As for example, Mary Aubin had been a Boarder in the Convent, and had a particular familarity with the Possessed; she knew a part of their secret, at least of what happen'd at first amongst them in respect of walking Spirits, as may be seen in the beginning of this History. She was an Orphan, Daughter of the late Seneschal de Monstreuil-Bellai; her Uncles Bourneuf, and Charles Aubin, had taken her from the Convent, to marry her to Havart Sieur de la Perriere, who was one of the Gend'armes of the King; He was a Man least scrupulous of all those of his Profession; he went one Friday in the Morning to visit his Mistress at the House of Charles Aubin, who was of the Reform'd Religion, and who invited him to breakfast with him on a broiled Leg of a Turkey, which he willingly accepted of. His young Mistress, who had no great affection for him, gave secret notice of it to her good Friends the Possess'd Nuns, into whose Bosom she pour'd out her Complaints against her Uncles who would force her to marry him; She went that day to see them, and aggravating the fault of the Spouse whom they design'd for her, the alledg'd his little Piety, and that on that very day he had eaten Flesh without scruple. The Nuns fail'd not in the course of their Conversation to get a Description of the Person of the Gallant, and of his Cloaths. He went that Evening to the Exorcisms. As soon as the Posses'd perceiv'd him, they cry'd out, O what a Villian! O what a wicked Wretch! He is worse then a Huguenot, he has breakfasted this Morning on the Leg of a Turkey! How resolute soever Havart was, he could not but he surpriz'd and confounded at this reproach; And as there was then in the House none but his Mistress and her Uncle, he would have believ'd that 'twas really the Devil who had discover'd that Secret, if his manner of living, and the little disturbance he gave himself about the Affairs of Devils and of Religion, had not immediately stifled in his Mind the reflections which that adventure had rais'd.

Sect. 62.

The Accounts we have, contain yet many other Discoveries of that Nature, by which it appears after what manner, and by how many Accidents the Possessed and the Exorcists acquir'd the Knowledge which they made use of for their purpose; but 'twould be too tedious to relate all here, and one may judge sufficiently by this last Adventure, what must be presum'd of the rest. We shall therefore mention only some Examples of the Mortifications, which the Curiosity of several Persons, too suspicious and little credulous, gave to these good Fathers, and their Possessed, in examining them too narrowly.

Sect. 63.

The Duke and Dutchess de la Trimouille were of this number; they were at Thouars in the Neighbourhood of Loudun, and they fail'd not to come also to see this Sight. The Dutchess, who was of the Reformed Religion, did not pour out her Secrets into the Bosom of the Exorcists, as Monsieur the Duke of Orleans had done; but on the other side, to the end that the Person whom the us'd might not be suspected, she spake a Word to the Almoner of the Duke her Husband, and made her self sure of this Almoner, by keeping him near her all the while that the Exorcist conjur'd, adjur'd, pray'd, and threatned the Devils, to whom he had at first promis'd to cause them to reveal the Secret. This Management lasted three Hours, and the Duke and Dutchess having had the patience to attend all the time, the Exorcists at last dismist them, telling them, that the Devil was obstinate and rebellious at that instant.

Sect. 64.

Those whom they exorcis'd at the Priory of the Castle, were put to a like Experiment by two Counsellors of the Court of Parliament, who agreed immediately among themselves upon a certain thing, whereof they gave no notice to the Exorcists, nor to the Priests nor Fryars, nor, by consequence, to the Devils; who could not satisfie them neither, nor discover to them, what they had too well conceal'd. The Exorcist freed himself from that Surprize, the ordinary way, which was to say, That there was a Pact of Silence, which restrain'd the Devil from speaking.

Sect. 65.

All these Accidents, and divers others, which 'twould be too tedious to recite, put the Favourers of that Possession much out of Humour; but they were yet infinitely more mortified by the Confessions which the Sister Claire and the Sister Agnes reiterated from time to time in publick. The acting the part of Demoniacks quite tir'd them and in the Fits of their ill Humour they often, since the Death of Grandier, made the same

Declarations, which they had formerly made when he was yet alive. Moreover, Sister Agnes being one day exorcis'd in the presence of a Physician of Chateaugontier, who propos'd to her some Questions ons in Greek, she answer'd ingenuously, That she understood not the Language, and that she bad never learnt it. The Exorcist quarell'd with her in Terms which shewed rather, that she had not well discharg'd her Duty, than in a manner which might incline one to believe that she was really possessed; and he continued afterwards to exorcise her with all his might; but she was out of all Patience, and cry'd out, That she never was a Demoniac; that for a long time they had tormented her in private, to oblige her to do all the things which she did in publick; That if God had not supported her, she should have despair'd; and that she was very unhappy in being in the Hands of those Persons. The Tears, wherewith she accompanied her Discourse, drew the Eyes of the greatest part of the Assistants, who believ'd not but that 'twas the Devil who had spoke thus through Craft, and only to cross the Exorcists.

Sect. 66.

The Sister Claire being exorcis'd in the presence of an Advocate of Saumur, and several other Persons, was burnt by the dropping of a Thread dipt in Brimstone, with which the Exorcist us'd to smoak out one of her Devils: When she felt the smart, she briskly withdrew her self out of the Hands of the Exorcists, bewailing her condition, and declaiming against the Tyranny of those who forc'd her to counterfeit a possessed Person; and she earnestly pray'd to God to take her out of the Misery wherein she was. The Devil who possesseth this Maid is extreamly crafty, said the Exorcist hereupon, and the God be invokes is Lucifer. That's false, reply'd she, I call upon the true God, Creator of Heaven and Earth. Being afterwards transported with Anger, she ran out of the Church, protesting that she would never return thither; but she was followed by a Lady of Quality, who was her Kinswoman, who allay'd her Passion, and brought her back to the Convent, having not been able to oblige her to return to the place where they perform'd the Exorcisms. Sect 67. About the end of the Year 1637, Father Surin was recall'd from Loudun, and in the beginning of 1637. Father Reces, also a Jesuit, was put in his place. These are the new Miracles which were wrought by his Ministry, as may be seen in a Book intituled, The Miraculous Cure of Sister Jane des Agnes, Prioress of the Ursuline Nuns of Loudun, by the Unction of St. Joseph. It was the Bishop of Poitiers who gave the Name of a Miraculous Cure to the Unction, whereof there is mention made in this Writing, as appears by the approbation of that Prelate, to whom it was dedicated, which he gave in these Terms: Having understood the truth of the Miraculous Cure, and c. We have judg'd it convenient for the Consolation of Pious Souls, that the Narrative made of it should be publish'd. That Narration contains, 'That Behemot being left alone in the Body of the Prioress, he had bound himself by a Confederacy with Asmodee, one of the Devils who possess'd the Sister Agnes; and that they had promis'd jointly to a famous Witch, to do some remarkable thing for the Confusion of the Church; That Asmodee should delude his Exorcist, telling him the Day and Hour of his going out; That he should deceive him, and expose him to the laughter of Hereticks; That Behemot, on his part, should trouble the Mother Prioress, and let her have no rest from the 8th or 9th of November, the Day of her Confederacy, until the end of the Year; But that God oppos'd the Designs of these Confederates; and that the Pact given to the Witch, which consisted in three small Branches of Mirtle, each whereof had three Leaves, was the 9th of the Month brought and put into the Mouth of the Superior; from whence it was afterwards, by God's Permission, pluckt out by her Exorcist; That the two Devils renew'd their Agreement; and Behemot being gone out of the Superior, to seek for a new Pact, the Nun's Guardian Angel seiz'd of him, and bound him for a Month, under the Picture of St. Joseph, which was in the Church, at the great Altar, under the Feet of the Sacrament; That all these things were reveal'd by a Vision to the Superior, who enjoy'd a great freedom of Mind during the Absence of her Devil, of whose return she was sensible, as soon as his Month was ended; That the Exorcist had no sooner perceiv'd him on the Countenance of the Possessed, but he ask'd him the reason of his Absence; to which he answer'd,' That he was not far off, that he had not gone out of the Temple of God, where he had continued under the Feet of Joseph; That a Spirit, which was the Maid's Guardian Angel, and was his Inferior in Nature, but Superior in

Grace, had bound him there for the Punishment of what he had attempted, not to leave her one Moment at Liberty all the rest of that Year; That he had broil'd near a violent Fire that had burnt him, that is to say, near the Sacrament; That since his Creation, be had not been so captivated, having not one Foot square for all his length. The Book adds, 'That the Ist Day of the Year 1637. that Devil was oblig'd to speak much during the Exorcisms, and to adore in a more venerable manner than usual, for the Edification of the Assembly, which was exceeding numerous and famous that Day; That the Exorcism being ended about five in the Evening, the Superior was constrain'd to go to Bed, and to submit her self to the violence of a Feaver which seis'd her, and caus'd her all that Night great Pains in all her Body, and particularly in her Left-side, which made the Physician judge that it was a Pleurisie; but that he was altogether astonished when he saw that the Blood was not spoil'd nor alter'd, contrary to the Nature of a Pleuresie; That Behemot being adjur'd to declare, whether he contributed any thing to the Sickness of the Superior, answer'd, That he did not contribute any thing hurtful, but that be bad receiv'd order from God by the Maid's Guardian Angel, to preserve the Blood entire; That that Declaration was made the 6th day of the Disease, after the Visit of the Physician; That Behemot being adjur'd again, swore by the Living God, That he had spoke the Truth; That the Physician speaking to the Exorcist in Latin, and sometimes also in Greek, of the danger wherein the Life of the Superior was, Behemot gave Intelligence of all their Discourse, with intent to fright her, which did not succeed, because she submitted her self wholly to the Will of God; That the Devil kept her employ'd a Night and a Day in thinking of all the things that befel her, to the prejudice and ruin of her Health, at least in appearance; such as were the Bleedings which were often repeated, and especially in thinking of the Order which was given her to abstain from the Communion, because they were obliged to make her take from time to time some Food, by reason of the weak Condition she was in; That the next day she complain'd softly to Jesus Christ, that after so turbulent a day and so tedious a night, he had refus'd to see her, and that then she had receiv'd him in an extraordinary manner by a spiritual Communion; That her good Angel taking her part, drew off softly the Glove of her Left-hand, and renew'd after the usual manner the Names of Joseph and Mary, leaving her at his departure a great Joy at the bottom of her Soul, in which her Confessor found her at that time; That the 11th day of her Sickness Behemot had the liberty to wander, and that then she began to be much better, and more chearful then usual, hearing something, I know not what, which said to her that she must shortly go and take the Air; Upon which Behemot coming to seize upon her Tongne, said, That had he been absent, she would have died, because all her Blood had been Corrupted; That he was ask'd, why he spake of Walking, and that he reply'd, That after having been bound in the body of the Nim, not to remove thence, he had now, as well as his Companions, the liberty to go and come from one place to another. That when

Behemot using that Freedom did beat about the Fields, there seem'd to the Superior that there parted something from her Head, which went off from her, and that in proportion to that retreat, her bodily strength diminished; which was an evident Proof that she had been supported by Behemot during her Sickness; That upon the Weakness which had been caus'd her by the Feaver, Pleurisie, and frequent Bleedings, there happen'd to her a flux of Blood, which cast her again into a greater weakness, but that this flux was a Crisis, which evacuated all her peccant Humours, after which she was no more sensible of her Feaver, but some little Fits from time to time; of which she took no heed, because she knew that they proceeded from the Operation of the Devil. But that the Feaver seiz'd her again on Sunday Jan. 25. with an extream violence, and redoubled the next day in the Morning, accompanied with pains of the Heart, frequent Vomitings, and intollerable Aches in her Right-side; That the Physician Fanton, who was of the Reformed Religion, having been sent for, he judg'd also that it was a Plurisie, that kind of distemper being at that time become Epidemical; That he caus'd the sick Person to be blooded, and tended her with very much care and diligence; That the Wednesday following her pain was very great, which the Devil perceiving, he appear'd to her about six or seven a Clock in the Evening in a frightful manner, and under a hideous form; That then seeing her fall into great Faintings, he believed that she was in an Agony, and gave her a terrible assault, of which she speaks in a Letter writ to Father Surin in these Terms.' The mischievous Behemot took that opportunity to give me a furious assault, for during the space of half an hour, be shew'd himself to me under a hideous and frightful form, with a great Throat casting out Fires and Flames as well at his Mouth as at his Eyes; he had great Claws which be stretch'd out upon my Head, telling me, that I was condemn'd by God to eternal Flames, and that he waited for the coming out of my Soul to carry it to Hell. He endeavour'd during that time to give me strong impressions of Despair, but our good God by his Mercy supported me in this Conflict, for I found my Spirit very much resign'd to whatsoever it should please his divine Goodness to dispose of me, yea even to go Hell, provided that it was not with his Malediction, and that I should there sing his Praises, and make it a Paradise. This is all the Answer that I had to make to that impious Spirit. In this manner are related the Words of the Superior in the Book of the Miraculous Cure, and c. wherein there is further added. 'That during that Combat she seem'd troubled and amaz'd, and notwithstanding she said twice or thrice, That must be, what God appoints; That her Confessor having been call'd to her assistance, she told him that Behemot, to overwhelm her with despair, had taken from her all the remembrance of St. Joseph and other Saints; That he had not left her the liberty to cast her self into the Arms of God, and to practise any act of Confidence; but that at last, at the end of half an hour she felt her Heart to throw it self upon the Providence of God, towards whom she turn'd her self saying, that he was her Father; after which she was quiet all the Night and the day following, but that her Sickness increas'd on Thursday in the Evening, even as she has exprest herself in the Letter already mention'd, which she writ to Father Surin, where she goes on in this manner:' About nine a Clock on Thursday in the Evening, that wicked Spirit began to give me great thwartings of Mind, and to represent to me the condition of all my Life since six years of Age, and brought into my Mind, by a discourse which he made in my Head, the least disorderly Actions wherein I suffer'd my self to be carried; especially be made great Instances upon the time of my Possession, and upon that mingling of the Spirit of the Maid and that of the Devil; And to tell you the Truth, I was then in a great Perplexity, and had nothing to say, unless that our good God had given me the Grace to acknowledge him by a more certain pleasing way, which was Contrition and Confession; and I believe if I had not made a Confession so exact to you, as that I have made, and that God had not supported me, I had upon that occasion lost my peace of Mind; but my sweet Love was not willing to suffer it, for which I am much obliged to him. His divine Goodness was so great, that after having seen me all the night in that Combat, he sent about five a Clock on Friday Morning my good Angel, to renew the Names of Mary and Joseph, and gave me great Sentiments of Confidence in his divine Majesty, whom I shall always Bless and Adore in all the Designs he shall have for me. The same Book of the Miraculous, and c. relätes further, 'That the Disease went on daily increasing, and that the Physician having seen a redoubling of it, which happen'd the Sunday following, said openly, that she was in danger of Death; but that the Exorcists, and even some of the Seculars maintain'd, that she would not die, grounding their Opinion as well upon the Providence of God in general, who seem'd much engag'd in the matter of the Possession, whereof the Mother Prioress was as the spring and foundation; as in particular upon the Promises which had been given of her deliverance before her death, and upon the impression of the name of Jesus on her hand; That the sick Person, declar'd that she would not require Extream Unction, upon her belief that she should not die; That this Confidence was augmented to her by an extraordinary way, viz. by a Visit which she receiv'd on Thursday in the Morning, and by a Voice which exhorted her to take Courage and Confidence, and which said to her, that her Disease would reduce her into a greater danger, but God would exert his Power; That she thought nevertheless the night following that her Confidence ought not to be too presumptuous, and that seeing that Men gave her for dead, she was oblig'd to put her self in the condition of a Daughter of the Church, having recourse to the Sacraments, which that Holy Mother causeth to be given to dying Persons; That having had this thought, she pray'd her Exorcist on Friday Morning to give her Extream Unction, in case that she relaps'd into the same condition, wherein she had been before, which he promis'd her; That on Saturday Morning about six a Clock, her good Angel was sent to her again to renew those Holy Names, and that she call'd one of the Sisters who were at the Grate, to be a Witness of what pass'd; That that Nun being upon her Knees at her side, there was heard distinctly a little Noise under the Coverlet; That the Mother's Glove was pull'd off, and put aside upon the sheet, the Left-hand withdrawn from the right, and brought low upon her Breast, and put in a posture sit to write, which was done without precipitation, and very leisurely; That since that her Glove was pull'd off, to that time that the Writing was renew'd, it seem'd that there was a little Dove which flew to and fro very softly and perceiveably; That its retreat was as visible as its entrance; That the Nun, who was present, put her Hand to the same place where she had heard the little Noise, but that she perceiv'd not the Motion of any thing; That the Characters having appear'd fresh after that Visit of the good Angel, the Fathers had taken a new occasion of Confidence; That the Physician, to whom they shew'd them, said, That it did not follow from these Marks, that the sick Person should not die, but that they would be useful to her for her Salvation; That the Disease was very much increas'd from the very day the Extream Unctions was brought to her by her Exorcist having on his Surplice and Stole, and accompanied by another Father, and by Demorans; That when they were ready to administer it to her, she desir'd to be given over by the Physician, and to be judg'd past recovery, according to Nature, but that before she had time to impart that desire to her Confessor, she felt that unperceiveably she begg'd of God to be left to the Mercy of his only Providence; That half an hour after making that Prayer, she was in an Agony, so that when the Physician, the Surgeon, and the Apothecary were come in, she fell into the last Convulsions of Death; That they saw in her Person all the Marks of a dying Maid; That she had a great oppression in her Breast, her Throat swollen, her Tongue and Mouth black, her Nostrils open'd and drawn back, her Eyes sunk, her Hands clutch'd, her Pulse Convulsive and intermitting, her Stomack and her Belly much swell'd, her Sweat cold, and the defluxion of her Brain impetuous; That when they saw her in that Condition, they judg'd her to be dying, and said, that she had not two Hours to live; So that they retir'd to make room for the Ceremonies of the Church; That at last the Physician being desir'd to inform Laubardemont with the condition of the Disease of the sick Person, he wrote to him this Letter.'

Sect. 68.

Sir, I have been obliged by the Gentlewomen Ursuline Nuns of the Convent of this Town, to give you notice of the condition wherein the Lady their Superior is in at present, who is in an estate af extremity, and without any appearance of Recovery, the said sick Person having not been able to spit, nor to give us any sign of a Cure by the discharging of any Excrement, and having at present a convulsive Pulse, and so great a difficulty of breathing as she never had before; and having her Belly much extended, without sufficient strength to admit of any Medicine, not even a Glyster, instead where-of we are going presently to give her a small Suppository; to endeavour to cause a part of that to come away; which swells her Belly, and throws her into an Oppression, which is so great it cannot be exprest. I shall add nothing more to the Circumstances above describ'd for fear of being troublesome to you, only I shall entreat you to believe, that she shall be assisted with the like Fidelity and Affection, as you shall be during my Life, by Sir, and c. From Loudun in haste, about seven a Clock in the Evening, the 6th of February 1637. Fanton Physician. 'Tis added in the Relation already cited, 'That they continued again the Prayers of the Ritual, and that they ended the Ceremonies of the Sacrament; That though all the Sisters had seen their good Mother in extremity, they wept not however, for the great confidence they had of her future recovery; That the Ceremonies being ended, as they approach'd the sick Person, she was restor'd to the late Condition wherein she was before the coming of the Physician, whom she presently after call'd to Mind, saying,' God will suddenly convert that Man, he has shew'd him at present all the Signs of my Death, what could he answer him if he be not converted? 'That she felt some time after a gentle but strong inclination to take rest, in praying at the Feet of her glorious Father Joseph, whose Picture she had before her Eyes; That this desire having been divers times interrupted, a Slumbering seiz'd her at last; But that she had scarcely slept one quarter of an hour, when the same Accidents, and some others coming upon her, she fell into the utmost conflict of Life; That the Exorcist and two Nuns ran to her, in whose presence she had one or two Convulsions, and like one a dying; That she had two visible stroaks of the Hiccup of Death; But that instead of the third, they heard a very strong Sigh, and that in a Moment she became sound and vigorous, and said she had felt her self depriv'd of all her bodily Senses, altho' she had always had her Judgment free, and that as she was in that Condition, she had seen a fair and great Cloud, in which was inclos'd on the Right-side her good Angel, of an incomparable beauty, as of a young Man of eighteen years of Age, with comely Hair, flaxen and very long, which reach'd to the Shoulder of the Reverend Father Reces, who was on the same side of the Bolster of her Bed; That this blessed Spirit held in its hand a fair Flambeau of Whitewax; That her glorious Father Joseph was on the other side of the Cloud, having a Countenance brighter than the Sun, and a Majesty more than Humane, of the Age of a Man between forty and five and forty Years, with a full Head of Hair, mighty bright, though of a Chesnut Colour; That she saw him look on the Companion of the Exorcists who was on the same side, after a fashion very pleasing and full of Majesty; That after that beholding her, he put his hand upon the Side where the principal Cause of her Disease had always been; That he anointed her with Oyl, or some other Liquor; That the place which was anointed was made somewhat moist; And that at that very instant she was cur'd, as she testified to them by these Words which she utter'd, I am heal'd, my good Angel and St. Joseph are come, he has anointed my side, and I have no more pain. That the Exorcist, having heard her speak of anointing, ask'd her if she felt any thing? She answer'd that she felt Moisture, and that having taken her Shift, she wip'd it presently without making any other reflection; That her recovery having been so sudden and momentary, they sung Te Deum; That the Physician having been sent for, came to the Convent without having heard any thing of that Miracle, and that he saw the Prioress come towards him cloath'd with her Nun's Habit, who smiling, related to him the Miracles of her Recovery; That his amazement was so great, that he continued some time without saying any thing, but that in the end he exprest these words,' The Change is great, but the Almighty Power of God can do any thing.

Sect. 69.

The Recital of that History being thus ended, the Author of the Book makes thereupon divers Reflections, in which he presupposeth that the Disease of the Superior was not feigned, neither in whole nor in part, but all real, true, and natural, and the Proof which he produceth as the most evident, besides that which he drew from the Testimonies of the Physicians, Apothecary, and c., of the Exorcists, Confessors, and of all those who saw or attended the sick Person, is the certain knowledge she had of the Quality of her Disease, and the Authentick Oath which the Devil had made, that this Sickness had its beginning iu Nature; and indeed he spake the truth; the cause was, in effect, in corrupted and perverted Nature. He proceeded next to the proofs of the Miraculous Cure, which are equally drawn from several Testimonies mention'd in the Relation, and also of the extraordinary and infinitely agreeable Odour, which remain'd in her Shift, wherewith that Unction had been wiped off from her Side; And in fine, the Virtue of that same anointing has since been manifested in sundry Diseases, and against the Devils themselves. For Confirmation of this last Argument, the Author relates, that the 10th of February Father Reces having caus'd a little Paper to touch that Unction, he went to the Exorcism of Frances Fillatreau, where the Devil Souillon, who smelt that excellent Odour, fell in a rage, and said, That be lov'd not to smell that, and that it was such a Balm, that the Person who had been anointed with it, ought no more to do any thing against the Will of God.

Sect. 70.

The 15th of the same Month, the same Devil, who doubtless was no Lover of Perfumes, felt also the Virtue of that Ointment in the Hands of Manouri the Surgeon, which made him withdraw, saying to the Surgeon, That he had touch'd something which displeas'd him. The Devils Cedon, Asmodee, Daria, and Baruc had the same Aversion; there was one which said, that 'twas the Father of God who tormented them, and others fell into Blasphemies against St. Joseph. That Saint was pleas'd that a Number of Miracles should be wrought by the means of that Shift, perfum'd with a Heavenly Ointment, which had gain'd a great reputation, and justly too, on Madam de Laubardemont, who being dangerously sick at Tours, eight days after the Superior was recover'd, and not daring to make use of Medicines, because of her being four Months gone with Child, her

Husband in despair, saw no other recourse, but that precious Relique which St. Joseph had left in the hands of his Kinswoman. He sent for it, and you may easily judge that 'twas not deny'd him. In effect, the 25th of February, Demorans carried the Shift into the House of Laubardemont, who went to Prayers with his Domesticks, after which the Canon presented to the Sick that excellent Remedy which he had brought, the only Smell whereof fill'd her with Joy, according to the Relation which the same Author makes of the Miraculous Cure, and c. But when an Application had been made to the Right-side of the sick Person she was perfectly cur'd, and was the same day, without pain, deliver'd of a Child which had been dead in her Body about a Month, according to the Judgment of Physicians. They us'd again that odoriferous Ointment to suppress the Vapours of the Matrix, which flew up to the Brain of the lying in Woman, which fail'd not to produce the desir'd effect, contrary to the usual Virtue of Perfumes, which excite that kind of Ailment, instead of asswaging it. After a Miracle so surprizing, wrought in the Person of the Intendant's Wife, there was at Tours a great Concourse of People of all Ranks, who came to visit, smell, and kiss the Celestial Relick, and to cause their Beads and Images to be touch'd with it. At last it was brought to Loudun, and there again it produc'd a considerable Cure on the Mother Angelica, a Nun also of St. Ursula, to whom it was happily apply'd in the extream necessity of a Disease, for which they could not find any other Remedy.

Sect. 71.

Upon the Credit which such Histories deserve, the Relation concludes boldly, 'That the Recovery of the Superior was miraculous, and as eminent as any other one can quote out of the Writings of any Author. It cannot be ascrib'd to Devils, without denying the Providence of God, nor be suspected for an Imposture, without calling into question the Miracles of Saints, whom the Church has canoniz'd, there being none better certified, than that although there is no obligation to believe it under the pain of an Anathema, being not inserted as those of the Scripture amongst the Articles of our Faith; But that it cannot be rejected without imprudence, nor misbeliev'd without rashness, and they who believe it not ought at least to suspend their Judgment, and be silent.'

Sect. 72.

If this Conclusion can be admitted in the Court of Rome, as tis the Design of the Society of the Nuns of St. Ursula. for the Glory of their Order, sure it would not have been long before we should have seen the Mother, Jane des Agnes, canoniz'd. But in spite of the Confidence, with which these Fictions and Visions have been vented for Truths, there were then, and always will be, some Unbelievers, who would overthrow all these Fables by a single Negation, seeing that they are not founded upon any Reason, nor upon any Proof, which may be in the least likely to be true, or which deserves to have the least regard. In effect, can one conceive any thing more strange, than to see God employ the Devils to do good to Mankind? And Behemot to become the Minister of Divine Grace in the Preservation of the Blood of the Superior, which would have been entirely spoil'd and corrupted, if she had been seiz'd with a real Pleuresie, and if she had felt in her Side the great Pain that she pretended to feel? Is it not also a thing wonderful and astonishing, that a Humane Body, such as is that of our Lord Jesus Christ, could be contain'd all entire and easily, under the Accidents of one Crumb of Bread? And that a Spirit should want room in the space of one Foot Square, under the Picture of St. Joseph? But the Testimonies of the Physician, Apothecary and Surgeon, are possibly more considerable Proofs, and especially that of the Physician Fanton, who was of the Reformed Religion, and who has writ a Letter full of Facts; which inter, by necessary Consequences, the Truth of the Miracle, when even the bad Reputation of Mannouri, with the former Proceedings, and the Stupidity of the Apothecary Gouin, might hinder them from being admitted of for unquestionable Witnesses. But the Physician told his Friends and his Children, and has left it in Writing; That the Nuns had deceiv'd him, in sending to his House very late in the Evening their Maid, to entreat him for Reasons, which to them were important, that he would write to Laubardemont, that the Sickness of the Superior was extream, and seem'd irrecoverable, saying, that he ought not to pry into their Reasons, which would prejudice no body; That they had a particular Interest which concern'd the Temporal

Affairs of the Convent, to oblige the Intendant to come to Loudun, which perhaps he would not do because of his great Employments, if they did not cause him to be written to, in that manner, by their Physician himself, who could not be suspected by him. The Physician further affirms, That the Superior was really bad enough by her Feaver, which had seiz'd her for some time, although he doubted not, but that extream Pain in her Side, where of she complain'd, was counterfeit; but that as he himself was uncapable of such a Dissimulation, he could not imagine that it could enter into the thoughts of another; That upon her complaints, he judg'd that the Disease might be a Pleuresie, which was then a Disease Epidemical: But the Blood of the sick Person which he had seen, had given him reason to doubt, and had even perplex'd him concerning the Nature of the Disease, having had no occasion to suspect any Intrigues and Cheats, as to the Declarations and Testimonies of the Devils touching the Causes of that Accident, because he had not had any notice thereof given him; That when he saw the Superior after her pretended Cure, she was in the same Condition as before, in respect of her Weakness and Feaver; That she was upon her Knees, because she could not support her self; That she was lifted up by two other Nuns, and that after having gone two or three Steps, she excus'd her self upon some remainder of her Weakness, and cast her self upon the Bed; where having felt her Pulse, he told her, that she was not so well recover'd, but that she needed to be put into it; but that seeing she was so well perswaded of her Cure, that was as much as to say, that she had no more need of a Physician, and that 'twas time for him to retire; which he did presently, and 'twas very lucky for him; for in going down the Stairs he heard a Voice, which was not unknown to him, and that he believ'd to be of Memin de Silly, who cry'd out to the Fryars, Jesuits, and others, who were in the Chamber, Why do you not stop him then? That was, as he was inform'd since, to make him sign willingly, or by force, the Attestation which had been already drawn up by Gouin and Mannouri; but far from doing it, and from being perswaded of the Truth of that Miracle, or from having said (concerning the Characters pretended to be renewed upon the Hand of the Superior) That those Marks might be useful to her for her Immortality, he continued all his Life-time a good Protestant, and so offended with the Cheat, that they would have put upon him, that he would never since put his Foot within the Convent of the Ursulines, notwithstanding the Sollicitations they made to him divers times, and even to the Year 1661, when he died; for he was an excellent Physician, and that notwithstanding his Religion, he always serv'd the greatest part of the other Convents, and the Hospital of the Town.

Sect. 73.

In the mean time Laubardemont came to Loudun, to promote that Miracle of St. Joseph, and to use all his Authority in conjunction with the Endeavours of the Ecclesiasticks, with intent to beget a belief of it in the Minds of Men. The 12th of February he sent for the

Physician Fanton, who was gone to visit some Persons in the Country: They believ'd that he conceal'd himself. The Lieutenant Criminal, who profest himself to be his Friend, came to acquaint his Wife, that this Course would ruin him, and do what he could, they should be sure to find him sooner or later. The next Day in the Evening Fanton being return'd, went to the Inn of the Sign of the Cross, where Laubardemont lodg'd, who supp'd that Evening in the Convent of the Ursulines. The next Day in the Morning he return'd to the said Inn; and the Intendant beginning to put Interrogatories to him, he answer'd, That if it was commanded him to give his Certificate touching the Disease of the Superior, he was ready to do it; which was the manner of proceeding upon the like occasion, the King's Edicts prescribing no other ways; and that therefore he could not submit to that new Custom, nor answer. Whereupon he was sent away for that time. The 16th of February the Intendant made an Ordinance, in which was contain'd, that the Physician should answer to the Interrogatories which should be put to him, upon the Penalty of a hundred Livres Fine. That Order was not signified, till the 27th of the same Month, with a command for Fanton to go to Tours, whither Laubardemont was return'd, to answer there to the Interrogatories which should be put to him; and for want of doing that, they summon'd him before the Council. Fanton appear'd at Tours the 3d of March: He was discharg'd of the Fine and Summons to the Council, upon the offer which he made to answer. In effect, having taken his Oath, and declar'd, That he was betwixt six and seven and thirty Years of Age; they ask'd him, if he had not visited the Mother Prioress of the Ursulines of Loudun in two Sicknesses which she had the first Day of the Year, and what were those Maladies? He answer'd, That he began to visit her the third Day of her first Sickness; 'That she complain'd of a Pain in her Left-side, seated below the Breast of the said Side, even to the Hypochondria; that he judg'd her to have something of a Bastard Pleuresie, having a continual Feaver, with daily Remissions; for which Disease he tended her during nine or ten Days, and caus'd her to be blooded three or four times; That on Thursday the 26th of the same Month of January, the Prioress sent for him early in the Morning, and told him, that about ten a Clock the Night before, there was fallen a great Defluxion on her Stomach, which had caus'd her a difficulty of Breathing, and an Oppression, with Pain on her Right-side; and that she had a Spice of a Feaver, which Distemper he had judg'd to be a true Pleuresie on her Right-side, followed by a Defluxion on the Stomach, which she afterwards voided by Spitting and Vomiting; which Evacuations the Sick Person caus'd to be kept in a Bason to be view'd, being Flegmatick, with a little Froth, and sometimes small Streaks of Blood, very red, like to that which she shew'd him also in a Napkin: He added also, that he continued to physick her, till about six a Clock in the Evening of Saturday, the 7th of February; during which time he had not observ'd any Signs of Concoction, neither in the Urine by Night, which they made to be kept for him, nor in that which she did spit; That having perceiv'd some Convulsion in her Arms, he began to make some bad Prognostication of the Disease; for the Cure whereof he had order'd a convenient Course of Diet, bleeding at the Arm seven or eight times, nine Ounces each time, except the last, which was to be three Ounces only, four Glysters, and some other Medicines; That he had not been present at the administring of any of the said Medicines, but that he was at most of the Bleedings. They ask'd him, if he had not said to divers Persons, that the Disease was Mortal? He reply'd, That he did judge that 'twas like to prove so, saving that 'tis common to hope, as long as there is Breath; That for the rest, he observ'd the swelling of the Belly of the Prioress to be less than usual the last Day that he saw her, and only a great Weakness; which oblig'd him to order her a Suppository, and to cause her to take two Yolks of Eggs. They ask'd him, if he did not own the Letter writ by him to Laubardemont? To which he answer'd, that he did own it. Being demanded, if an Hour after he had writ it, he did not go to the Convent, and saw the Prioress up, drest, and in good Health? He said, That he went indeed to the Convent two Hours after he had writ the Letter shew'd to him; That being enter'd into the Chamber, where he had visited the sick Person, and not finding her in Bed, he believ'd at first that she might be dead, but that they shew'd him her kneeling against the Wall, with the greatest part of the Nuns of the Convent; That two Nuns lifted her up under the Arms and follow'd her; That she came towards him, being but the length of an Ell from him, that she walk'd very slow, saying to him, I thank you for the Assistances you have given me, I am much oblig'd to you; That he felt her Pulse, and found it very weak, and that she pray'd him to excuse her, if she laid her self upon the Bed, because of her great Weakness; That after he had again felt her Pulse, he went out of the Chamber, and return'd to his own House; That the next Day about four in the Afternoon, she sent to him a Maid, who entreated him on her behalf, to come and see her; but that he answer'd, That he pray'd the Superior to excuse him if he did not, after having been told in her Chamber, that she was well, being nevertheless well inform'd of the Condition wherein he had left her the Night before. Being ask'd why he answer'd not the same things to the Interrogatory which was put to him by Laubardemont the 14th of February? He answer'd, That he might not be oblig'd to contradict plainly the noise that was spread abroad of that Cure, he had pray'd him to be satisfied with the Certificate he should give concerning the Disease. Whereupon they ask'd him, if seeing the Prioress perfectly recover'd, he did not say, That there was something extraordinary in it, and that the Physicians in their Prognostications never exclude the Power of God? And if, in effect, he refus'd not to go see the Prioress, out of a design to exempt himself from giving his Testimony of what he acknowledg'd extraordinary and supernatural in her Recovery, for fear of displeasing the Party of those of the Pretended Reformed Religion? He said, That he had not found, and much less judg'd, her recover'd, as appear'd by what he had already said, and that he went out without having utter'd the Word Extraordinary, nor any other like it;

That the Physicians never exclude the Power of God for the Cure of Diseases; That, on the contrary, they have recourse to him as to a Sovereign Physician, without whose Blessing upon Food and Physick, they believ'd not any Cure possible; That he never refus'd to give his Certificate concerning the Diseases of the Prioress; That the Letter of the 7th of February, written at the Request of the Nuns, contain'd many things which might be declar'd and set forth by a Certificate, but that it contain'd them not so precisely, having not been oblig'd to be so punctual and strict in a Letter requir'd of him, and writ in haste, without circumspection, and which ought not to bear so good Testimony in a Court of Judicature, as a Certificate made by Order of a Judge, and subscrib'd by him; That for the rest he had not writ the Letter in compliance with the desire of the Nuns, but to give notice to him (Laubardemont) of the condition of the said Prioress, because of the assurance which they had, that he would give more credit to what should be writ to him by a Physician, then to what should be writ to him by others, believing that the design of the said Nuns was only to cause him to come to Loudun, which they said would be much for their interest; They ask'd him again if he own'd not that the Contents of his Letter to be true? He reply'd, that they were in some sort true, not so exact as things ought to be declar'd by a Certificate; It being usual for Men to take more liberty in a Letter to express themselves, which is not fit to bear Testimony in a Court of Judicature, as when one is to set down a Truth to be certified and affirm'd. The Intendant ask'd him in fine, how he judg'd that the Prioress had been able to pass from that condition of Extremity represented by him, to that in which he saw her an hour after? He answer'd, that her Condition was not so very extream, but however that might happen, as 'tis every day to be seen in the Motions of Nature, by the evacuation of some sensible humour, or by the excretion which is insensibly made through the Pores of the Body, or else by the removal of the humour from the place where it causeth such accidents, to another part less considerable. That moreover some troublesome Symptoms which are produc'd by the humour being in one certain place, may be seen asswag'd without necessity of changing the part, which happens by the mitigation of the humour allay'd by Nature, or by the coming of another humour which is less acute, which may take off the Acrimony of the former; That the manifest Evacuation is made by Urine, by Stool, or by Vomits, Sweats, and loss of Blood; That the insensible Excretion is when the parts are insensibly discharg'd, which kinds of Excretion are oftener made in Diseases, which are caus'd by hot Humours, and chiefly from Choler, without any signs of Concoction, which precede such Excretions, although it may be for the discharge of Nature, and by way of a Crisis; And that for the cure of Diseases, there ought naturally to go out of the Body less Humours, when they are evacuated by Remedies, which not only carry off the antecedent Cause of the Diseases, but also the present; and that the Humours in their Motions observe certain regular Hours.'

Sect. 74.

These Answers which contain'd so long an account of the Maxims and Practices of Physick, being not what Laubardemont sought for; 'He continued to interrogate Fanton, and ask'd him, if he did not take notice that the Prioress had not had any Crisis from the time he writ to the time he visited her again, and that the alteration of her condition, represented by his Letter, could not have been so quickly wrought by natural Causes, and even by those he had mention'd in his last Answer? To whom he answer'd, That he was not able to judge of that, having but just gone in and out the last time he saw the Prioress, and having not examin'd what had pass'd during his Absence; But that very often it happens to a Physician, to see such, whom he had despair'd of, to become better two Hours after; Whence the Latin Hyppocrates, Celsus, relates that sometimes there happens wonders in Physick. The Intendant, not finding yet his account in these Answers, ask'd him, if he had not conferr'd with Duncan about what he was to answer concerning the Sickness of the Prioress and her Recovery? He answer'd, not, and that he had not seen him since the 14th of February, and had not held any communication with him by Letters; That in Truth he had seen him before that day, but that he had neither ask'd him any advice touching that matter, nor had he really receiv'd any. Laubardemont then reproach'd him that he had not fully told the Truth, that he had involv'd it in a great number of Words, to the end that it might be less understood, having been induc'd to do it by those of the Pretended Reform'd Religion, and that he advis'd him to tell the whole Truth. Whereupon Fanton declar'd that he had told it, and that he had not spoke of that affair but by meeting accidentally which some of his Kindred and Friends, whom he had never call'd together for that purpose. He said further, that he remembr'd not that the Prioress seeing him, the 7th of February in the Evening, had said to him that God had miraculously Cur'd her; That indeed a Jesuit, whom he believ'd to be her Exorcist, told him, when the Prioress was laid upon the Bed, that wonderful things were done by the intervention of St. George or St. Joseph [which of the two he knew not] and that the Father had added, that he was neither a Prophet nor a Prophet's Son, nevertheless that he knew well what would happen, and that he had often spoke to him of it. He was ask'd if before the Extreme Unction was given to the Prioress, ne was not ask'd, whether she were in such a condition, that they ought to give it her? He reply'd, that the 5th or 6th of February, going out of the Prioresses Chamber, he was follow'd by Demorans and one of the Jesuits, who enquir'd of him, if he judg'd that it was necessary that the Prioress should have the Extreme Unction? Whereunto he answer'd, that his Judgment ought not to be follow'd, being of a Religion which was mistrusted by them, and that however to content them, he said, that he had seen it given to them, who were not more sick than she. All the Interrogatories above mention'd, and his Answers having been read to him, he sign'd them, and Laubardemont dismist him.'

Sect. 75.

Fanton's Answers do sufficiently shew; that he was a little deceiv'd in his conjectures of the Superior's Sickness, and that he had thought it greater then it really was, upon the relations that she made him of what she felt as well in her Side, as elsewhere, upon the difficulties of breathing that she mention'd her self to have during the few Moments that he was by her; upon the quality of the Excrements, Blood, and other things which they caus'd him to see, as if she had really voided them, and that they had not been alter'd and put for him to see, in such a condition as they ought to have been, that they might make him give such a Judgment as they desir'd; or else whether they did shew him the Excrements of some other sick Person, and he always affirm'd since in his Family, and to his more particular Friends, 'That the matter must needs be so, because he had never seen any Exrements that the sick Person had voided in his presence; That as he was uncapable to commit an imposture, he did not imagine that they would put one upon him, whatever occasion he might have to think so, by the reflections which he ought to have made upon the Intrigues of these Nuns, and by the Delusions of which they had been suspected by the Publick; That he ought to have consider'd, that the Superior knew well how to make her Throat and her Tongue to swell, and to make extraordinary Contorsions during her Exorcisms; She might as well make her self swell, and feign an oppression before her Physician, and counterfeit a retraction of her Arms, which however it was, they remain'd still in the same condition after he had given over visiting her; That for the rest, during the time he had visited her, she had a very violent Feaver, and all the signs of a great Sickness upon her Countenance; That this is all the certain Testimony that he could give, nothing having been more easie then to cheat him in the rest, as well because the Circumstances of the matter might permit it, as because he had not any suspicion of the Cheat, and that he had not made any particular examination of those circumstances upon that account; But that he durst not reason so boldly in his Interrogatories upon the suspicions he then had, or upon the easiness that there had been to delude him upon that occasion, nor upon the apparent signs that there were that they had really cousen'd him; And that he was content to say only the truth upon the matters which were propos'd to him, because it would have been dangerous for him to have done otherwise, and that the consequences would not have fail'd to be very fatal to him and all his Family.'

Sect. 76.

The following Year 1638. the famous Father Tranquille died. He was a Capucin Preacher, the most renown'd of all the Exorcists then remaining. He made, a little before he died, horrible Cryings out, which were heard by all the Neighbours of the Convent of the Capucins, and the report being quickly spread abroad in the Town, there were a number of People, who went towards the Convent, and into the nearest Streets, to the intent they might hear his Cries, and to be Witnesses themselves, if what was said of it were true. There went not any Person who was not convinc'd, nor ought there to be any at this day unsatisfied of the Truth of that matter, who considers the relation of the circumstances of his death, which was publish'd by a Capucin, and whereof this is the Extract.

Sect. 77.

'Father Tranquille was a Native of St. Remi in Anjou; He was the most famous Preacher of his time. His Vow of Obedience call'd him to the Exorcisms of Loudun. The Devils dreading this Enemy, went to meet him to frighten him, if it had been possible for them; and they made him feel such a Weakness in his Legs upon the way, that he thought to stop, and go no further. He was four Years in the Employment of an Exorcist; during which God purified him by Tribulation, as Gold in the Furnace. He thought at first that he should quickly expel the Devils, being supported by the Authority which the Church has receiv'd of our Lord: But having found by Experience that he was deceived, he resolv'd to have Patience, and to attend the Will of God. He was willing to abstain from Preaching, fearing that his Talent should be a Snare to him, and to raise Pride in him, and he gave himself wholly to Exorcism. The Devils seeing his Humility, conceiv'd so great a Rage, that they resolv'd to incamp in his Body. All Hell assembled for that purpose; and nevertheless it could not cause him to be either besieg'd or fully possess'd,

God having not permitted it. 'Tis true, that the Devils threw themselves into his inward and outward Senses; they overturn'd him on the Ground,; they cry'd out, and sware by his Mouth; they made him thrust out his Tongue, hissing like a Serpent; they bound his Head, press'd his Heart, and made him endure a thousand other Pains: But in the midst of all these Evils his Spirit kept united to God, and with the assistance of his Companion he readily routed the Devil which tormented him; who cry'd out sometimes by his Mouth, Oh, how I suffer! The other Fryers and Exorcists pitied Father Tranquille in his Sufferings, but he was pleas'd with them wonderfully; and there was this difference between him and Job, that God suffer'd not the Devil to touch the Life of the last, whereas he gave up to him the Life of Father Tranquille. When he felt the Temptation of the Flesh, he resisted readily the deceitful Allurements of Satan; he cry'd out extreamly to his Confessor, he entreated him to have pity on him, and was not asham'd to discover to him the Assaults of that stinking Owl of Hell, and that he might effect it more easily, he cast himself into the Arms of the Virgin, his particular Advocate, for whom he had so great a Devotion, that he had put an Iron Chain about his Neck, in the Quality of her Slave, to the end that he might say in truth to that Queen of Virgins, My dear Mistress, I am your Slave; Alas! suffer not that your Enemies and mine should ever seize on him who belongs to you. When the Devil of Pride tempted him, he conceal'd from the Eyes of Men, as well his Sufferings as his Actions of Virtue, and he call'd that, Hiding his Life in Jesus Christ. Then he took

St. Joseph for his Patron, whose Life has been in such a manner conceal'd, that many Ages are past without People's having been inclin'd to invoke and reverence him according to his Merits. He requir'd not that it might be permitted him to do publick Penances above the common Sort, to the end that he might not seem more perfect than others: And to obtain a more profound Humility, he took for his Advocate the humble St. Francis, his Seraphick Father. Having been sollicited by a great Minister of State to quit his Employment, to serve God and the King in a place where he should bring forth more Fruit, he answer'd him, That it behov'd him to overcome, or die in the Field of Battle, where his Obedience had planted him. His Humility was so great, that he said, he thought himself unworthy of all Consolation. The Devils have often been desirous to beget in him a disliking of his Perfection; but their Attempt was in vain; and his Courage was so great, that le often pray'd his Seraphick Father St. Francis, to give him part of his continual Sufferings, but not of his Consolations, which he wholly renounc'd, because he deserv'd them not. In fine, when he was provok'd to Anxiety of Mind by some Devil of Impatience, he invok'd presently the Glorious St. Bonadventure, with the Blessed St. Francis de Sales, who were rendred famous to the World by their Meekness and Affability. The Devils having resolv'd to kill him, the Magicians redoubled their Sorcery, and God, by a Secret, but very Just, Judgment, suffer'd them to do it. They assaulted him more vehemently than ever upon Whitsunday, when he was to preach; and the time for his Sermon being come, he found himself not dispos'd. His Confessor commanded the Devil to leave him at liberty, and the Father to go up into the Pulpit upon his Obedience; which he did, and preach'd more to the satisfaction of his Auditors, than if he had spent whole Weeks in Study. He did Wonders upon the Descent of the Holy Spirit; and 'twas then that he rendred to the same Holy Spirit the fiery Tongue which he had receiv'd, because that was the last of his Sermons. After that Sermon the Devils afflicted him more than before. He said Mals three or four Days, at the ending whereof he was constrain'd to keep his Bed till Monday, when he died. He vomited much Filth, which was judg'd to be so many Pacts, from the Expulsion whereof there was still hop'd some Relief; but the Surgeon found him very ill, and said, That if God did not suddenly stop the Course of that Diabolical Operation, 'twas impossible that he should subsist; for as soon as he had taken any Nourishment, though with an Appetite, the Devils caus'd him to cast it up, with such violent Palpitations of his Heart, that the soundest Person might have burst. They caus'd him Pains in his Head and Heart, of such a kind, whereof there is no mention in Galen or Hyppocrates; and to express their Nature well, one must have suffer'd them like that good Father. They cry'd and roar'd out of his Mouth; but in the mean time he had always his Judgment free. All these Torments were join'd to a continual Feaver, and to divers other Accidents, which cannot be comprehended by those that have not seen them, and who have not the Experience of the ways by which the Devils act upon Men's Bodies.

The Devils encreas'd exceedingly the Pain of the Patient the Night before his Decease; which they hop'd to hasten, by causing him to render his Soul by an approaching and extraordinary Vomiting, to the end that he might die without being perceiv'd; their Intention being to tarnish also the Lustre of his Death, and to avoid themselves the Lash of the last Remedies, which the Church has been accustom'd to make a devout use of, upon these occasions. They did then what they could to make him be left by the Fryer that watch'd with him: They made a continual Noise on one side or other in the Infirmery, which would quickly have put to flight one less resolute than that Fryer, who, in spite, of them, continu'd firm and couragious to assist the sick Person in the violence of his Vomiting, wherein he cast up much Filth, stinking so horribly, and which was so intolerable, that they were forc'd to throw it out of the Window without delay, so much it did infect the Chamber. The next Morning his Brethren, the Fryers, perceiv'd that God would give way, and take off his Restraint on the Powers of Hell over the Life of their Patient, who pray'd them to give him the Extream Unction, when they saw he should have need of it. About Noon one knocked at the Door, to know, if what the Devil had newly declar'd at the Exorcism were true, viz. That Father Tranquille was departing, and that he could not hold out longer; which being found true, the Extream Unction was given him; after which his blessed Soul took its flight to Heaven, to receive there the Crown which one may piously believe was prepar'd for him, after having fought so Couragiously, and conquer'd so Gloriously. For if those are the cruellest who destroy the Life of any one, because he maintains the Glory of his God and his Master, so is he so much more excellent, there being not more subtle Tyrants than the Devils, who were the Executioners that put to death the humble Tranquille, for supporting the Glory of God; and because of the Charity which he had for his Neighbour, he could not consequently be more excellently Martyrized, and afterwards more gloriously crown'd. It was thus that he died in the 43d Year of his Age, and the 23d since his Admission into the Religion of the Capucins. He was visited, during his Sickness, by a number of Persons of Honour, who return'd greatly comforted with his Words. His Patience was so great, that he desir'd not even the things for which he had an Inclination, but he took all indifferently that was prescrib'd him. The Devils, inrag'd to see so Heroick a Virtue, cry'd out often by his Mouth in these Words, O, how I suffer! I suffer more than all the Devils together, and than all the damned. In brief, it was a very War in Hell to them, to find a Soul so generous in the Body which they tormented. He was open'd after his Death, to see if there remain'd in his Body any Effects of Sorcery, but there were none found. The time of his Interment being come, they carry'd his Body into the Church, which was fill'd with People. They had no sooner set him down to perform the Service, but the People flew upon him to touch their Beads: Others cut off pieces of his Habit, which they kept as precious Relicks. The Croud was so great that they broke the Coffin, and mov'd the Body from I know not how many places, every one drawing it to him, to have his piece: Insomuch that he would really have been left stark-naked, if some Persons of Honour had not interpos'd themselves round about, to secure him from the indiscreet Devotion of the People, who having cut in pieces his Habit, might possibly have committed some Excess upon the Body it self. A Jesuit made the Funeral Oration: The Priests of the Town came in Procession at his Interment: The Regulars and Seculars offer'd the Sacrifice of the Mass for the Repose of his Soul. And one of the Magistrates having got leave to set a Tomb over his Grave, he put this Epitaph upon it; Here lieth the humble Father Tranquille of St. Remi, a Capucin Preacher. The Devils being no more able to endure his Courage in his Employment of Exorcist, they caus'd him to die by their Vexations, induc'd thereto by the Magicians, the last of May 1638, The said Writings contain'd also other considerable Particulars of the Sickness of that Exorcist, with what follow'd after his Death, which well deserve to be inserted here: Which is, 'That when they administred to him the Extream Unction, the Devils, feeling the Efficacy of that Sacrament, were oblig'd to raise the Siege: But 'twas not to go very far, forasmuch as they entred into the Body of a good Father, a very Religious Person, who was there present, and whom they have ever since possess'd, whom they vex'd presently with Contorsions, and very strange and violent Agitations, with thrusting out of his Tongue, and very frightful Howlings, redoubling also their Rage at each Unction that they made upon the sick Person, and encreasing it again at the sight of the most

Holy Sacrament, which was sent for, because the Real Presence of that Man and God altogether, forc'd them to let him die in Peace, for whom in this last Passage they would willingly have laid some Snare. Also at that very instant of his Death, out of Fury and Rage that they could no longer lay claim to him, they cry'd out horribly, He is dead; as who would say, All is done, there is no more hope for us of that Soul. Afterwards rushing upon the other poor Fryers, they agitated him so strangely and so horribly, that although he was held by a great many Fryers, they could not however hinder that he should not kick out with his Feet toward the deceased Person, till he was carried out from thence; And he continued thus strongly and cruelly agitated Day and Night till after the Burial; so that they were constrain'd to leave always some Fryers to attend him. The next Day after the Burial, a Devil being adjur'd to adore the Providence of God in the death of Father Tranquille, he threw the Person possessed against the Ground, and said, I adore the Providence of God in the death of his Saint Father Tranquille, who has always gloriously triumph'd, even to the end of his Life. Another Devil being likewise exorcis'd, went upon the Grave, which he trampled with his Feet, after clawing with his Hands, and throwing the Earth from side to side, as if he would take him out; and casting upon him great Stones, with a furious Look he utter'd these Words; Come out you Hangman, come out there. Whereupon being ask'd, why he persecuted him thus after his death? he acted a long while with the Hands of the Maid, and after an extreamly inrag'd manner, the same Postures, which a Person doth who kneads Dough: He was urg'd to explain himself clearly by Words: 'Tis, said he, because he dealt thus with me. As if he had said, I persecute him after that manner, to testifie the rage that I have against him, because he doth now by me, as the Baker doth by his Dough, who tosses and tumbles it as he thinks good; to which he added, He burns me more than ever. He swore also, That 'twas they and the Magicians that kill'd him, but that they were all much out in their reckoning, because in doing that, they imagin'd they should oveturn one of the Principal Supports of the poor Possessed Maids, and of the best Protectors they had with God and Men; But that at present be supported them more powerfully and more effectually than ever, because of the great Power which he had with God; so that thinking to gain much, they had lost all. Besides that, he attested with an Oath, that the Seraphic Father St Francis was at the Bolster of the dying Father, where he receiv'd his Soul, and put it into the Hands of the Virgin, who presented it to her Son at the Foot of the Cross, because he had born it; that before God he was a Martyr, whom Hell had Martyriz'd, and that as he had been Tranquille in his Life, and his Death, he was also Tranquille in his Glory. At last the Exorcist having condemn'd him to do an honourable Penance, and to ask pardon in the name of all Hell, of him whom they durst put to death; in the end he obey'd, after much resistance, Kissing the Grave in two places, which answer'd the two parts of the Body where they had most cruelly afflicted him, the Head and the Heart, saying, That his greatest pain had been there;

Then coming to the Foot of the Grave, he kist it again, and prostrating humbly before it, he said, I, Leviathan [thus this Devil call'd himself, who is the chief of all the Devils of the Possession] I ask pardon in the Name of all Hell, of that Servant of God whom we have caus'd to die.'

Sect. 78.

What ground for Reflection doth not that History printed the 29th of August 1638. furnish the Incredulous with? They conclude, that that vexation of the Devils, if it were true, or at least the torments of Father Tranquille, which were but too real, and which could not proceed but from the remorse and agitations of a tortur'd Conscience, were very sensible Marks of the Severity of the Judgments of God, who permits that the Devils, or the Ideas of Devils and of Hell should thus torment at the hour of death these pretended Exorcists, who whilst they liv'd, so impudently mock'd both Hell, the Devils, and God himself; That otherwise supsing that the Devils had acted after a sensible and immediate manner upon this Capucin, the Consequence which his Panegyrist drew from thence to prove the Sanctity of the Deceased, was false and that it ought to be retorted upon him: Because there are found in the Scripture but two Examples, at most, of the faithful immediately afflicted in their Persons by the Ministry of Devils, viz. job under the Old Testament, and possibly the Apostle St. Paul under the New, which shews that God suffer'd very rarely that that should happen. That if sometimes he employ'd those evil Spirits to afflict his Children, we do not read that he made use of them to take away their Lives, and there is no appearance that he permits the Devils to attempt it, because the Life of the Righteous is too precious before him, to give it them for a Prey. That seeing that they allow that the Devils were the Executioners, who had put to Death the humble Tranquille, it must necessarily be concluded that he had well deserv'd to be their Martyr. Likewise, that he wonderfully delighted himself in sufferings, which happen'd to him upon their Account, and preferr'd them before all the Consolations which might have come to him from elsewhere. But whether that so many horrible Oaths, so many dreadful Blasphemies, and so many other words of Despair having been utter'd by the Operation of Evil Spirits, and that they did really torment that unhappy Father, when he exprest them, and that he cry'd, thrusting out his Tongue, and hissing like a Serpent; Whether he has done all these things by the only perverseness of Nature, and without being otherwise possess'd than by his Despair, his condition had far less resemblance to that of a just Person, who never fails to have recourse to his God when he is under Sufferings and an Agony, than to that of a Reprobate, who testifies that his Punishment is greater then he can bear, as it appears by the frightful Words which that unhappy Person spake, Ah! how I suffer, I suffer more than all the Devils together, and than all the damned. Words worthy of the rest of his Actions, his Thoughts, his Devotions, worthy of a dying Man, who amongst so many Patrons that he chose, forgot and left out Jesus

Christ the only Mediator, whom the Father had given him. Words, in fine, worthy of a Man who renounc'd Spiritual Consolations and the Sweetness which they produce in the Soul. In the mean time, because it pleas'd the Monks to bestow upon so many horrible Things, I know not what, false Lights of Merit and Sanctity, in attributing boldly the name of Virtue to Vices, and that of a quiet death to a death most terrible; to a death accompanied with horrible torments and dreadful Cries; The People suffer'd themselves not only to be surpriz'd with these weak allurements, but they seem'd persuaded and prepossess'd to that degree as to run in Crouds to the Coffin of the dead Man, and to tear his Habit in pieces, which had an extraordinary Stench and Nastiness, because besides the Vomitings and Ordures of his Decease, there happen'd to him yet other Accidents after his Death. The Relations above mention'd evidence the Truth of these Matters, and all the most sensible Persons of both Religions, who were then alive, and some of whom are living at this day, have attested the most considerable things, which could come to their knowledge, assuring that it was with an Astonishment and Indignation which cannot be exprest, that they saw the furious fits of the indiscreet Devotion.

Sect. 79.

After the death of that Heroe, the Possession produc'd no more Miracles. The possessed Seculars went to the Exorcisms at certain hours, as some go to take a Walk; when they were ask'd on the way, if they were yet possess'd? Yes, said they, Thanks be to God. 'Twas advis'd sometimes to ask the other Bigots, who went daily to behold that Sport, if they were not also possessed, they answer'd, We are not so happy, God has not lov'd us enough for that. But the fatal Blow to that diabolical Inrtigue was the cutting off 4000 Livres Pension, which the King gave for the charges and expences of the Exorcists. This cross accident proceeded from this, that since the death of Grandier, Cardinal de Richelieu had no more a particular concern in that affair; and from what Madam de Combalet his Niece had assur'd him, that this Game was so ill play'd, that he must be a very Chouse to believe it, which made the Cardinal conclude, that if he suffer'd it to continue a longer time, that would serve but to discover further the Injustice which had been committed in the death of Grandier. Besides, he did not much concern himself in the design which the Monks had to establish a kind of Inquisition; Possibly also that in his Heart he did dislike it, and that he had not allow'd of all their management both at Loudun and at Chinon, and in many other Places of France, but that he might not discontent them, at a time when he might have need of them; being assur'd that he could easily stop them, when he judg'd it fit, and when they should become useless or inconvenient. Besides the Fathers Lactance and Tranquille, the two Principal Supporters of the Possession, who had had a very great reputation both by themselves and by Father Joseph, who protected them, were no longer in being, and the manner, in which they ended their days, had been so strange, that almost all those who were engag'd on the behalf of the Possession, how resolute soever they had always been before in the pursuit of their designs, did not fail to be shaken, and to make some reflections, which troubled them and put them into disorder. If there were some who could persist yet, and not be touch'd by the examples which they had before their Eyes, they were much concern'd at the loss of the Pension, which made them at last resolve to take no more such extraordinary Pains, which were like to be so ill recompenc'd. Mignon also, whose hatred was satisfied, and revenge glutted by the death of Grandier, was glad to see the end of so dangerous an Intrigue, from which he was not to hope any further advantage to himself. For he had too much Wit not to know that the Possession was already but too much decry'd, and that the applause which it had whilst the Government was favourable to it, was very much diminish'd, when 'twas known abroad that it would be no more supported by their Authority; and that the Court seem'd inclin'd to be no further concern'd. They brought no more the Possessed so often to the Exorcisms; and they left off at last by little and little to bring them, upon a Pretence that they would no more exorcize but in private. In effect, the Superior having not been conducted to the Tomb of the Bishop of Geneva, God provided in secret for her Cure, because Men neglected to do their endeavours in it. Behemot was driven out with little noise, and without other Witnesses than the Exorcists and Confederates in the Possession; amongst which number there were some Magistrates with Laubardemont, who, altogether secretly, and without the knowledge of the Publick, made Verbal Processes of the pretended Miracles that were wrought at the going out of this last Devil, to be put amongst the Papers, which might one day be useful for the Canonization of the Superior of the Ursulines of Loudun.

Sect. 80.

But the Possession at Chinon having had its beginning much later then that of Loudun, it continued also a little longer time. For in the Year 1640 there was one of the Possessed named Beloquin, who being provok'd by some violent Passion against a Priest call'd Giloire, or sollicited by some of his Enemies, caus'd a Pullet to be bought by a Woman, her Neighbour, and having let out the Blood, she preserv'd it in a Viol, and eat at night the Pullet in the Company of that Neighbour who bought it, and of another Man, one of her Friends, whom she had invited, to whom, without doubt, she did not impart her design. The next day she went very early into the Church of St. James, as it were to perform her Devotions and finding no Body there, she went to the Altar, and pour'd the Blood out of the Glass upon the Linen-Cloth which cover'd it. When Barré the Curate of that Church came thither, and went to the Altar, he made great enquiries to know how that Blood came there; Whereupon receiving no information from Men, he interrogated the Devil of Beloquin, who being urg'd by the Exorcism, answer'd that it came from the Maid her self. That it was the Priest Giloire, who being inform'd by Magical Art, met the Maid in the Church very early in the Morning, as she came to perform her Devotions, and that he had ravish'd her upon the Altar. That Declaration, which caus'd a horrour in all good Catholicks, and which at first held some others in suspence, open'd the Eyes of her Neighbours who had bought the Pullet; She discover'd her suspicions to another Friend, who could not hold her Peace, so that the Report thereof began to spread abroad till it came to the Ears of the Lieutenant Criminal. This Magistrate making a very strict enquiry, came at last to the very rise of that Report. The Friend and the Neighbour of Beloquin, who had eaten the Pullet, were sent for and interrogated; They declar'd what they knew and what they suspected. The Verbal Process of their Examination was taken in writing and sent to the Archbishop of Tours. Beloquin who had notice of it, took at a Pewterer's House of Chinon a leaden Buckle, which she put into her Matrix, and bound it in with a Napkin, complaining bitterly of the Pains she felt by stoppage of Urine, which was caus'd her by the Sorceries of certain Magicians. She desir'd afterwards of the Ecclesiasticks, who were Exorcists at Chinon to be conducted to Tours before the Archbishop, to receive from that Prelate, by the Authority of the Church, some relief to the Pains she endur'd. But some Spies amongst the Friends of Beloquin having been misinform'd, gave her false advice, and the Archbishop favourable to the Possession, was not to be met with in his Diocess. The Coadjutor, who supplied his Place, heard quietly the afflicted Person, and promis'd to assist her, and for that effect to use all the means which should be in his Power.

Beloquin took courage again, and comforted her self for the unlucky Absence of the Archbishop. The Coadjutor, to perform his Word, caus'd two lusty and strong Men to be call'd, whom he commanded to hold her, and two Midwives, whom he order'd to search her. That search discover'd the Cheat, at which the Coadjutor, being exceedingly offended, caus'd the pretended Possess'd to be put in the Prison of Chinon, and went himself quickly after to the same Town, where having made an information against her, and against all the Cabal of her Confederates, he sent for the Judges of Richelieu and Chinon, to proceed to Judgment in that matter; which was carried on with so much Vigor, that none doubted but that the Guilty would be severely and exemplarily punish'd. But the sollicitations of the Kindred of the pretended Possessed, the most part whereof belonged to considerable Families of Chinon and especially to the Family of the Counsellor Chesnon, who was of the number of the Judges; the Orders of Cardinal de Richelieu, who desir'd that the Business of the Possession should end without noise, least it should call to Mind what had formerly happen'd. These Orders, I say, and these Sollicitations hindred the Punishment from being so terrible and exemplary, as it would otherwise have been. Barré was only depriv'd of his Cure and his Prebend, exil'd out of the Diocess of Touraine, and confin'd to the Town of Mans, where he kept himself conceal'd to the end of his Life, in a Convent of Monks: And the Maids whom he Exorciz'd, were condemn'd to pass the rest of their days between four Walls.

Sect. 81.

Since this Sentence was given, and that it had dissipated that Cabal, there was no further talk of Possession, Exorcism, or Devils. 'Tis true, the greatest part of the Possessed, as well Seculars as Nuns, and even the Superior, being tir'd with the Trade which they drove and the Pains it had given them; they were not displeas'd to see them end quietly, especially when they heard of the fatal Success of the Possession at Chinon, which gave them occasion to reflect upon the danger which they had run, if they had been examin'd with so much Severity and Rigour, as these last. Therefore they receiv'd with Joy the Condition of remaining in quiet, and enjoy peaceably the Riches they had acquir'd by a way so extraordinary and so dangerous. But they were not wanting to manage all the other advantages which they could expect, endeavouring to make profit of the Reputation, which their pretended Possession had procur'd them with all the good Catholicks, whom the Monks persuaded every where, that these good Maids were the most illustrious Examples of Virtue and Piety, and at the same time, of Pains and Sufferings; which had ever been in the World. Which found more or less credit according to the proportion of the distance of Countries. For as in the Neighbourhood of Loudun there were but few Towns, from whence there came not a great number of Spectators, to behold the Wonders of that famous Possession, there were also in those Towns a great many Witnesses of the little Edification which they receiv'd, the report where of gave a great Check to the Relations publish'd by the Monks. But 'twas not so with those who liv'd far off. All the Conversations of devout Persons ran upon this Subject. The Assurance with which the Story was deliver'd to them, and the Character of those who publish'd it, suffer'd them not to doubt of it. The Books which were given them, fill'd with Facts related with the utmost boldness, the Quality of an Intendant, Commissary of the King, by whom these Facts were attested, and the dreadful punishment they had caus'd a Parson to undergo, confirm'd them entire in their persuasion. 'Tis true, that there were few places, where there were not also some Unbelievers, who told the News of what they had heard or seen, but the number of those afar off was so small, and the Proofs of the contrary seem'd so strong, and were after such a manner authoriz'd, that in general all the good Catholicks gave Credit to it; and in particular those of the Province of Bretagne, where the People are very superstitious and credulous, even to that degree, that there was then a Superior of another Order of Nuns, who writ to the Superior of the Ursulines, That if she had liberty to dispose of her self at her own Choice, she offered her self willingly to come to Loudun, to serve the Possessed who were so dear to God and to St. Joseph, and especially to pass the rest of her days near the illustrious Mother Prioress, upon whom God had made so great an effusion of his Graces; in whose Person there were seeen so many Miracles wrought, and who had been so particularly favour'd by the great St. Joseph, that he had been so ready as to come himself to assist at her Recovery, and to bring her a Heavenly Ointment for that effect. So the Ursuline Nuns were every where famous; their Reputation flew into all Parts, and Strangers, as well Incredulous, as others, who pass'd by Loudun, fail'd not to go and see the Names of Joseph, Mary and Jesus, which had been writ by the Devils upon the Hands of the Superior, and the Characters whereof were often refresh'd by the Ministry of her good Angel, who came from time to time to visit her, and to perform that Service to her; in acknowledgment whereof she did not fail to give him the Glory of it; for she refus'd not, during a certain time, to shew these Names to all the Curious, whom she took care to entertain with the Visits of that Spirit, and the Favours with which she was honour'd: But at last the Spirit grew weary, or by some particular dispensation, was not able to work that Miracle any longer; Or rather, to speak more intelligibly and more truly, when the wrinkles of old Age had made her Hand dry and lean, the Druggs which were employ'd to renew them, were no longer able to imprint them. The good Mother said then, that God had granted upon her Prayers to suffer those Names to wear out, which were the cause that a Multitude of People came to importune her, and to withdraw her often from her Acts of Devotion.

Sect. 82.

If there be any place in the World, where People can well keep a Secret, it is in the Convents, when there is a Concern for the Catholick Party in general, or for the

Order, and the Convent in particular. So that one has not been able to learn any thing of the State of the Possessed after the end of the Possession, unless it were, that they made some Verbal Processes of new Miracles, which had been wrought in the Person of the Superior, of one of which there was some Knowledge gain'd by means of the Magistrates who attested them, especially by those who had been sollicited to do it, (as the Counsellor Tabart) refus'd notwithstanding to attest one Event, whereof they had not been Witnesses, and upon the bare Relation of the Mother Prioress of the Ursulines, who said, she had heard a sorrowful Voice, first in the Dormitory, and then at the Door of her Chamber; where, after many Groans, she saw a great dead Body all in Eire come in, who came from Purgatory, whether it were to go into Paradise, or to desire the Succour of some Masses for his Ease: For the Magistrates, who refus'd to subscribe that Miracle, and have made that Report, were not so exactly informed of all its Circumstances, as they who saw and sign'd the Verbal Processes which were made thereof. The Superior was exceedingly frighted at the sight of that dreadful Object, which presented it self to her. She ran to her Holy-Water-pot, she took Holy-Water and threw it upon the dead Body, to oblige him by virtue of that Water to retire. The Water made the same noise as when it falls upon a Bar of red-hot Iron. It rebounded upon the Hand and the Cheek of the Superior, where it raised some Blisters, the Scars whereof, 'tis not doubted, would have continu'd all her Life time. So considerable an Accident which is pretended to have happen'd in the

Convent, could not continue so conceal'd from the Boarders which were there. There was one who was of a merry Humour, and who apparently was not satisfied with the usage she had receiv'd from the Superior who said, that 'twas very easie to make the like Scars; and that she doubted not but that the Superior us'd for that purpose the Beggars Herb, a Name which is given in that Country to a certain Herb, with which the Beggars rub themselves, to make Sores to appear upon their Bodies, with intent to excite more Compassion, and of which there grew a great quantity in the Garden of the Convent. They were not then able to keep the Secret in that particular, as in the rest of the things which were done to obtain one Day the Canonization of that Nun. One cannot also say any thing of the manner wherein the ended her Days; but 'tis well known what was the End of almost all the Authors and Favourers of the Possession, and of the Witnesses who testified against Grandier. We shall not however report here the Particulars, because those kinds of Relations find little credit: Or if there were incontestable Proofs of them, such Events would be ascrib'd to Chance, and to the ordinary course of things of this World. However, were it expedient to enter into a particular Account of them, there would not be wanting Proofs, both within the Country and without, seeing that the greatest part of those People liv'd a long time after the Possession ceas'd, and that the Circumstances of their Death were well known by a number of Persons, yet living at this Day. But, at least, I may be allow'd to quote Monsieur Patin, and relate here what he says concerning

Laubardemont, in his 37th Letter dated at Paris, the 22d of December 1651. Page 130. of the Edition at the Hague. 'The 9th of this Month, at nine of the Clock at Night, a Coach was set upon by Robbers: The Noise which they made caus'd the Townsmen to come out of their Houses, as well possibly out of Curiosity, as Charity. They shot on both sides: One of the Robbers having receiv'd a Shot, fell to the Ground, and a Lacquey of their Party was seiz'd. The others fled. The wounded Person died the next Day in the Morning, without saying any thing or complaining, and without declaring who he was. However he was known at last to be the Son of a Master of Requests nam'd Laubardement, who condemn'd to death in 1634. the poor Parson of Loudun, Urban Grandier, and caus'd him to be burnt alive, under the pretence that he had sent the Devil into the Bodies of the Nuns of Loudun, whom they had caus'd to learn some Tumbling Tricks to persuade Fools that they were Demoniacks. May not this be taken for a Divine Punishment of God upon the Family of that unhappy Judge? to expiate in some manner the cruel and merciless death of that poor Priest, whose Blood still cries for Vengeance.'

Sect. 83.

Those who know the circumstances of the death of Mannouri, and many others of those unhappy Caballers, and in what condition several of their Families are at present, have reason, as well as Patin, to acknowledge and admire the Judgments of God, and to say, that the

Blood of Grandier has cry'd for Vengeance a long time after his Death, and possibly to this very day.

FINIS.

www.ingramcontent.com/pod-product-compliance
Lightning Source LLC
Chambersburg PA
CBHW071235160426

43196CB00009B/1067